AF348619

ZHANG ZHAOYING

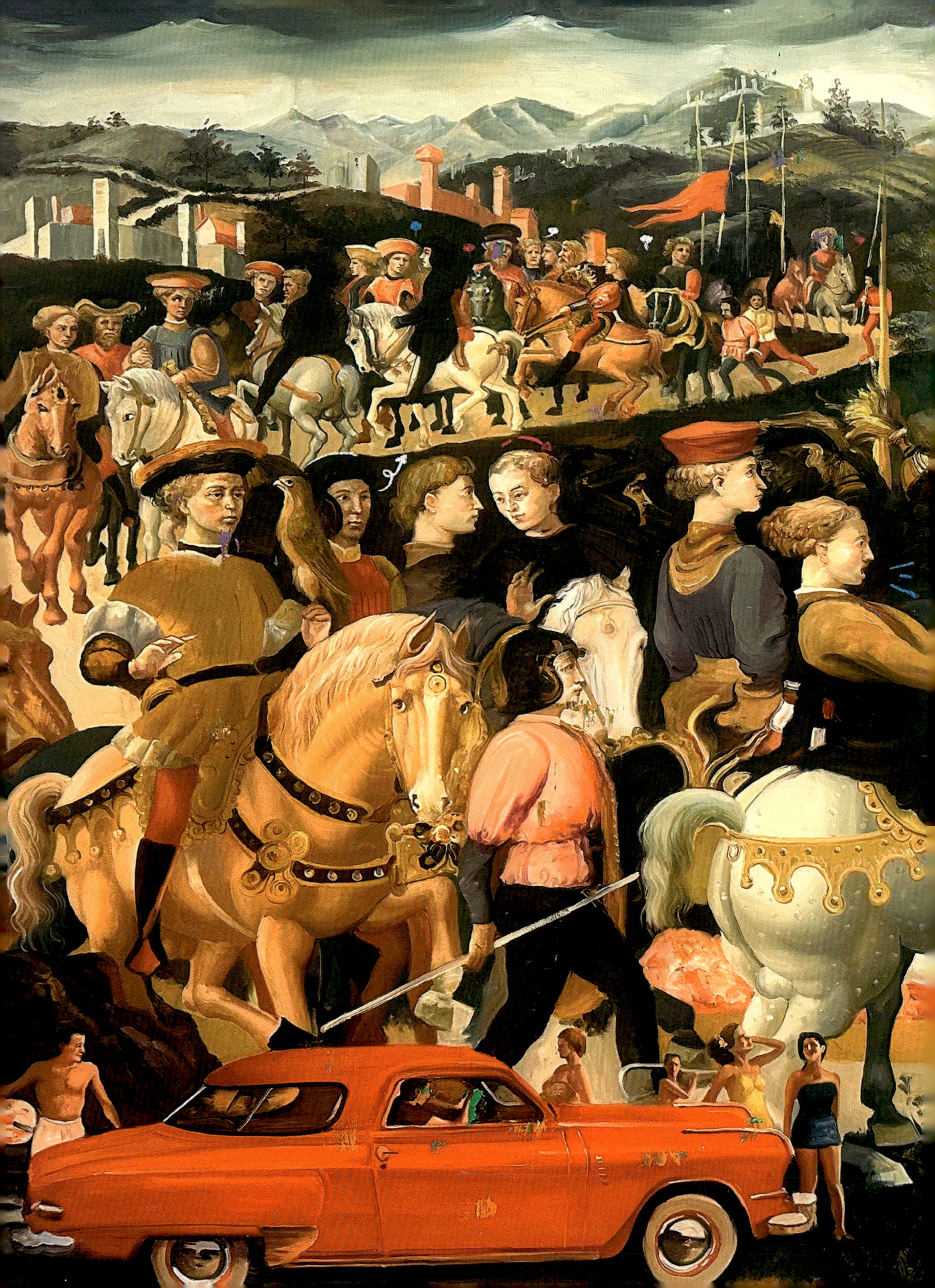

ZHANG ZHAOYING

edited by Lü Peng

SKIRA

LÜ PENG

The Temptation of Giorgio de Chirico: Zhang Zhaoying Painting Exhibition

The Historical Context of Zhang Zhaoying's Painting

By 1988, the year Zhang Zhaoying was born, the Guangzhou modernist group Southern Artists Salon had already been active for three years. By the time he entered the Sichuan Fine Arts Institute to study painting, the market for Chinese contemporary painting had already reached its high water mark. Before this, paintings by the instructors at the Sichuan Fine Arts Institute, mainly born in the 1950s, and those of the younger artists born in the late 1960s and early '70s, whom they had educated and cultivated, had already become important components of Chinese modern and contemporary painting history in the 1980s and '90s. Apart from the modernist art of the 1980s, a long list of names – Shen Xiaotong, Xin Haizhou, He Sen, Chen Wenbo, Zhao Nengzhi, Feng Zhenjie, alongside China Academy of Art graduates Zhong Biao and Tu Hongtao – was backing the emergence of the new contemporary painting phenomenon. In fact, entering into the 2000s, critics following contemporary art instinctively began to shift their sights to artists born in the 1970s, with the painting of Li Songsong, Qin Qi, Li Dafang, Yin Zhaoyang, Zhang Xiaotao, Yang Mian, and Xie Nanxing beginning to attract attention. Around the year 2007, the term "new painting", which critics had previously used unconsciously, became a deliberate critical term to describe the constantly emerging phenomena within the medium. By 2015, when Zhang Zhaoying graduated from the Académie royale des Beaux-Arts and returned from Belgium, a new batch of artists was emerging on the art market. The ambiguously defined term "new painting" became a hot topic in the art scene and was also quickly adopted by the market, used to denote newly emerging painters born in the 1980s and even the '90s. Objectively speaking, the turbulent history that began in 1978 – the point in time at which new painting became a political possibility – had already come to a close in the first decade of the 21st century. In recent years, although the market has continued to promote emerging painters – Huang Yuxing, born in the 1970s, being a notable example – when analysed from the perspectives of history and the evolution of the media, this period of market popularity for abstract works has also been a low point for contemporary painting in China. It is worth noting, then, that the works of Zhang Zhaoying and other artists born in the 1980s and '90s like him are forming a new chapter in the history of this form of art. This is not to say that the work of this newest generation of artists is not connected to history. To the contrary, the decisive efforts of many artists in this field over the past four decades have provided the very foundation for a renewed contemporary language, allowing a young generation, free of systemic limitations, to engage in new experiments within a new globalised era.

Rooted in historical logic, an analysis of the context of Zhang Zhaoying's generation of artists is an important pathway to understanding today's young painters.

Those who have experience or basic knowledge of the twenty-seven years of Chinese history from 1949 to 1976 will know that when Chinese artists (represented by Wu Guanzhong) advocated for "formal beauty" and "abstract beauty" in the 1980s, it was not due to the influence of Clement Greenberg's views, but was rooted in the unique historical context. In this historical context, the constant debates about such artistic issues as "form" and "abstraction" did not follow the same linguistic progression as it did in European modern painting – for example, it was not the kind of linear thread from Courbet to Manet, Monet, Matisse, Kandinsky, and Dalí seen in European modern painting. When painter Wu Guanzhong proposed the question of so called "formal beauty", it was nothing more than painters – at this time they represented virtually all artists – having experienced cultural repression for too long, making a reserved confession to their yearning for freedom. The difference from the earlier historical circumstances was that Wu Guanzhong and the other defenders of "form" and "beauty" were not branded rightists, anti-party clique or bourgeois artists. They did not lose their physical freedom, and in fact their call for freedom sparked criticism of the despotic era and came to shape a new political and social context. At virtually the same time, backed by the sentiments of Scar Art's "exposure" of political darkness, and modernist appeals such as the *Stars Art Exhibition*, all of the ideas and expressions not in keeping with "laudatory" art and its corresponding system of thinking began to sprout like spring shoots after the rain. These artistic ideas and modes quickly gained partial political legitimacy. During this time, the nationwide criticisms of spiritual pollution and bourgeois liberalisation that emerged in 1984 and 1987 had a repressive influence on modern art. These two official ideological suppression campaigns, however, can be seen as intra-party conceptual conflicts and strategic reform initiatives. Overall, no matter how severe the inertia of the old ideology, there was no wavering from the theme of reform, and the liberation of ideas was a legitimate political expression in the 1980s. As a result, Western philosophy, politics, literature, art, religion, and other forms of humanities became a massive force for a change in the old ideological logic. Gradually, many artists born in the 1950s and '60s no longer followed or employed the official artistic thinking and methods of their predecessors before 1976.

After 1987, the art world began discussing the true place of the soul, and what the new linguistic logic of art would be. "Neo-classicalism", "purified language" and "the great spirit" were the key words of the day. Artists and critics, however, did not reach a consensus on what constituted the future of art. The Tiananmen Square Incident of 1989 ended modernist efforts in art. And yet, once this Pandora's box of ideas was opened, the resulting effects were unstoppable. The Tiananmen Square Incident of 1989, however, demonstrated the severity of systemic power.

Another equally important event was Deng Xiaoping's speech on the occasion of his southern tour, the core of which was that the economic reforms must continue. Deng Xiaoping was of course aware that the June 4th Incident was the result of bourgeois values and ideology, but in order to develop the economy and suit his international political needs, he asked the party and society in general to avoid discussing sensitive political topics such as the differences between capitalism and socialism, thereby placing once sharp ideological conflicts on ice. The national leadership instructed the people to continue implementing the guiding principles of the Third Session of the 11th Party Congress – to develop the national economy. As a result, official art media did not engage in criticism of modernism, and the market opened up space for life. The market economy society launched an entirely new operating model of artistic production, just as described in the foreword to the privately organised Guangzhou Biennial:

> *In terms of the operating economic background,*
> *investment has replaced the patronage of the past; in terms*
> *of operating subject, private enterprises have replaced*
> *the art institutions of the past; in terms of operating formalities,*
> *legally binding contracts have replaced the memorandums*
> *of the past; in terms of operating academic background, juries*
> *of critics have replaced the artist-run selection committees*
> *of the past; in terms of operating objectives, comprehensive*
> *effectiveness across the economic, social, and academic*
> *spheres has replaced the monolithic, narrow, and endlessly*
> *contentious artistic success. These characteristics of*
> *the Biennial demonstrate the fact that the Chinese art history*
> *of the 1990s is now fully under way.*

This was an operational strategy for art rooted in market economics thinking, demonstrating that the Chinese art ecosystem had begun to accept the conceptual changes of market economics or consumer society. As a result, modernist essentialism was dispelled, and metaphysical concepts and discursive systems lost their influence. This was precisely the environment which produced the representative artists of Cynical Realism so familiar in the West – Fang Lijun, Liu Wei, Yue Minjun, Yang Shaobin, and the others. Meanwhile, artists such as Wang Guangyi in Wuhan, as well as Li Shan and Yu Youhan in Shanghai, took a skeptical, satirical attitude toward familiar images and signs as they rearranged them without historical logic, cutting off the logic and context of historical images. This is a case of the use of historical and current images preceding Zhang Zhaoying's generation. For instance, in the *Great Criticism* series, Wang Guangyi juxtaposed Cultural Revolution imagery with capitalist signs, semi-consciously producing a semiotic symbol: this is today's China. Their works show that artists had begun to choose Chinese signs, and that painting had shifted from the modernism of the 1980s to appropriation and semiotics.

The appropriation of historical images became an important model for a new generation of artists. Yue Minjun's "grin" ignored the anger and unconscious of the modernism that came before, but did this artist's production of a "grin" amount to discarding his individual standpoint? It would be better to ask, what is the basis of a standpoint? This attitude legitimised the exaggeration and alteration of images for Zhang Zhaoying's generation. Having endured the purgatory of modernism, Zhang Xiaogang has constantly pondered whether we can abandon our responsibility to inquire. In historical films, he discovered the rewriting that results from time and distance, and discovered that the reevaluation of history can serve as a method for escaping essentialist inquiry. Due to complex psychological motives and experiences, Zhang Xiaogang filtered out the expressive logic of Western contemporary art – demonstrating to his generation the importance of maintaining consciousness and inquiry. As one of the earlier painters to employ Expressionist vocabulary, Zhou Chunya's answer was to provide an entirely new definition of "temperament" not subject to the constraints of any traditional thinking. The slightly younger Zeng Fanzhi used a special "mask" to symbolise subtle tragicomedy playing out between capitalist market economics and socialist ideology. In his later "chaotic brushstrokes", Zeng told the critics and young artists that so-called "painterliness" should not be a drag on contemporary painting.

Soon after, painters born in the 1960s launched Kitsch Art, which appropriated current images and engaged in other painting experiments that focused on images of everyday life. At the time, many of the painters who broke with the modernist attitude and invented new images were from the southwest. In the late 1990s and early 2000s, the market was particularly fond of southwestern painters from this period, to the point that people would often ask, "why the southwest?" At this time, there were many examples of new painting that cast off realist traditions and modernism. I once wrote in an essay:

> *The place where the term "new painting" applies is in the area of Cynical Realism, Political Pop, and the confluence between them. If we must find a commonality between them, it is this: there is no essentialist inquiry, but there is the revelation of real issues; there are no Western-centric standards, but there are universal globalised attitudes; they no longer attack specific targets, but they do raise conflicts through juxtaposition; they do not discuss what art is, but they do hold fast to art-historical stances; there is no singular interpretation, but there are distinct concepts.*[1]

The symbolic traits of 1990s painting have been considered the outcomes of cynicism, the China card, international coupling, and postcolonialism. In terms of conceptual and thematic connotations, people tend to sum up these phenomena as painting that plays the China card, while in terms of language and technique, it has been regarded as a rejection of traditional "painterliness" for an emphasis on conceptuality

1   "The Historical Context of New Painting" (2007), in *The Landscape of Art History* (Beijing: The Commercial Press, 2023).

and semiotics. At the same time, people noticed that the simple conceptual dichotomies and tastes such as East and West, tradition and modernity, national and global that had been so frequently recurring in the 1980s completely disappeared from the artistic concepts and styles of the new artists.

After 2000, influenced by Western ideas and grounded in a deeper understanding of Chinese reality, the tendency towards free painting was in full swing. A richer array of individuality and questions emerged in the works of different painters, marked by great vitality. What many critics in the new century described as "conceptual painting" actually amounted to artists setting out from a more individualised starting point, except that now the freedom of thought was fully open. For many artists, painting had become part of a unified whole of individual unfolding, alongside video, installation, and sculpture. This was the precondition that made it possible for the critics to once again begin using the traditional analytical vocabulary of painting, terms such as "allegory", "symbol", "expression", and "depiction". When confronting the grand and microscopic narratives, essential and phenomenal depiction, social and psychological issues, signs and expressiveness, human and individual experience, this vocabulary allowed them to nimbly adjust the scope and direction of analysis. The themes, techniques and resources of painting were fully engaged.

Today, the point of departure and linguistic possibilities of new painting stem from the stimulation and acceleration of globalisation. Painting today has become a vital product of the complex issues of the era of globalisation. Unlike the metaphysical and the macroscopic, its effect has been to compress the artist's abstract conceptual logic, and to shift the question to specific phenomena taking place around us. For instance, *Titan's Banquet*, which Zhang Zhaoying completed in 2013, appears to be a sweeping scene, but in fact the artist intentionally used an apparently complex image to respond to the abstract painting of this period. His point of departure is the question of form in art itself, but he has woven a hypothetical dramatic scene, drawing the viewer's attention to a game of visual play. Though during these years Li Songsong, as well as the northeastern painters Qin Qi and Ji Dafang, also had an impact on the art scene through the defamiliarisation of images and scenes, Zhang Zhaoying's works from this period already clearly reveal his innate sensitivity towards image and form. The point of departure for this sweeping composition is actually very specific.

The *Cathedral* series, completed in 2016, is evidently the result of the influence of European painting and the cultural environment Zhang Zhaoying encountered while studying art in Belgium. There may be a question about how much internal basis Europeans have today for their religious faith, but religious traditions and their cultural power certainly remain a strong presence. The artist has interpreted this power as a spiritual need, and not necessarily a specific religious faith. The unconsciously altered *Cathedral* form serves as an expression by the artist on questions of spirituality. In this series, Zhang Zhaoying's choice of technique is evidently a parody of the tendency towards constant abstraction in painting. In works such as *Museum of Treasures*, he likewise uses toys reminiscent of cartoon characters as a playful path of resistance against pure formalist painting. *Mystery Party*, which was featured in the Anren Biennale, makes wholesale use of compositions and source material from European painting history (the Ghent Altarpiece) as a metaphor for an unsettling imagined reality, the adoration of the mystic lamb revealing a scene of crisis. To a great extent, this work by Zhang Zhaoying (as well as the earlier *Museum of Treasures No. 4*) presaged the arrival of the Covid pandemic in 2019 – the bird-masked physician, the steampunk props, and the viral cells seemed to foretell of complex, unavoidable problems on the horizon for humanity.

His pandemic period works are meditations on the meaning of existence. When a cool, monotone grey becomes the universal perception, the value of life and art is posited anew. In fact, the inner appeal of such artworks as *Lifelong Learning* and *Going to Work* is the artist weaving and positing familiar scenes and figures in search of potential meaning within bleak historical periods.

Unlike earlier straightforward Surrealist painters from the '85 New Wave period, such as Meng Luding, as well as various artists in Nanjing (such as Ren Rong, Xu Yihui, and Xu Lei), Zhang Zhaoying's Surrealist compositions have developed into a complex and comprehensive exercise in iconographic history across time and space. This is particularly manifest in recent works such as *Lifelong Beauty – The Temptation of Giorgio de Chirico*. The starting point for this work was the religious path of the ascetic monk Saint Anthony. The artist hoped to reveal the modern incarnations of medieval puritanical religious views by presenting this path beset by temptations. Along Saint Anthony's path, however, images from Italian metaphysical painter Giorgio de Chirico are laid out like so many stage props: the melancholy street, figure models, and the *Song of Love* transforming the saintly markers of suffering into art historical aspirations. Evidently, the artist's aesthetic response to the temptations of De Chirico is like that of Saint Anthony. De Chirico's compositions and narratives are themselves displays of melancholy and meditative exhortations. Through clearly visible image appropriation, rearrangement and alteration, Zhang Zhaoying illuminates spiritual issues of contemporary society, even the new temptations and desires people face in the 21st century. The artist says, "Society has begun to pay attention to depression, to individual existence, to meditations on the times. From an-

HIS PANDEMIC PERIOD WORKS ARE MEDITATIONS ON THE MEANING OF EXISTENCE. WHEN A COOL, MONOTONE GREY BECOMES THE UNIVERSAL PERCEPTION, THE VALUE OF LIFE AND ART IS POSITED ANEW.

cient times to the present day. Though faith and religion are no longer the mainstream, temptation has never disappeared, and desire comes right behind it. This is the shadow of us all, like a tiny little theatre of the desires of contemporary society."

Due to unique historical context, Zhang Zhaoying's painting inherits the evolutions of Chinese painting across various periods since the 1980s, touching on numerous traits of Realism, Impressionism, Expressionism, Surrealism, and Pop Art, but at the same time, his painting has discarded unitary schemas in painting language, nimbly piecing together a unique methodology of his own, marked by free techniques and highly controlled painting. When we analyse his painting language, it is not difficult to grasp his artistic traits as long as we understand their historical context.

January 28, 2025 (Tuesday)

ZHANG ZHAOYING

works

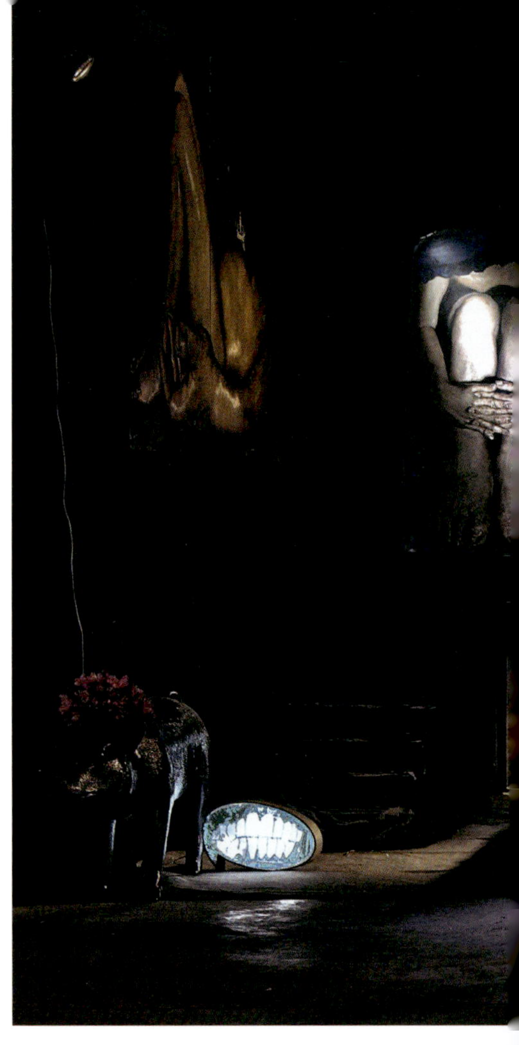

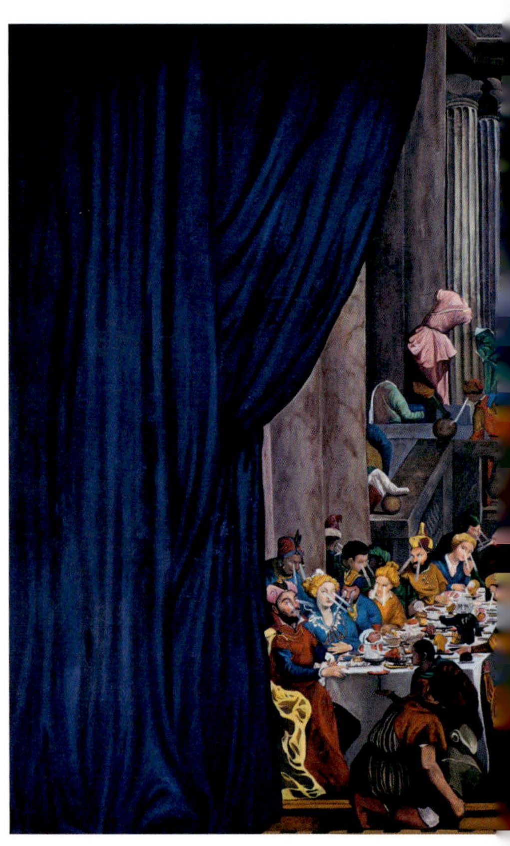

Titan's Banquet, installation view, 2013
Titan's Banquet, 2013   oil on canvas, 120 × 200 cm

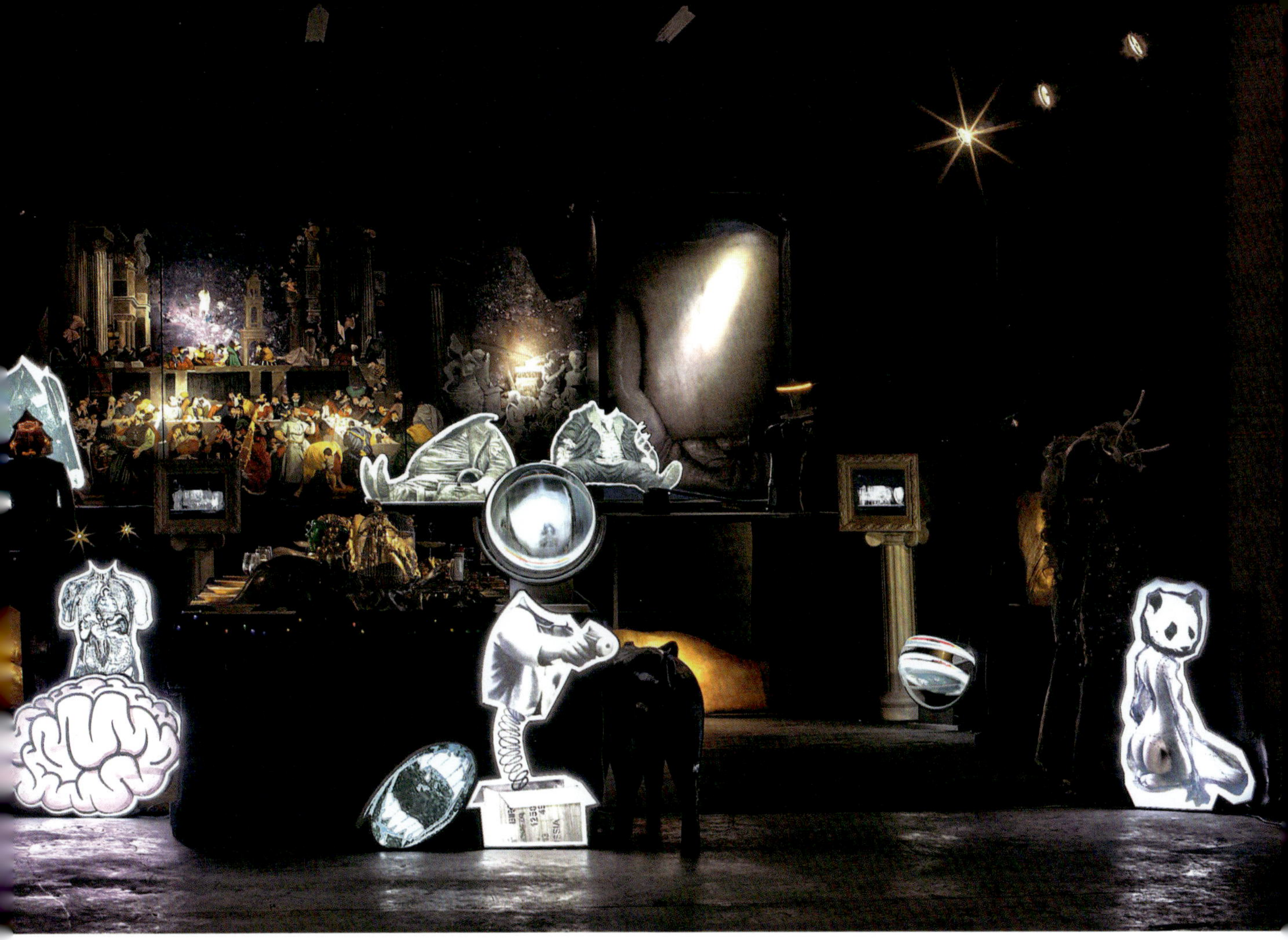

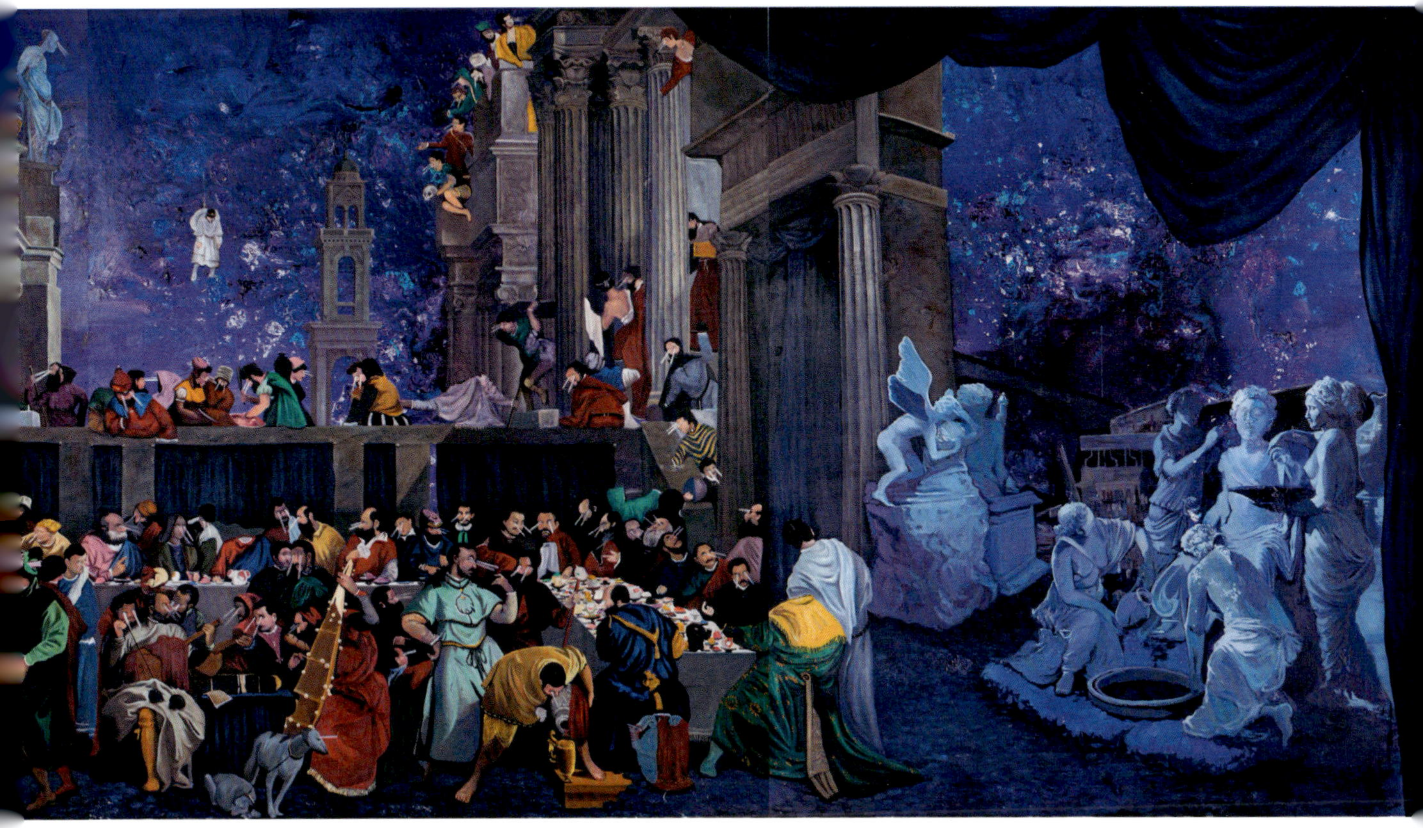

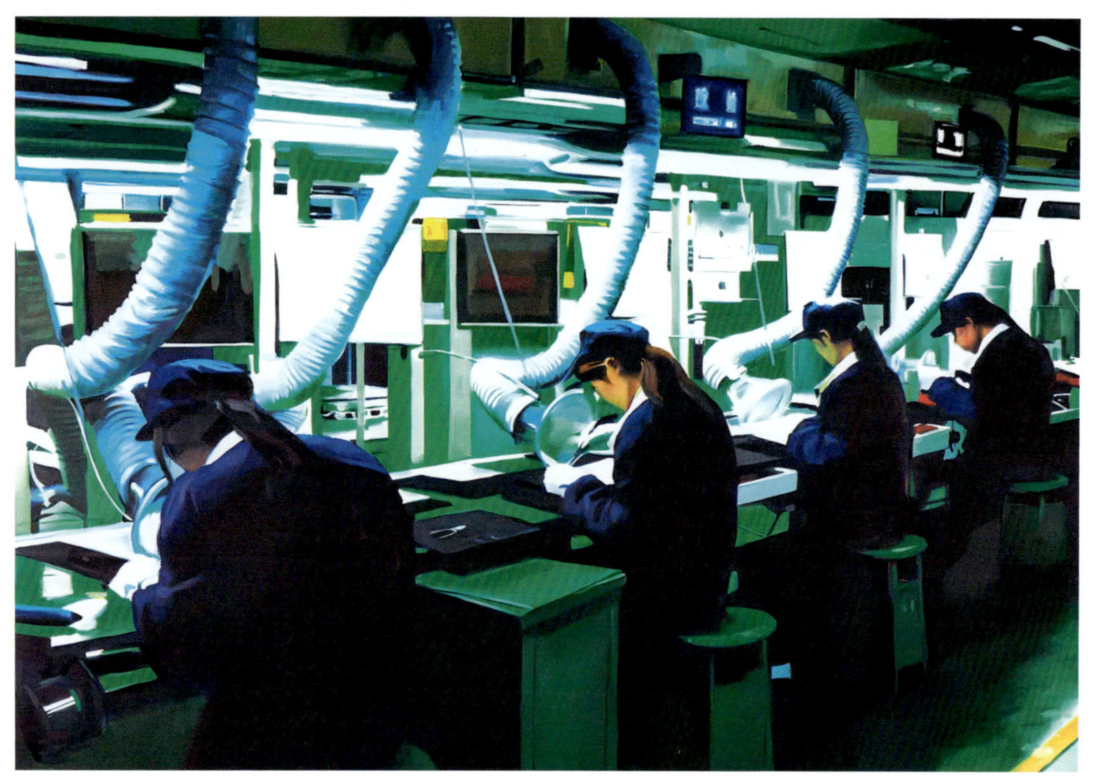

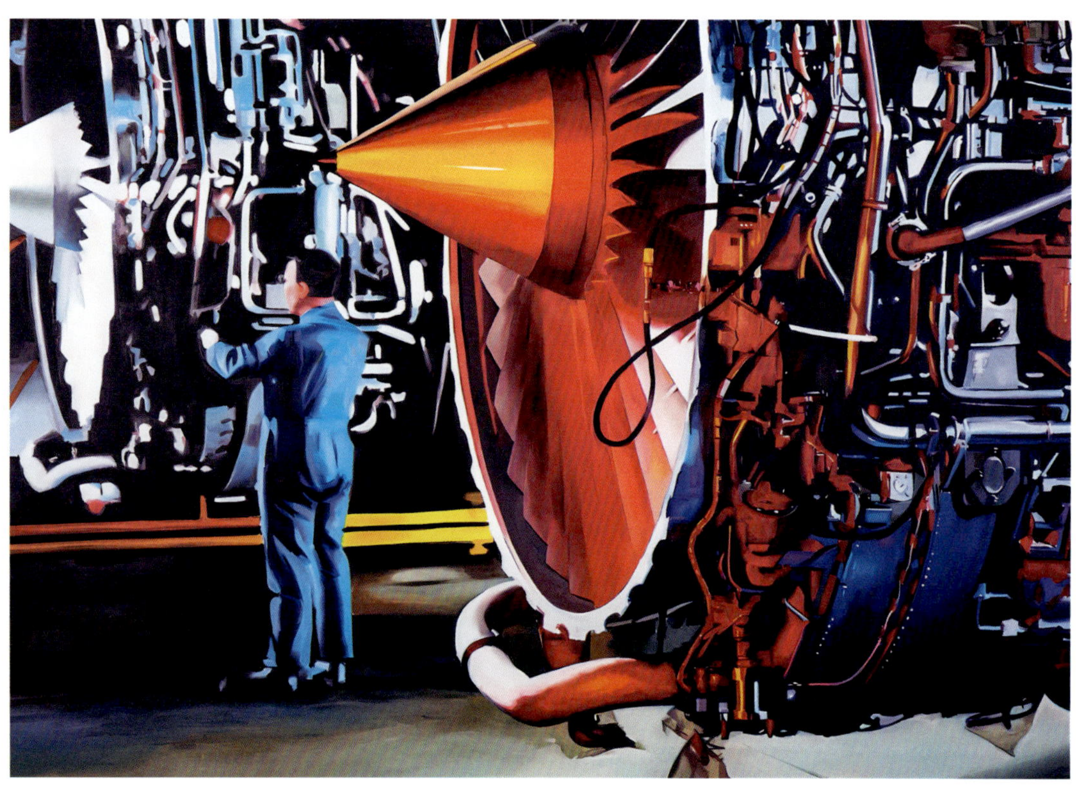

Large-Scale Production No. 1, 2014
oil on canvas, 180 × 250 cm
Large-Scale Production No. 3, 2014
oil on canvas, 180 × 250 cm

Following pages   *One Small Theatre a Day*, 2015–16
oil on canvas, 365 pieces, 30 × 40 cm each

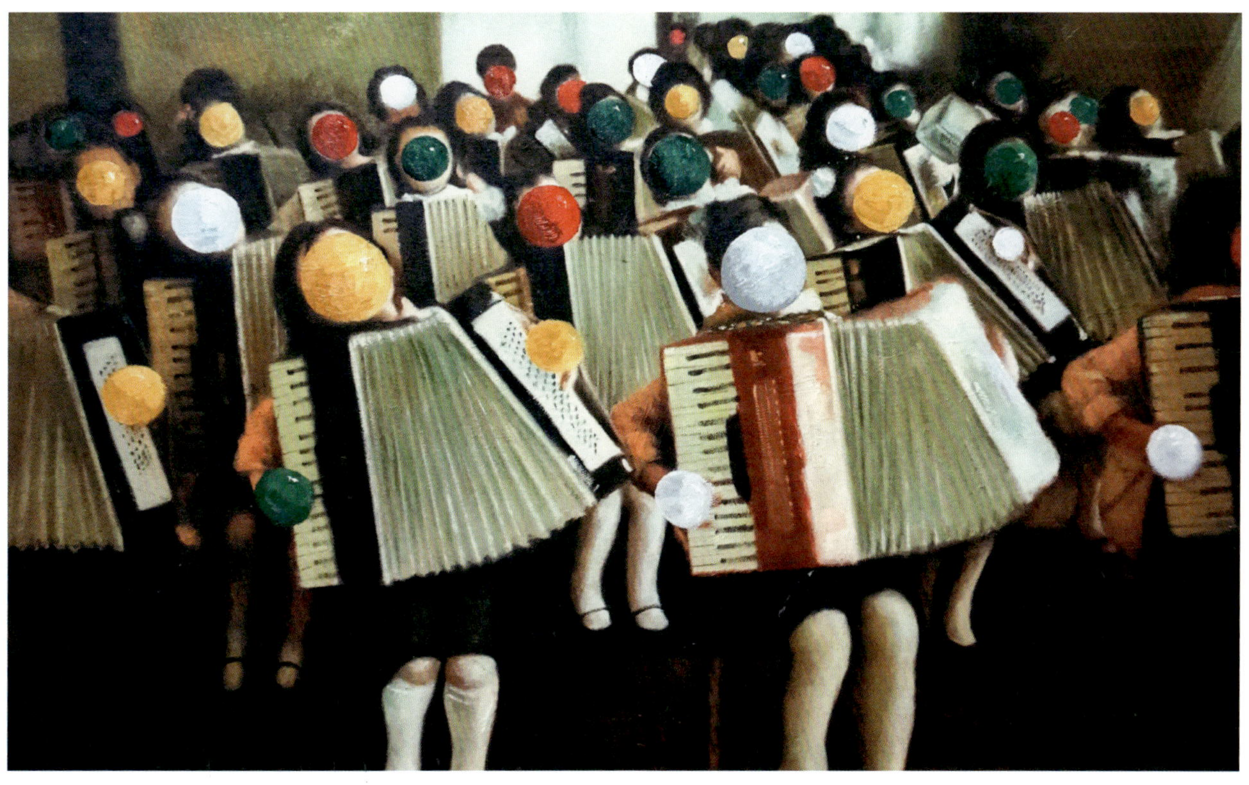

    Custom-Made Youth No. 21, 2015   oil on canvas, 60 × 80 cm

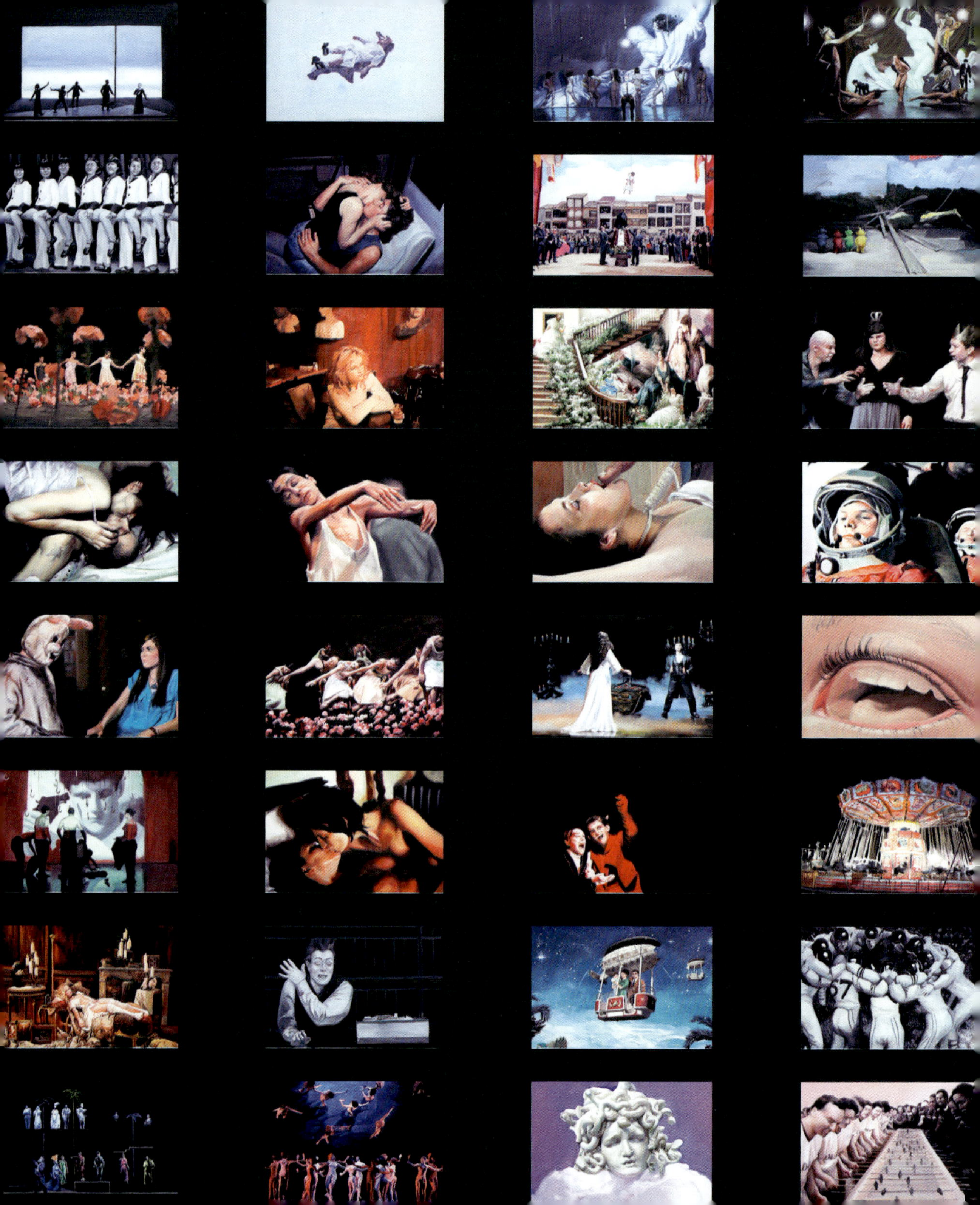

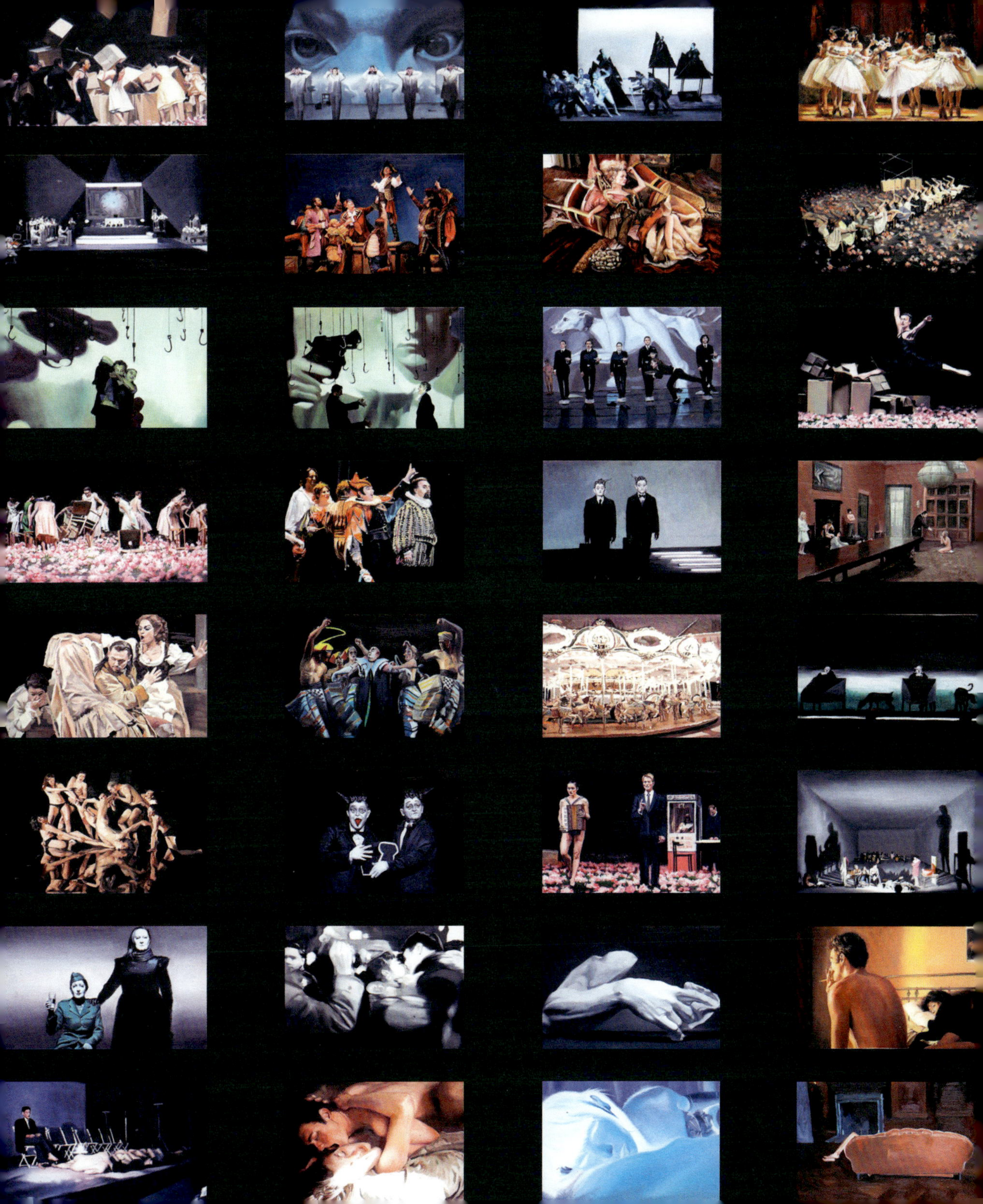

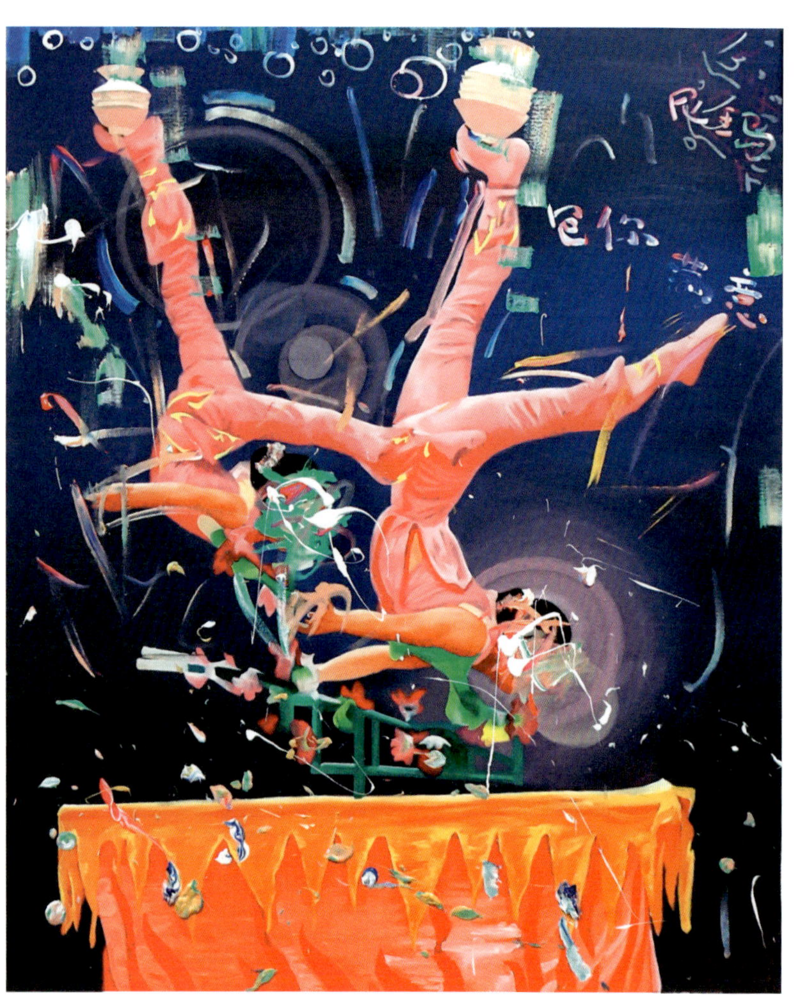

People's Square No. 3, 2016   oil on canvas, 120 × 100 cm   **22**

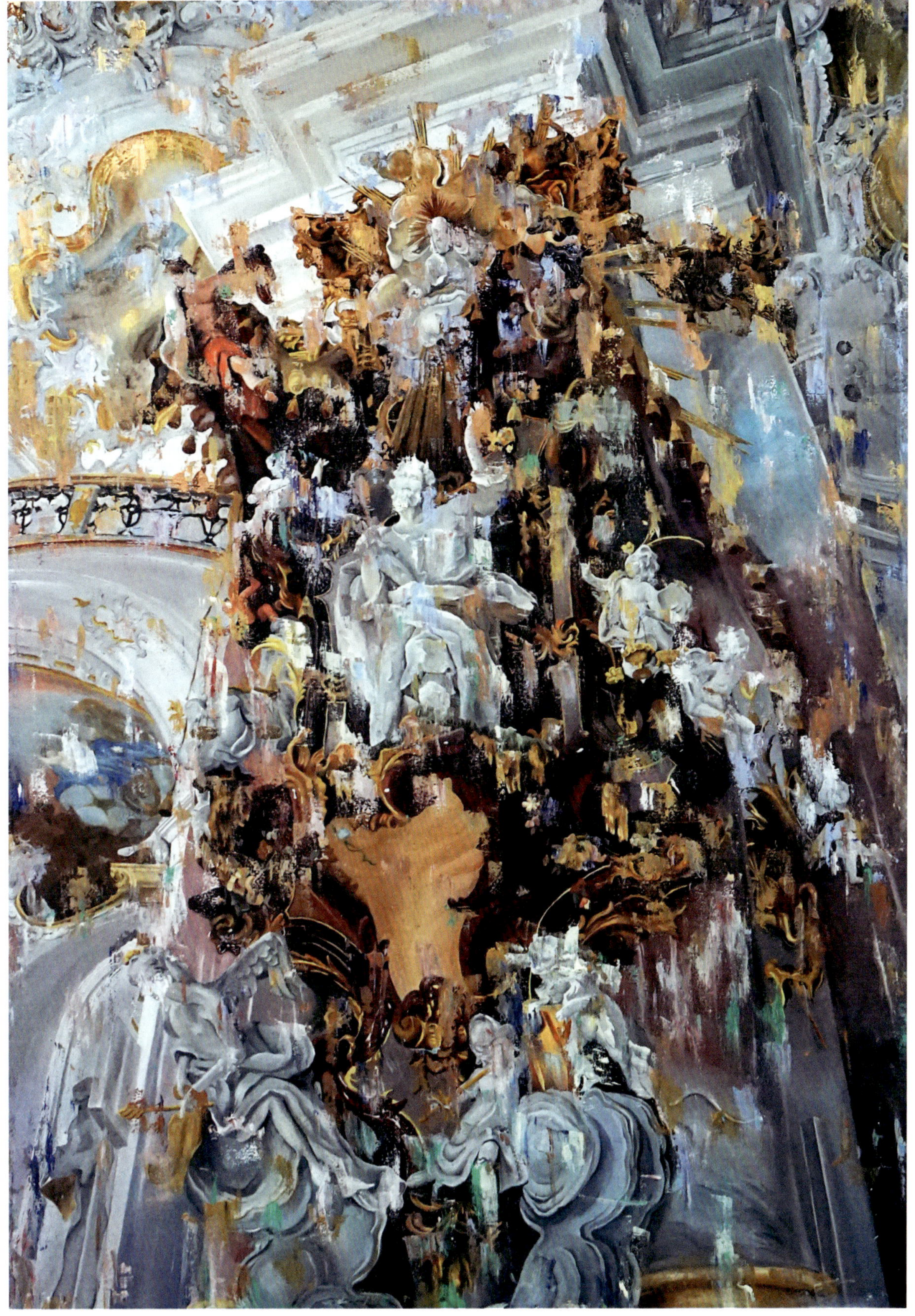

   Revelation, 2016   oil on canvas, 180 × 120 cm

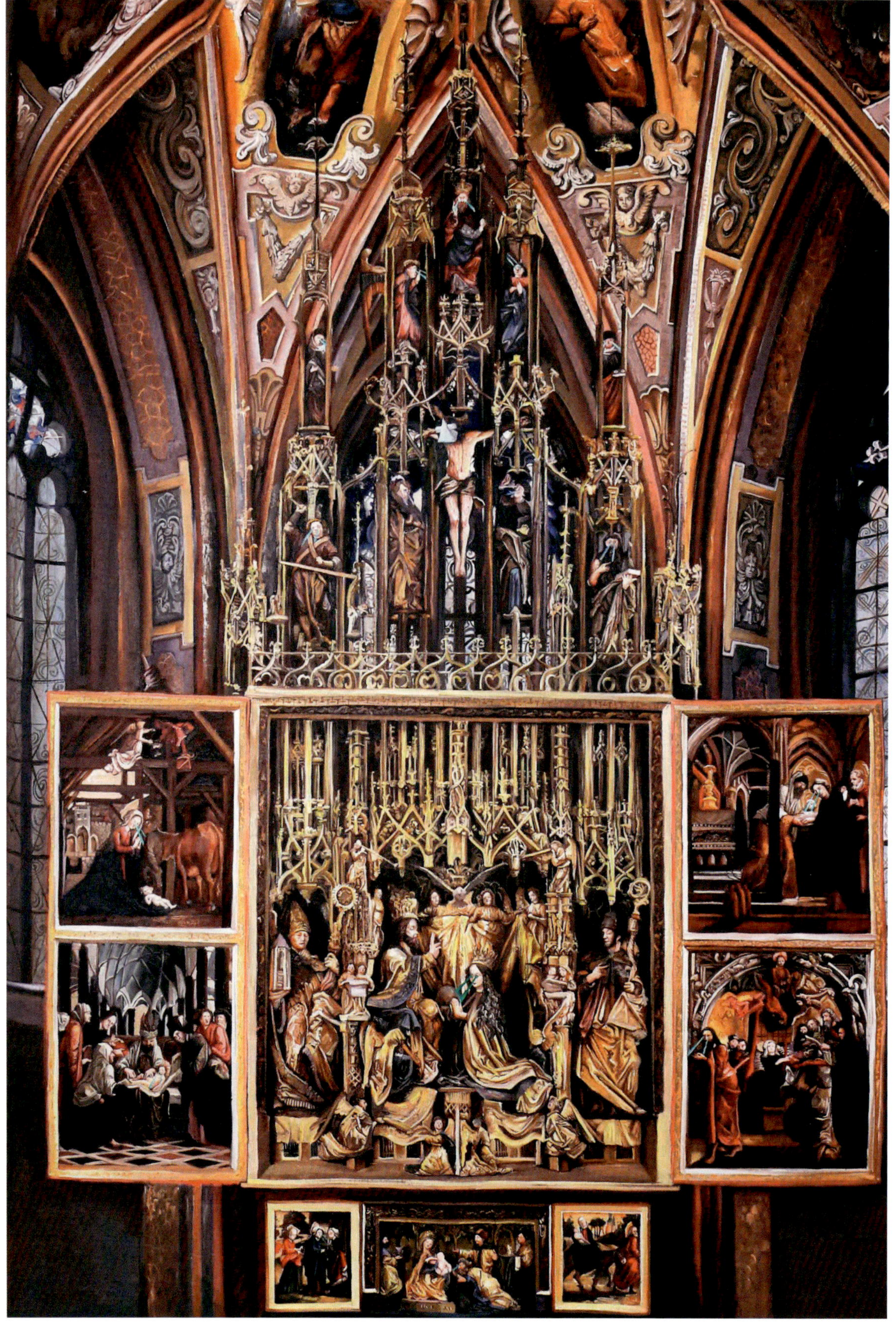

Gothic Biography (Adaptation C), 2016   oil on canvas, 270 × 180 cm   **24**

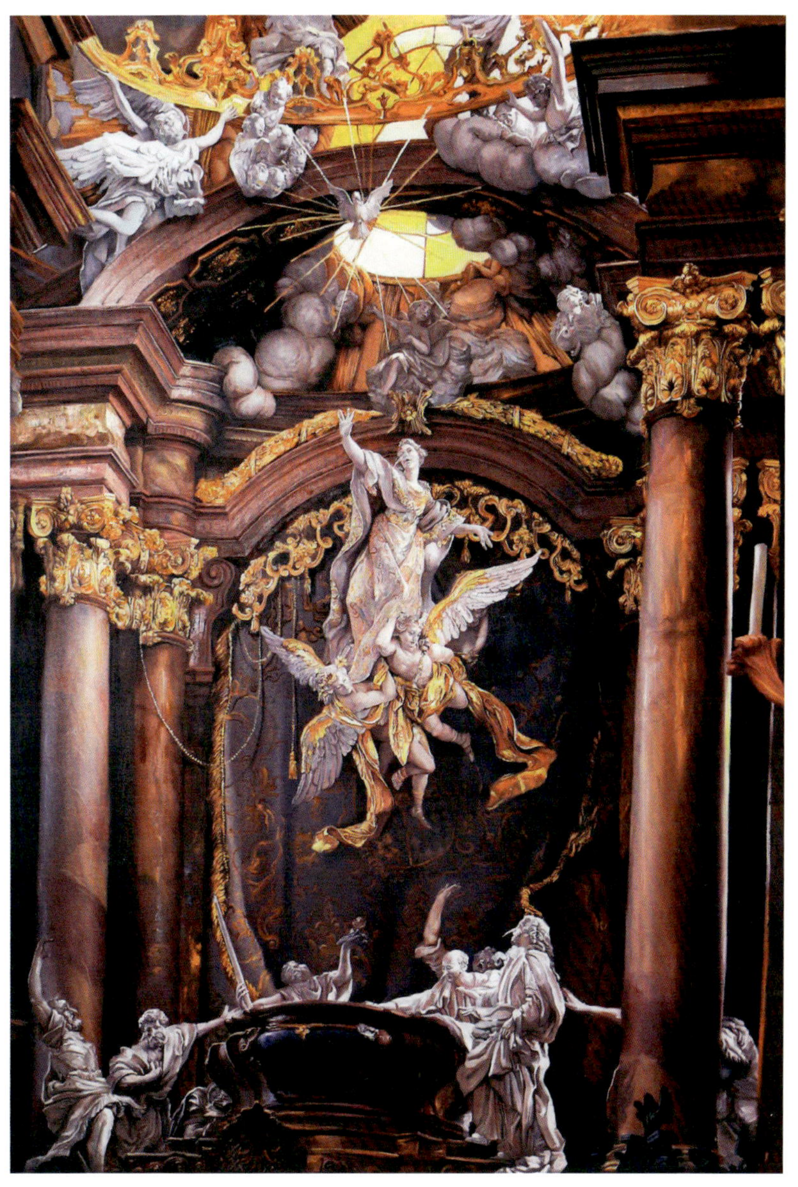

     Gothic Biography (Adaptation E), 2016   oil on canvas, 270 × 180 cm

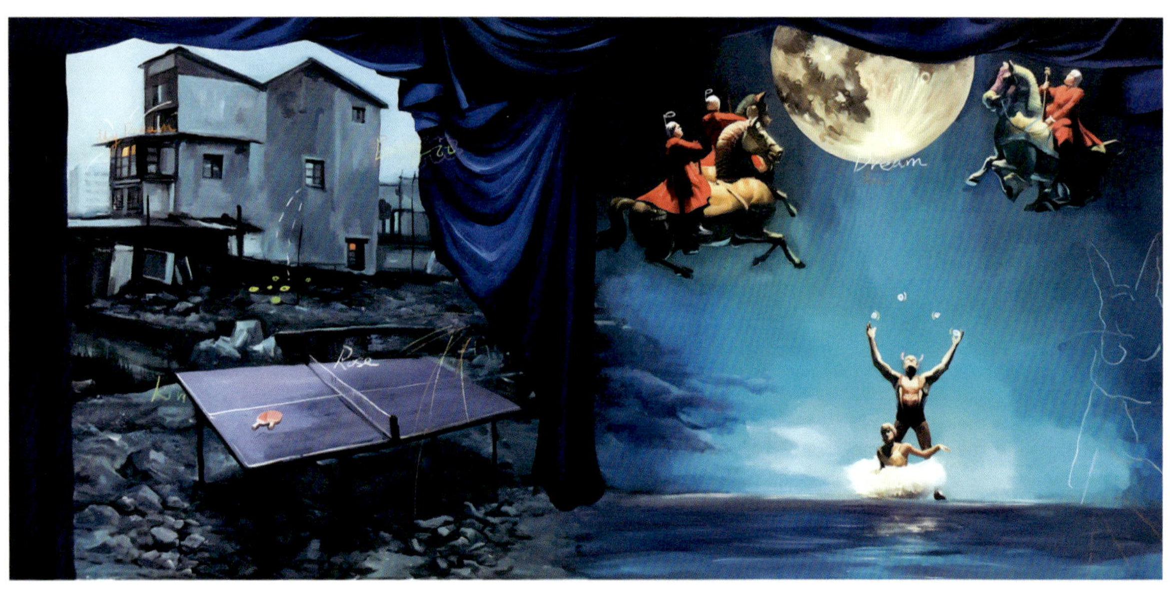

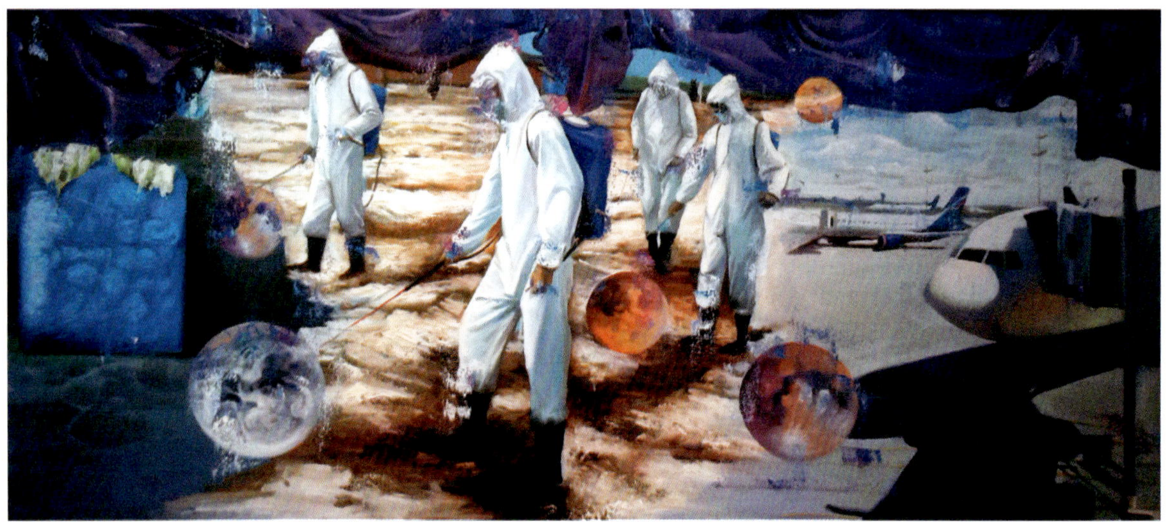

Museum of Treasures No. 1, 2016   oil on canvas, 100 × 200 cm
Museum of Treasures No. 4, 2016   oil on canvas, 100 × 200 cm

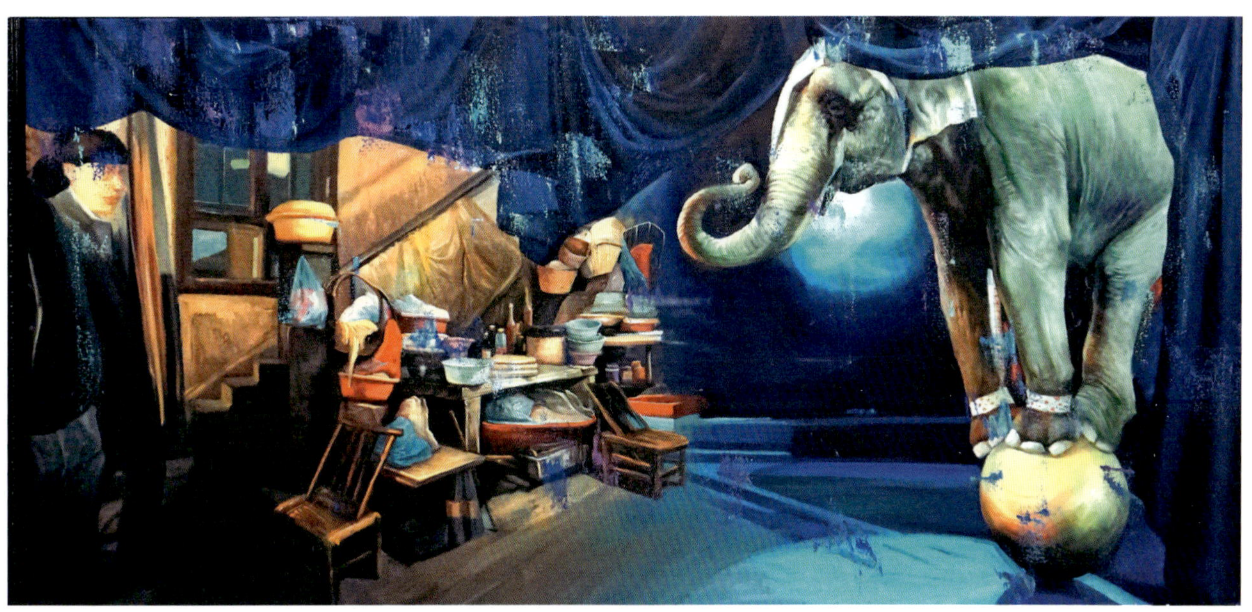

    Museum of Treasures No. 5, 2016   oil on canvas, 100 × 200 cm

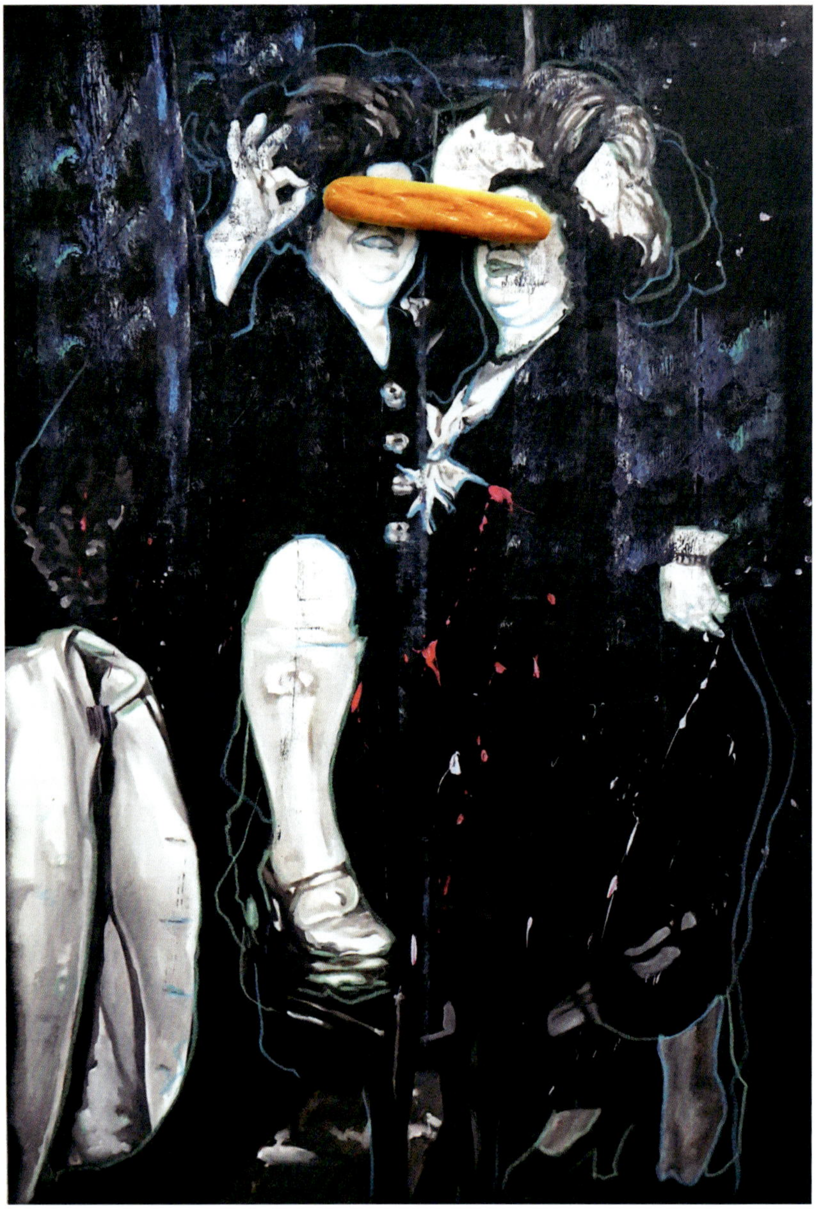

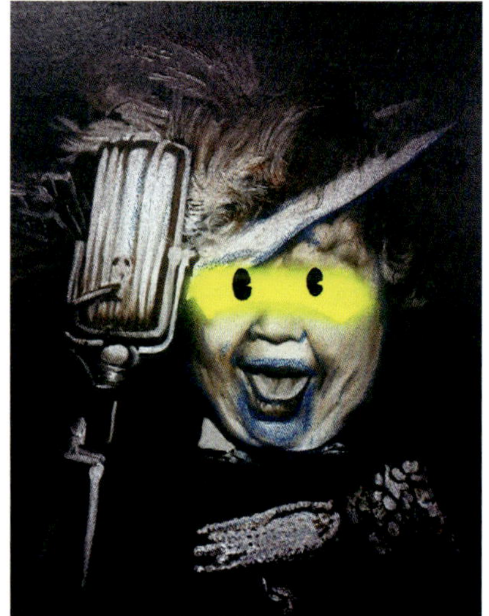

Two and a Half Wealthy Ladies, 2017
oil on canvas, 150 × 100 cm, 40 × 30 cm

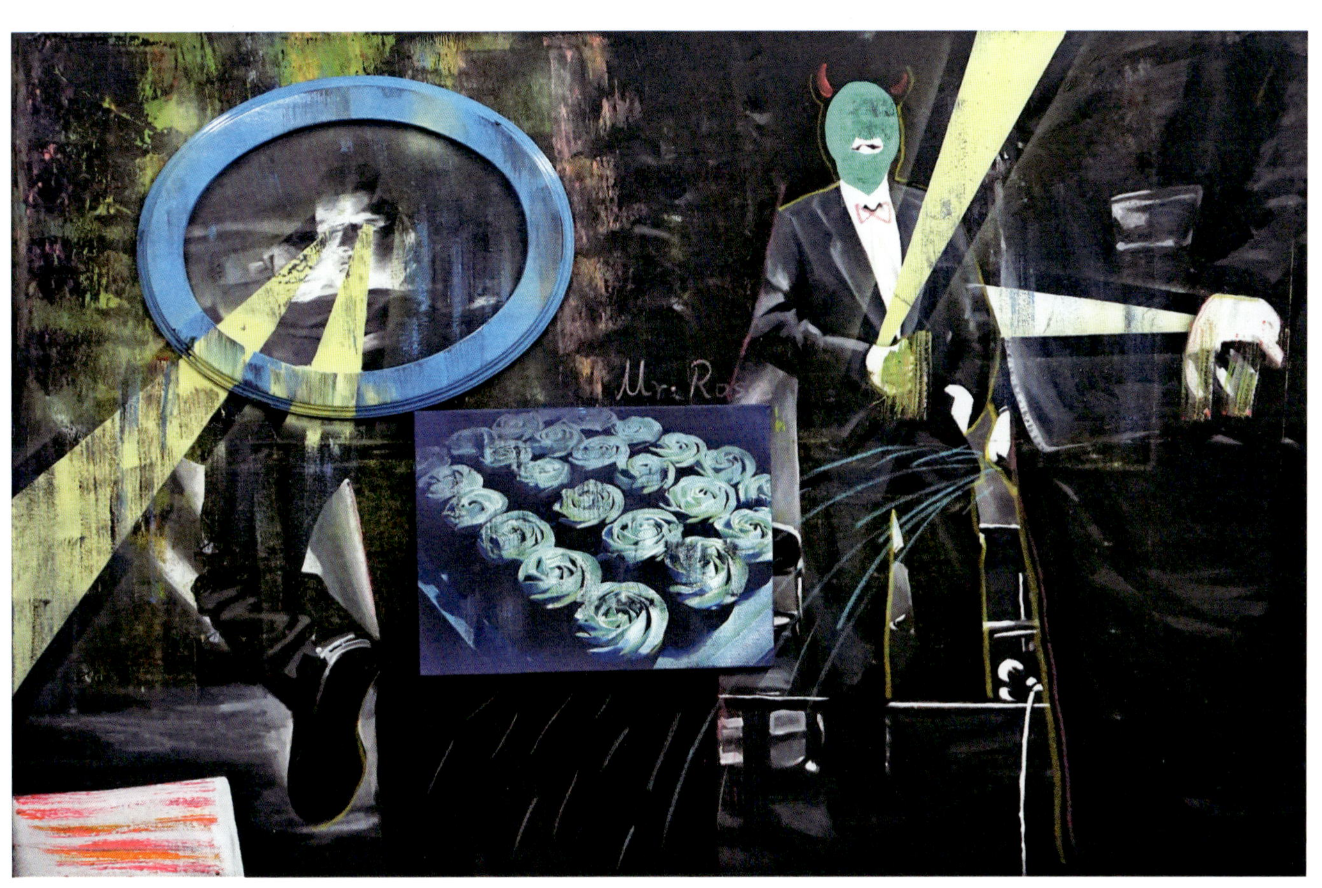

Only When the Lights Are On Can You Find What You Want, 2017
oil on canvas, 100 × 150 cm

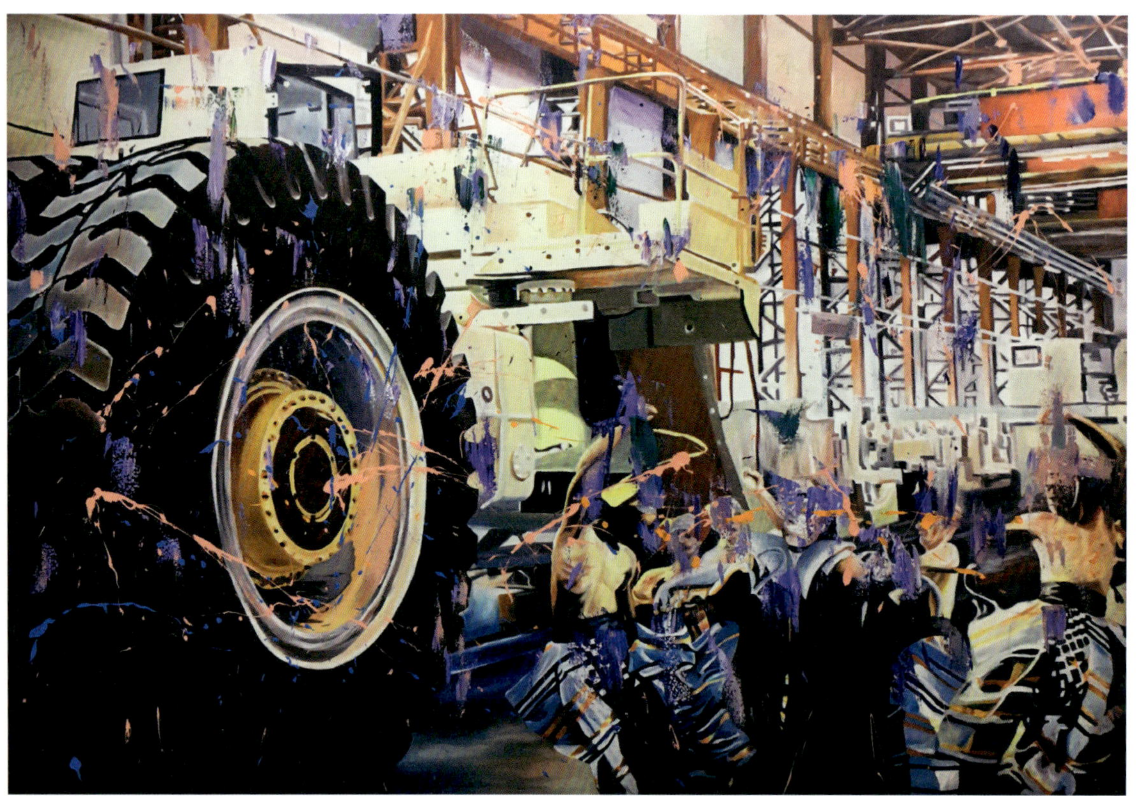

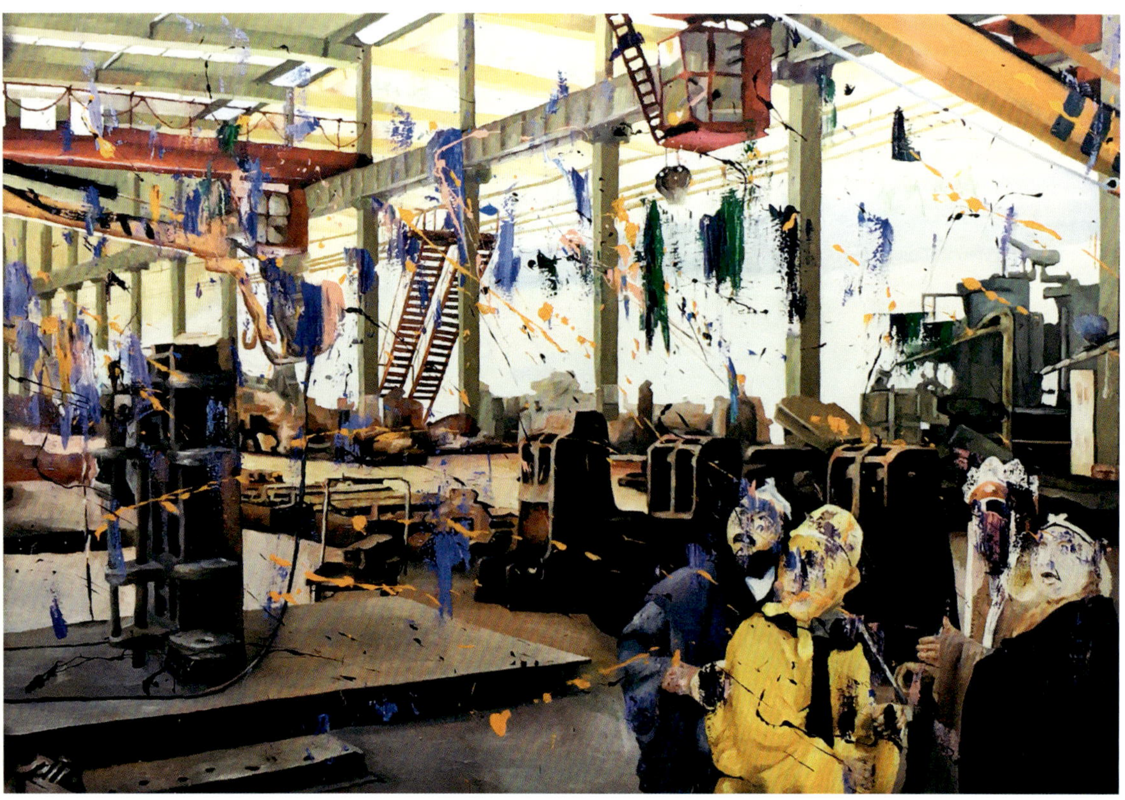

Big Winner of Production No. 6, 2017   oil on canvas, 180 × 250 cm
Big Winner of Production No. 8, 2017   oil on canvas, 180 × 250 cm

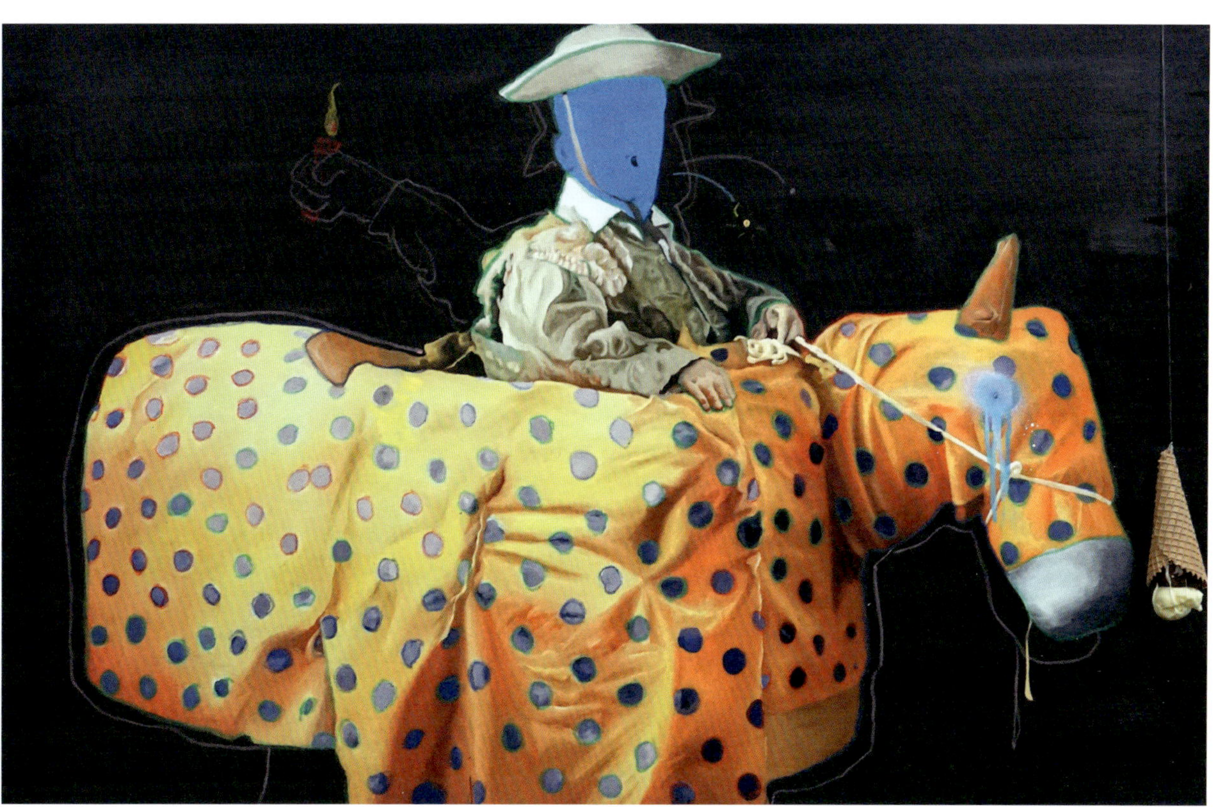

   A Real Horse? Not a Horse!, 2017   oil on canvas, 100 × 150 cm

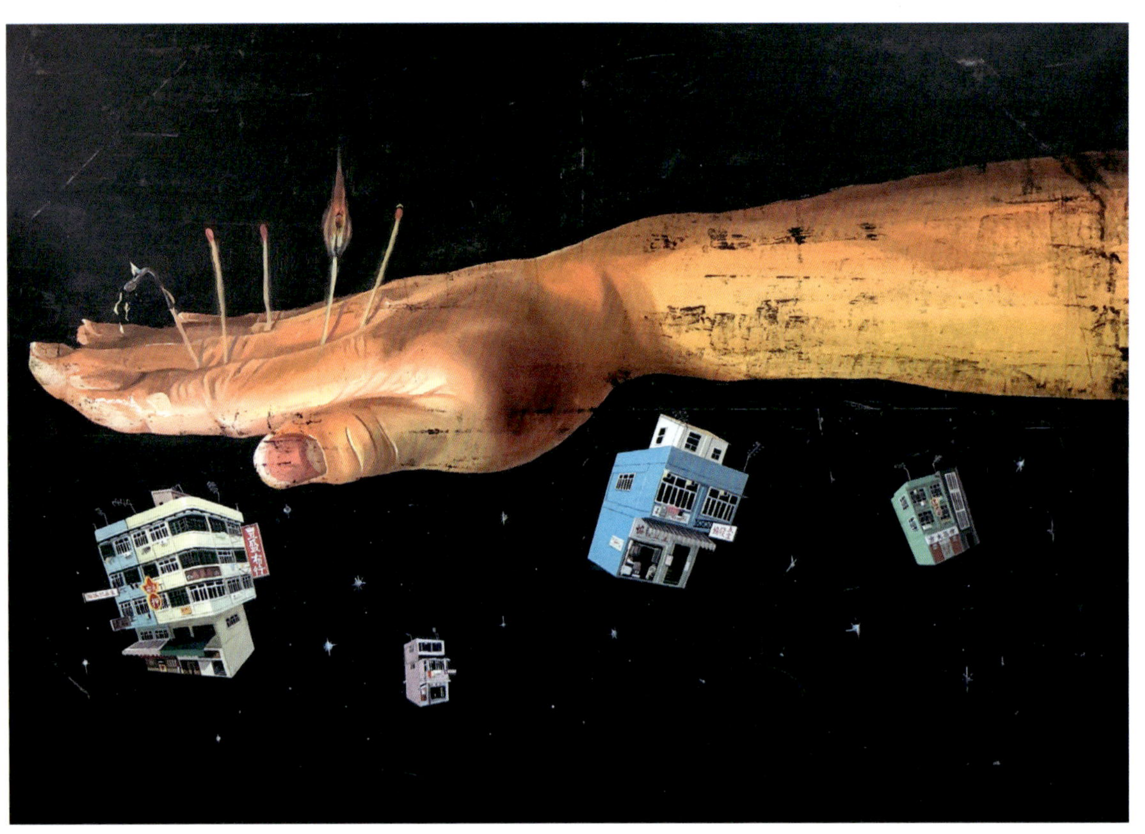

The Hand as Protagonist – Matches, 2017–18
oil on canvas, 120 × 165 cm

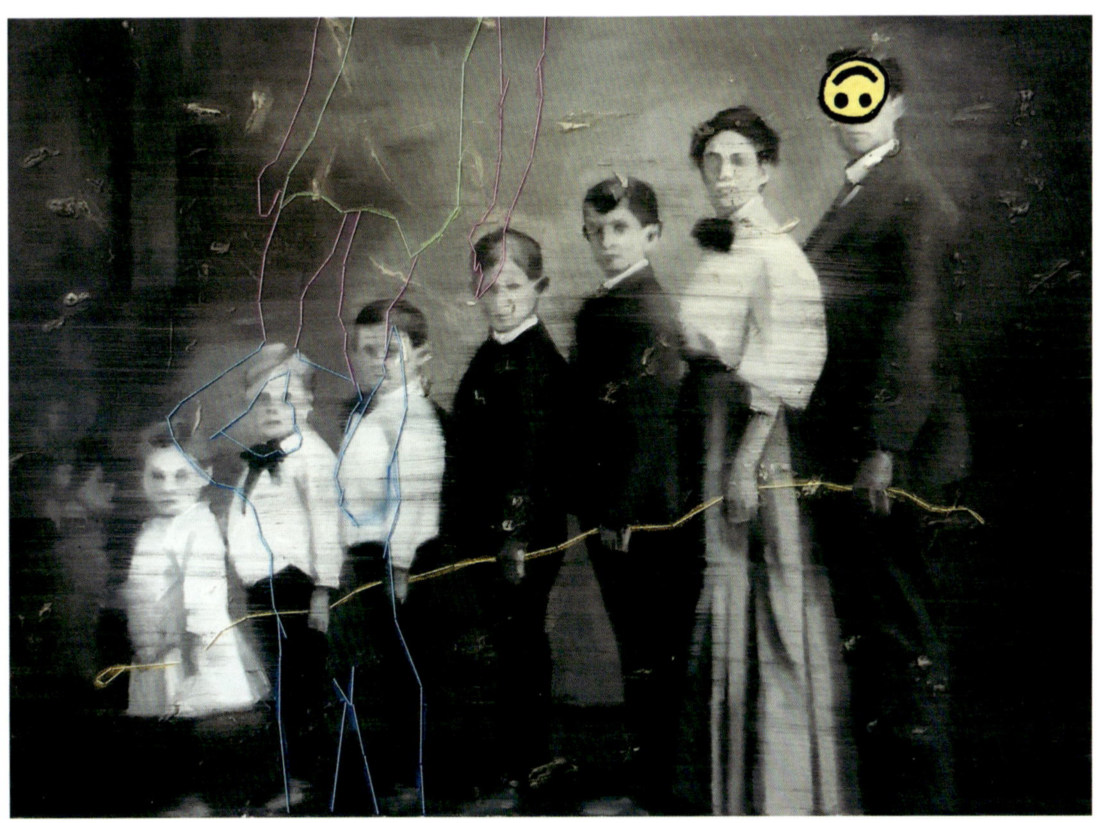

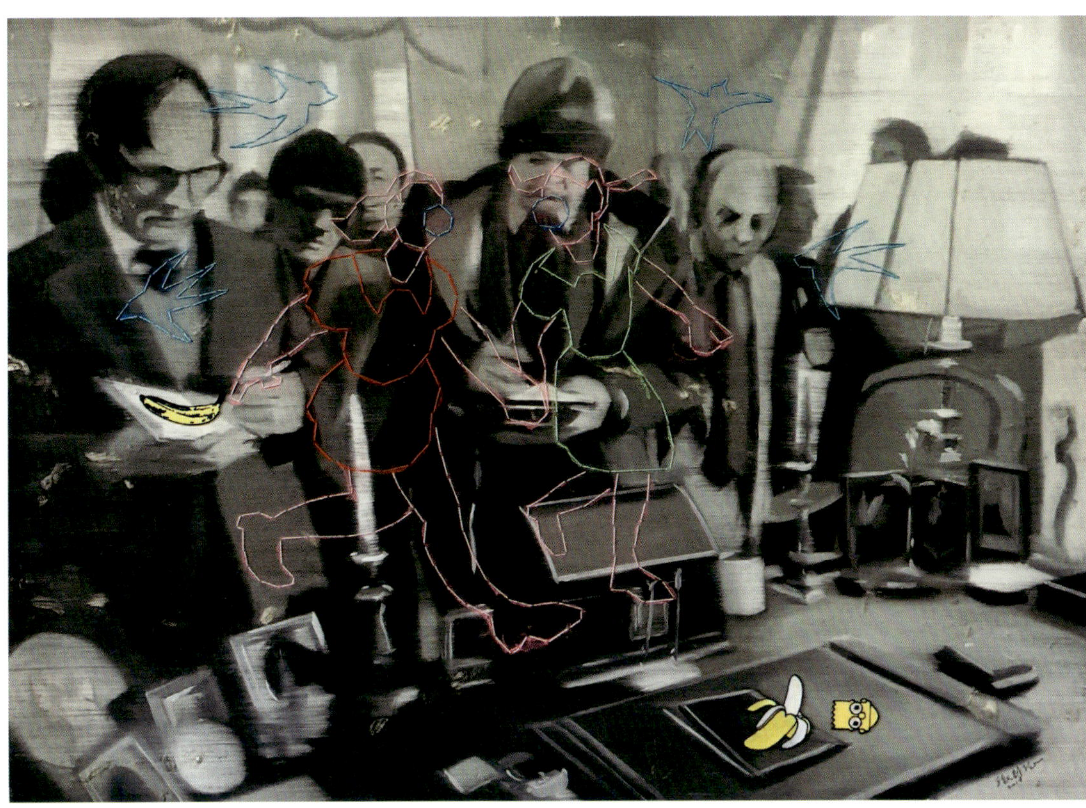

Embroidery Soap Opera – Heritage, 2014 and 2018
oil on canvas and embroidery, 90 × 120 cm
Embroidery Soap Opera – BOSS, 2014 and 2018
oil on canvas and embroidery, 90 × 120 cm

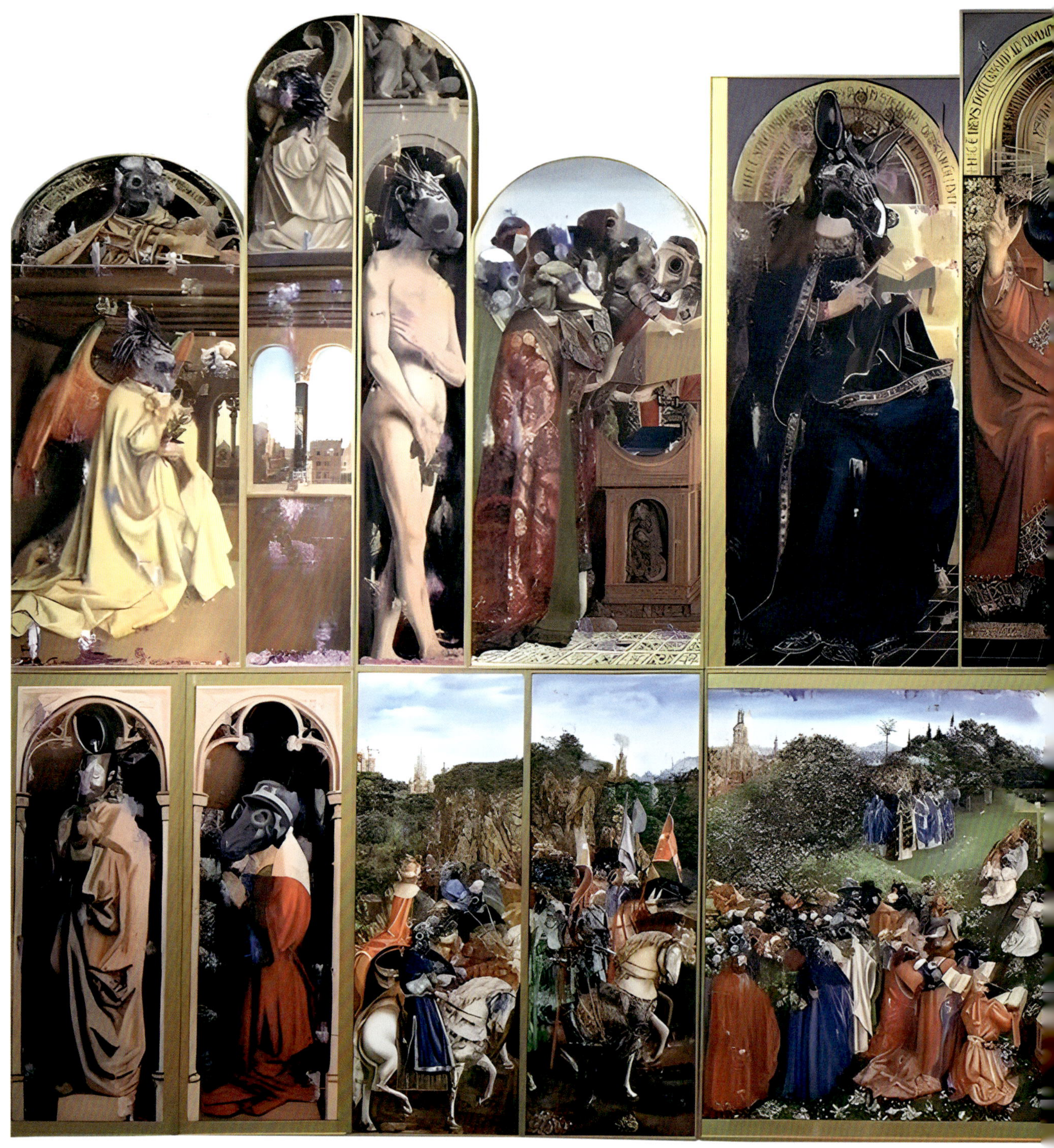

Mystery Party, installation view, 2017   oil and mixed media on canvas, 370 × 570 cm
Collection of Mart – Museo di arte moderna e contemporanea di Trento e Rovereto

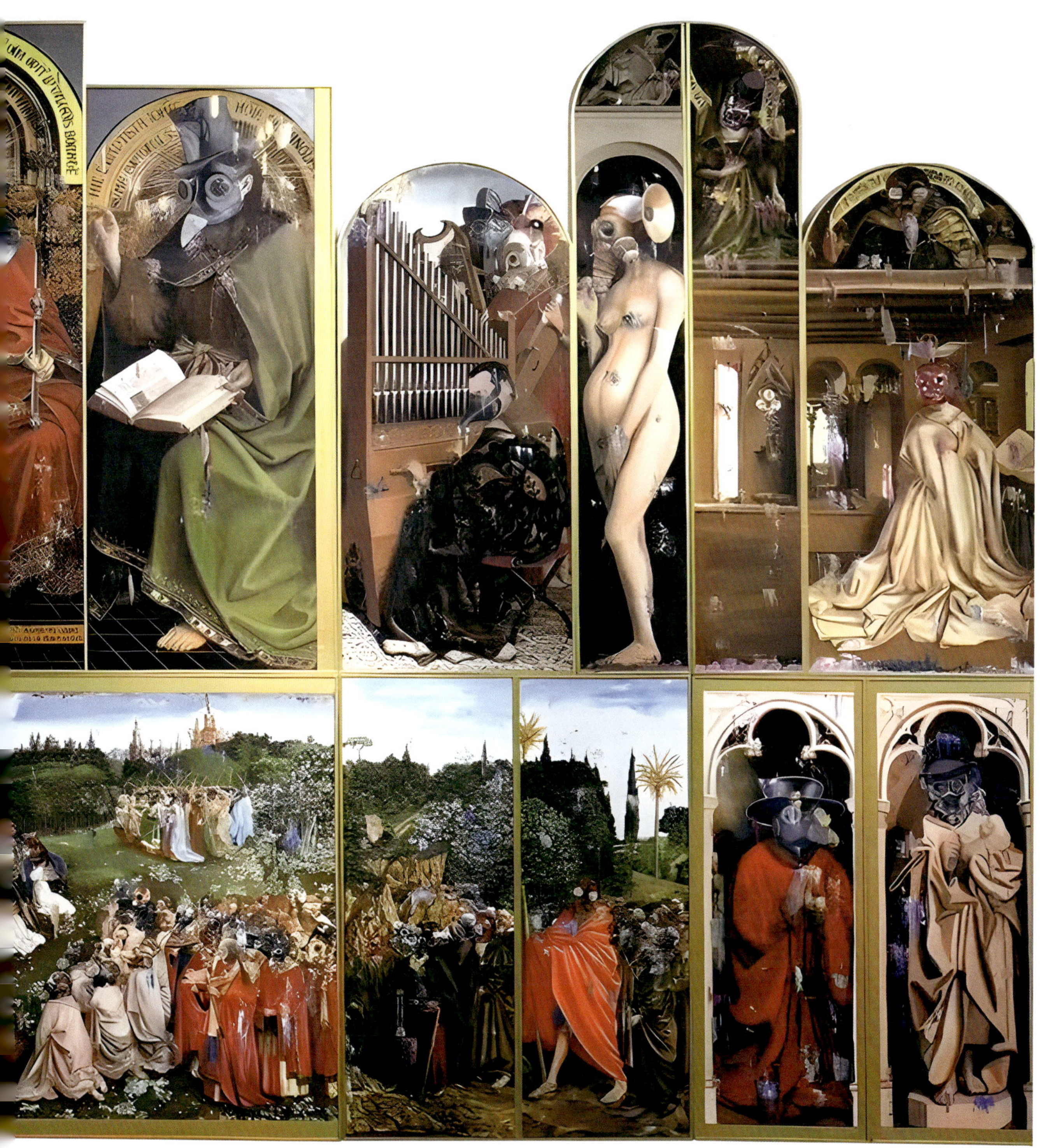

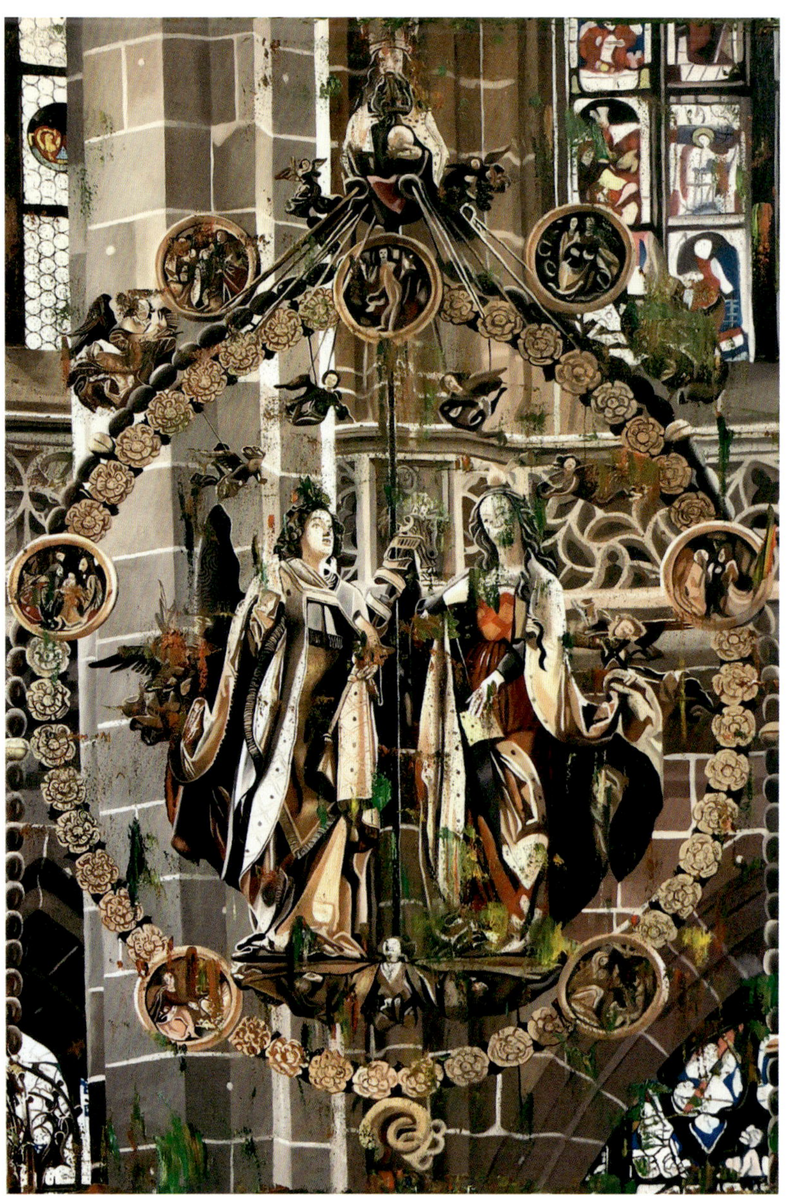

Myth Party - Learn to Fly, 2017-18   oil on canvas, 100 × 60 cm   **36**

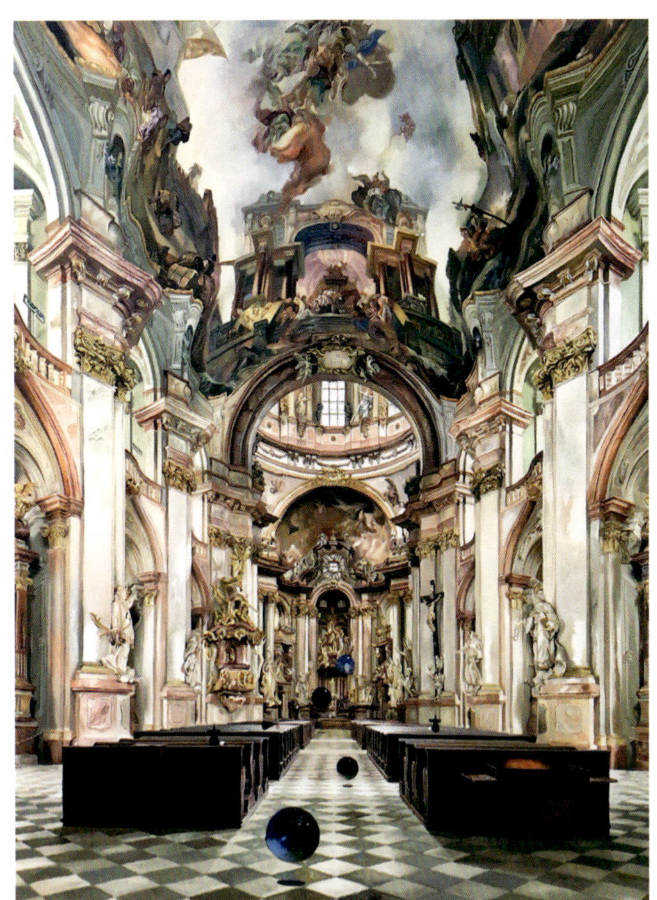
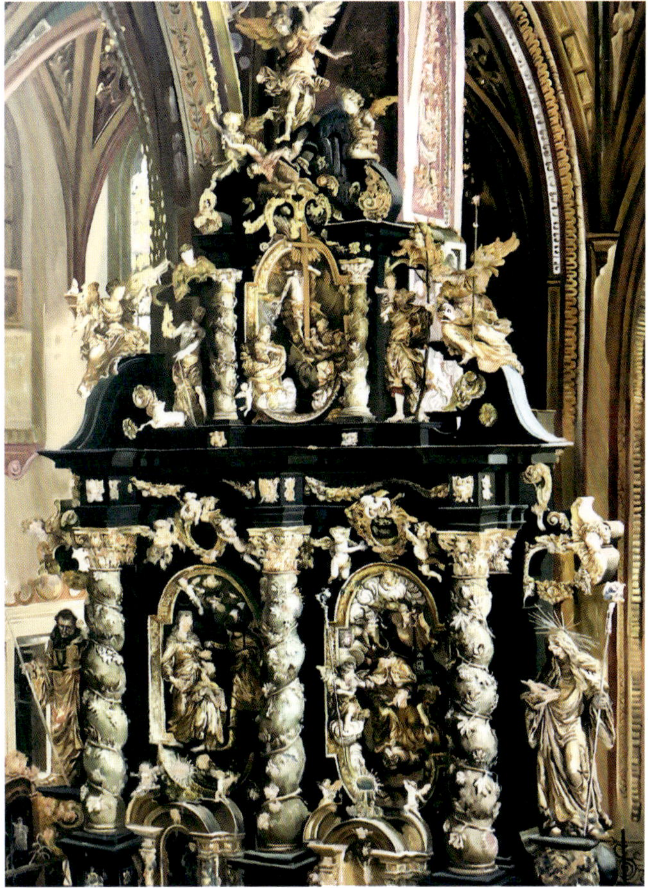

Myth Party – Achievement, 2018–19   oil on canvas, 180 × 118 cm
Myth Party – Light Harvesting, 2018–19   oil on canvas, 180 × 120 cm

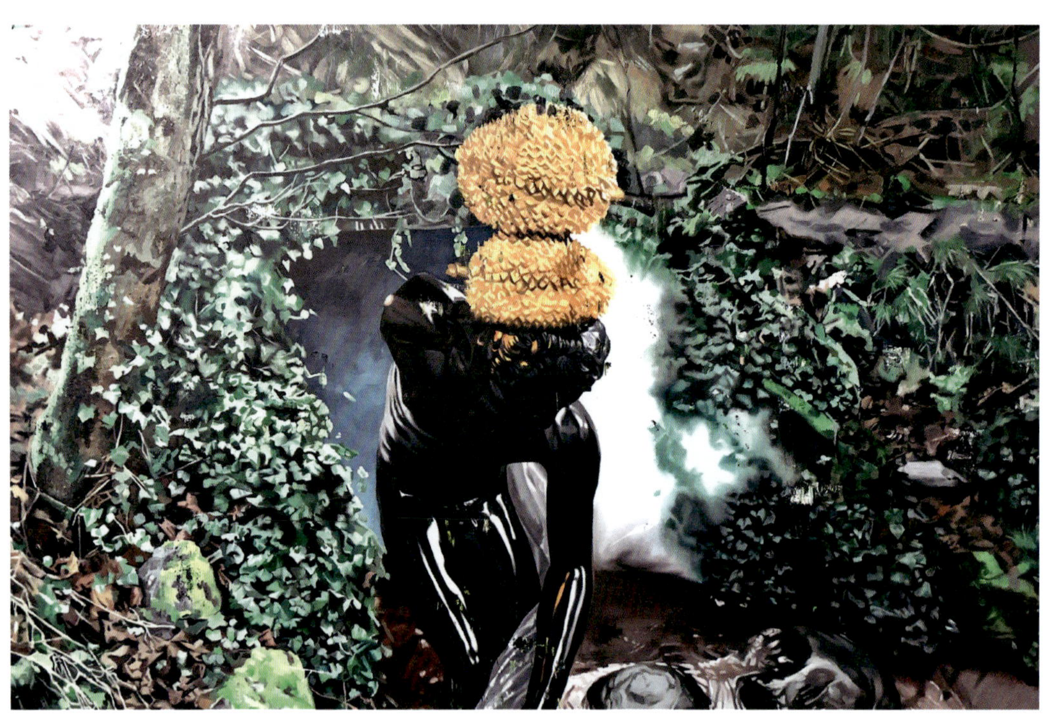

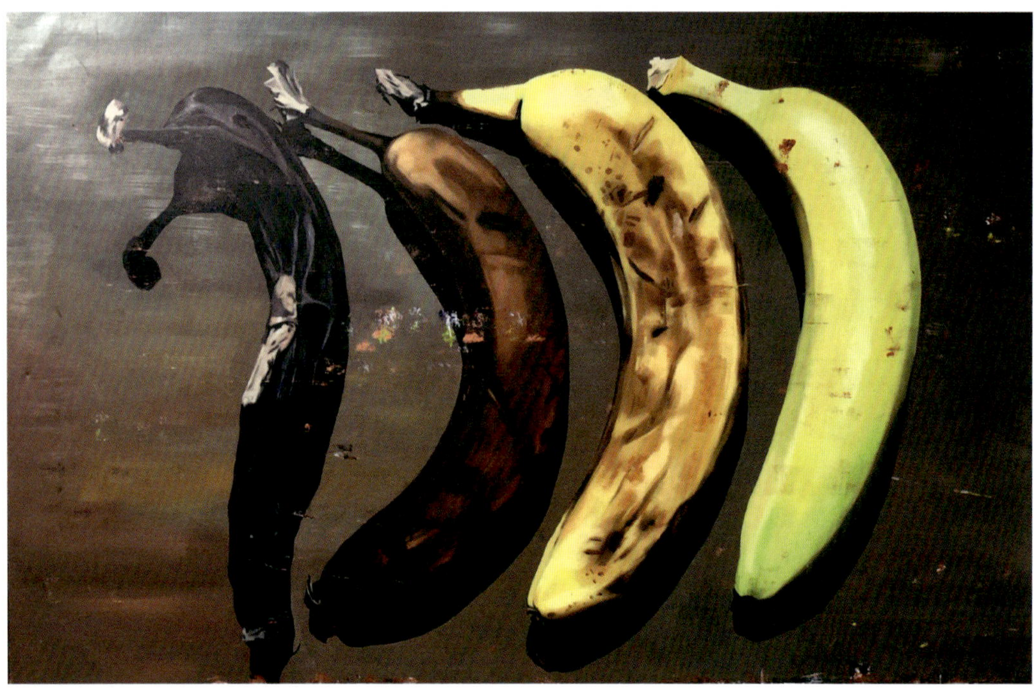

Faith Props – Durian, 2018–19
oil on canvas, 120 × 170 cm
Faith Props – Living Every Day Well, 2018–19
oil on canvas, 120 × 170 cm

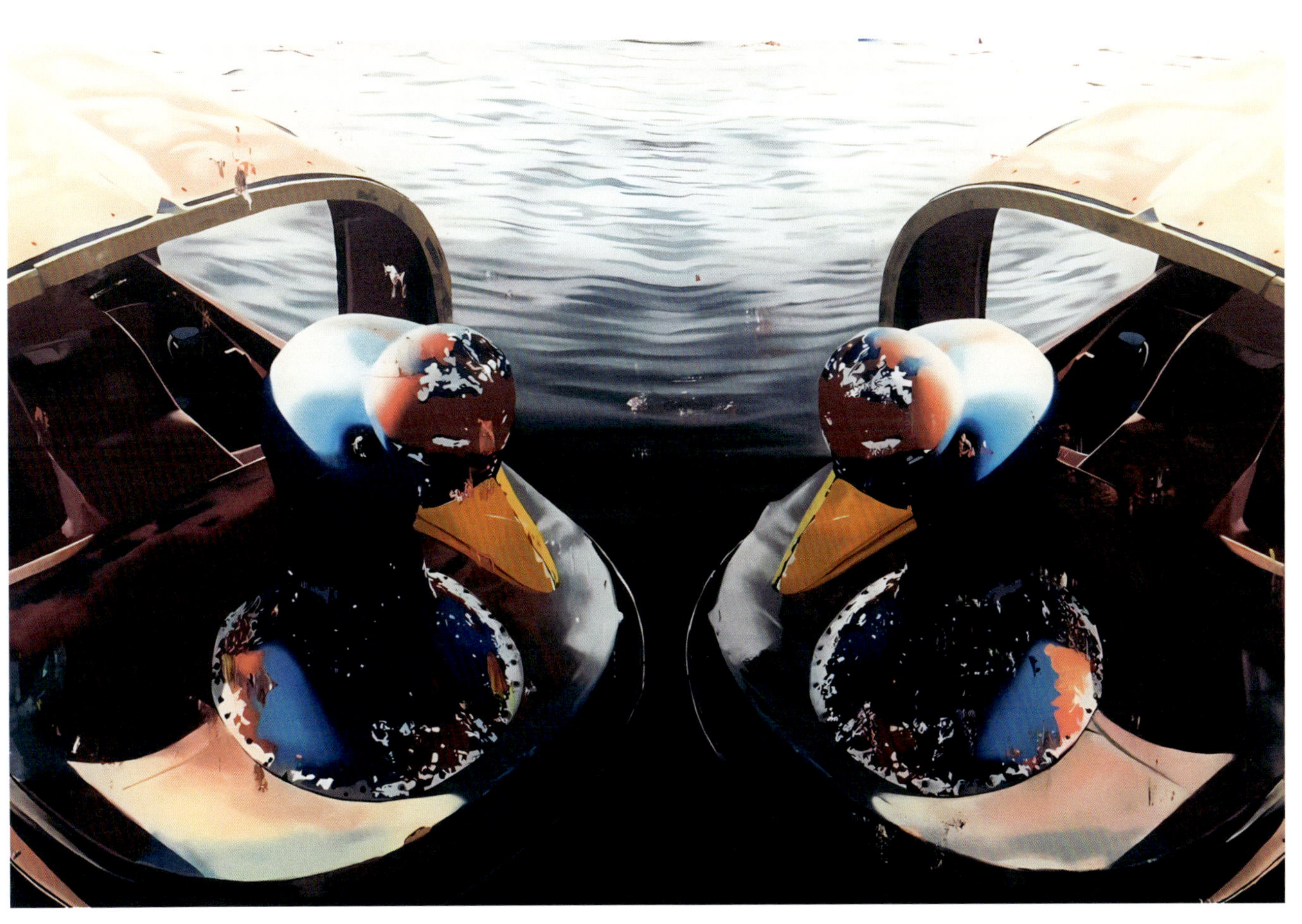

Faith Props - Mandarin Ducks, 2018–19
oil on canvas, 120 × 170 cm

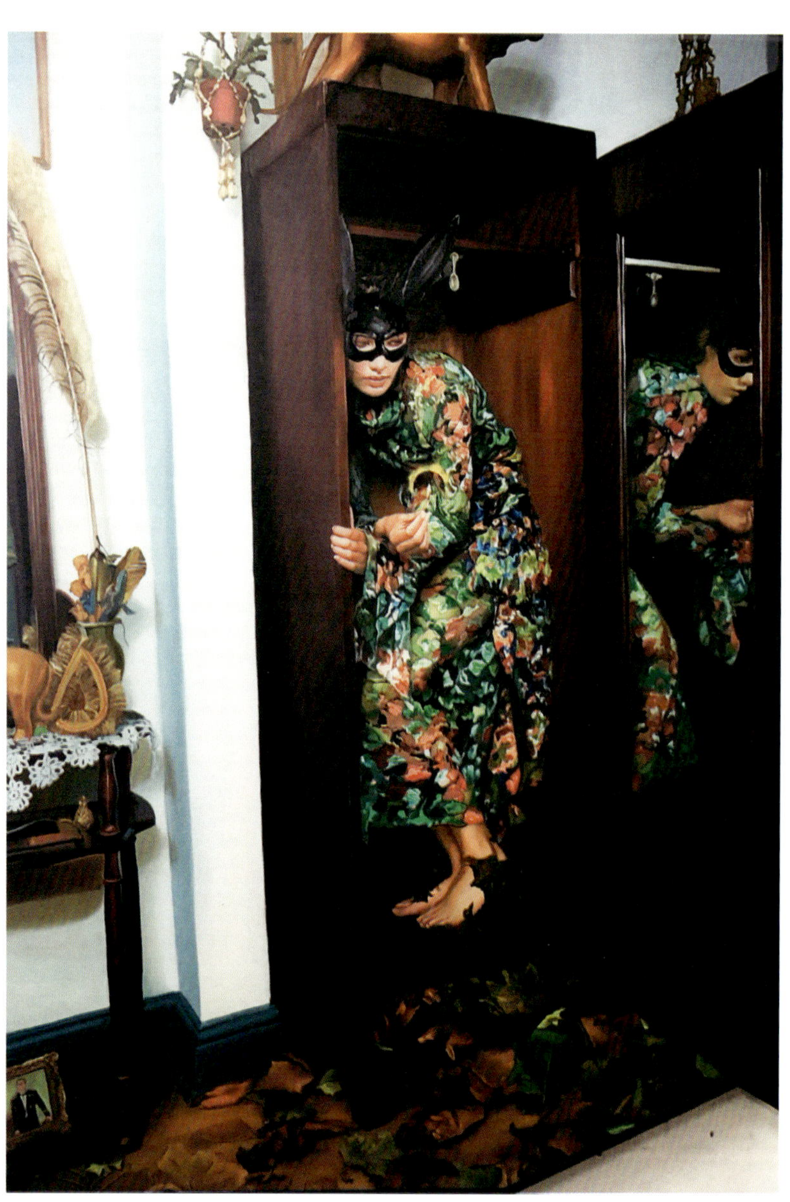

Letters – The Rabbit's Secret, 2019   oil on canvas, 200 × 133 cm

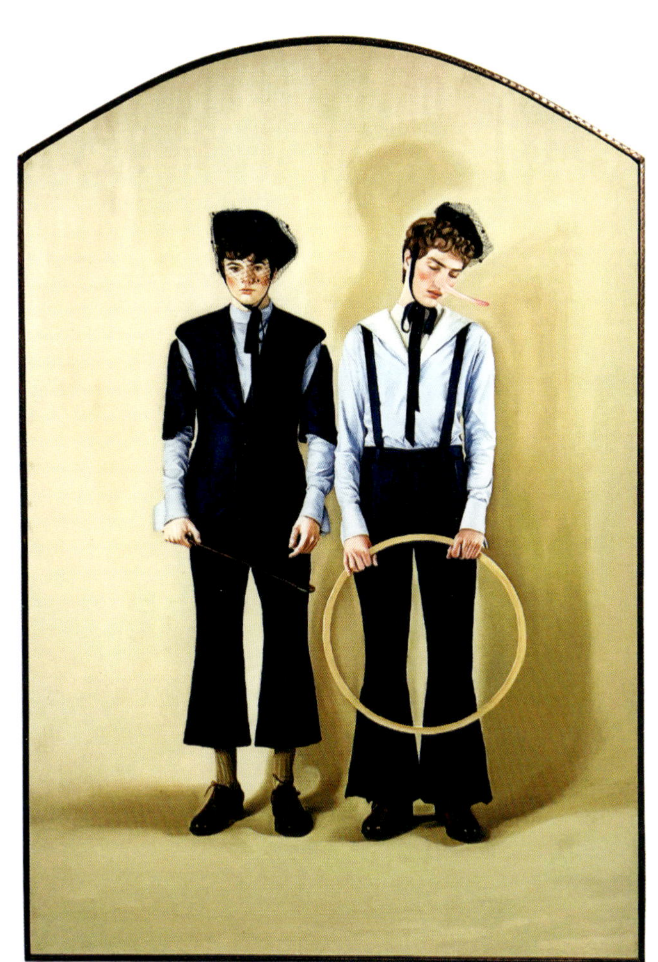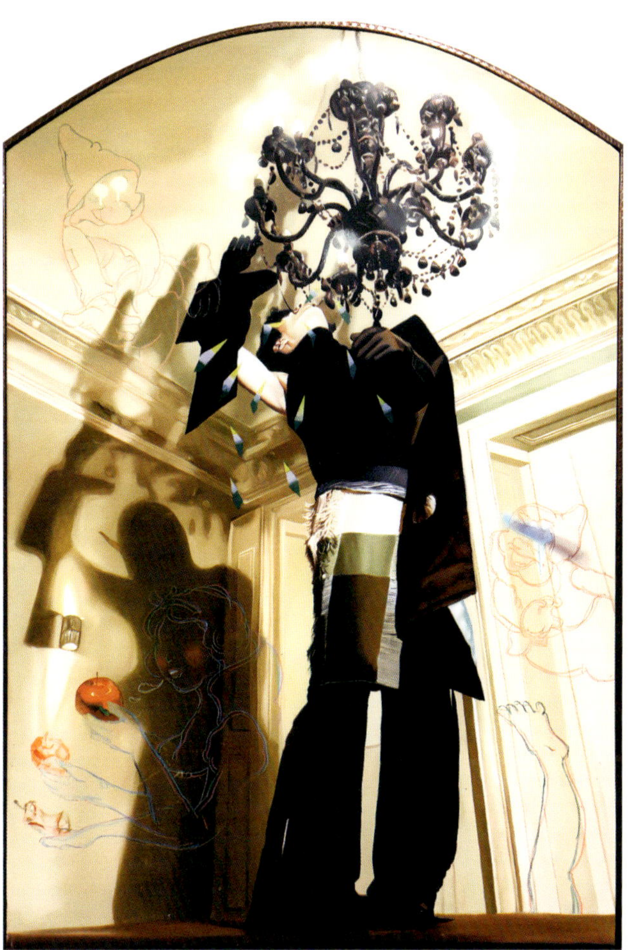

Letters – Pinocchio and a Boy, 2019   oil on canvas, 200 × 133 cm
Letters – Young Dalí, 2019   oil on canvas, 200 × 133 cm

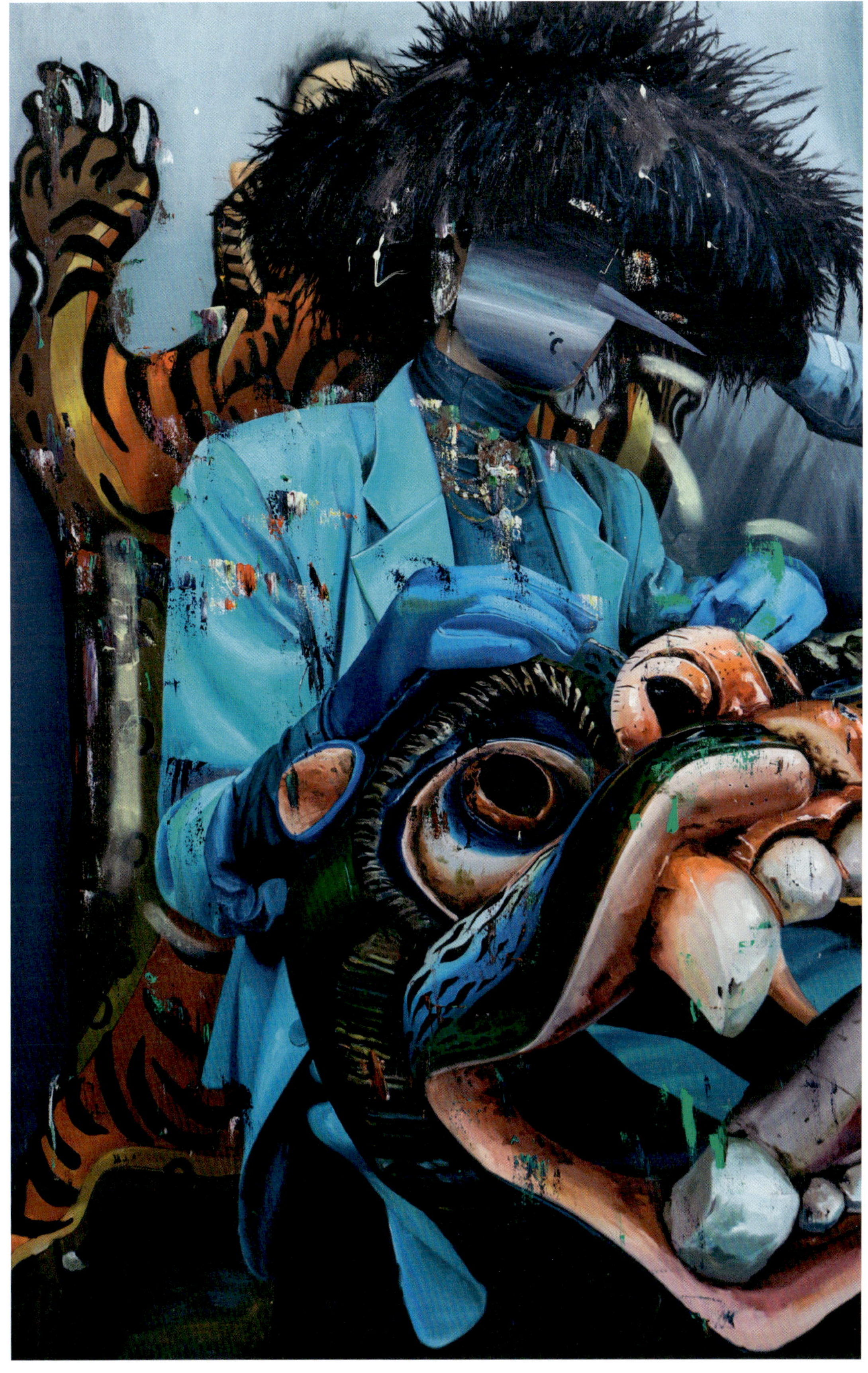

   Letters - Aristocrat, 2019–20   oil on canvas, 160 × 100 cm

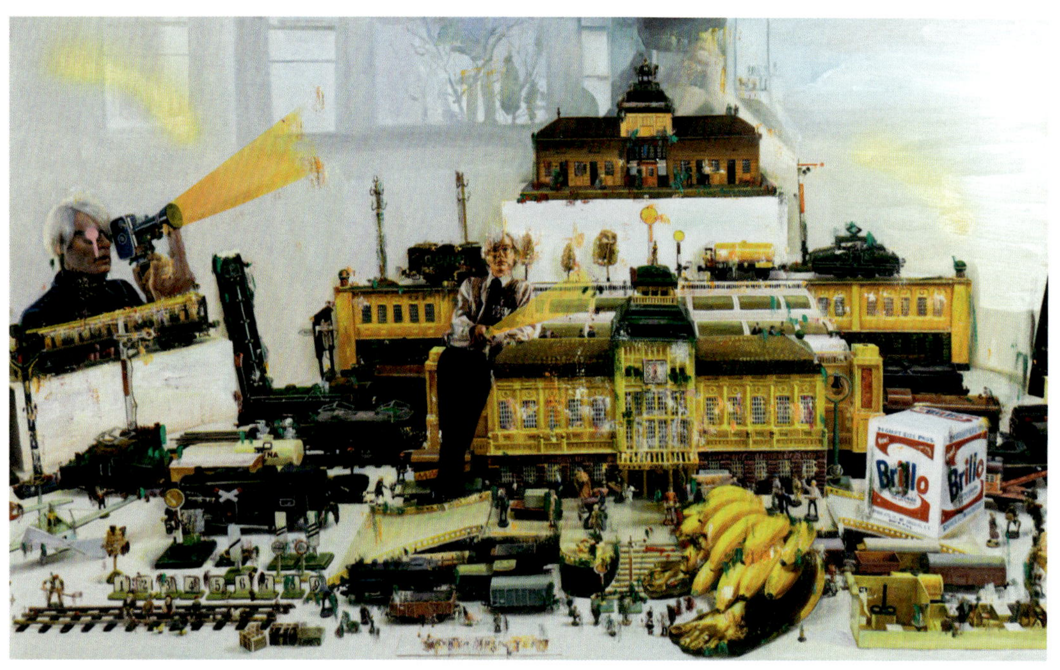

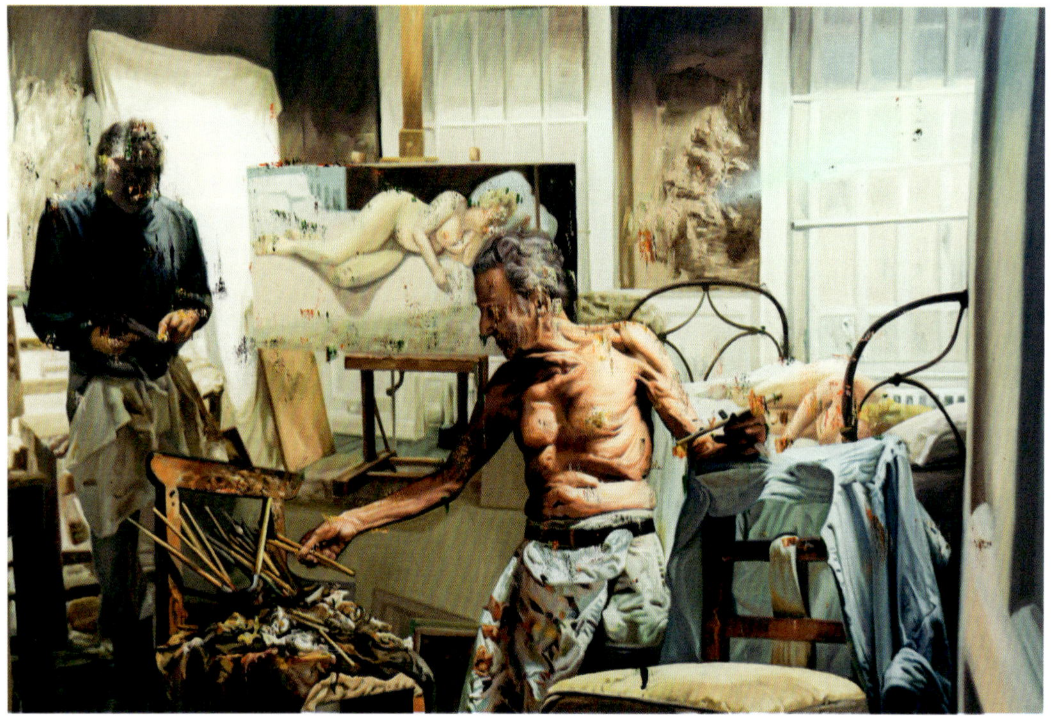

Lifelong Learning - Andy's Yellow Station, 2019–20
oil on canvas, 112 × 180 cm
Lifelong Learning – A Lifetime, 2019–20   oil on canvas, 150 × 220 cm

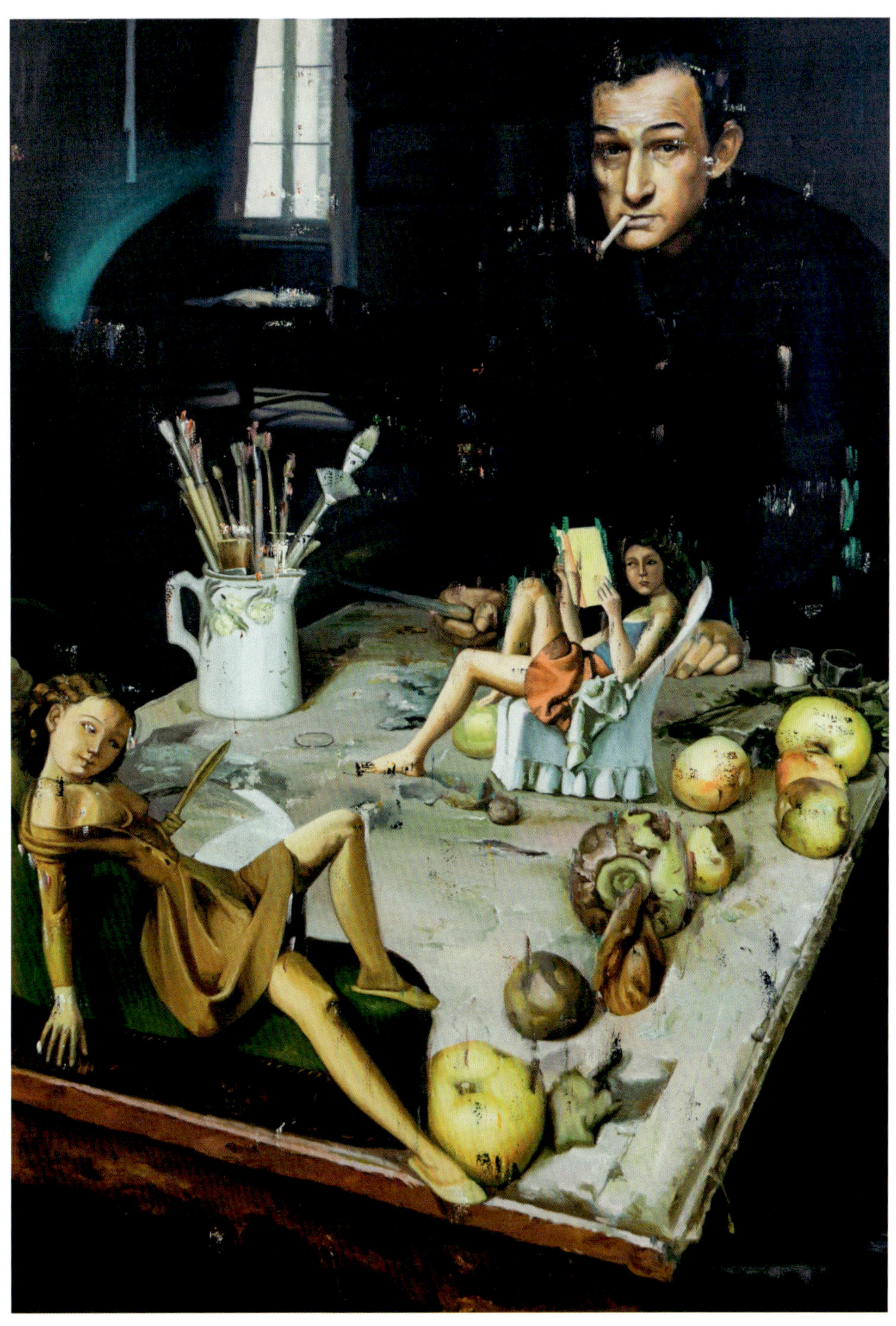

Lifelong Learning – Balthus' Workbench, 2019–20
oil on canvas, 200 × 135 cm

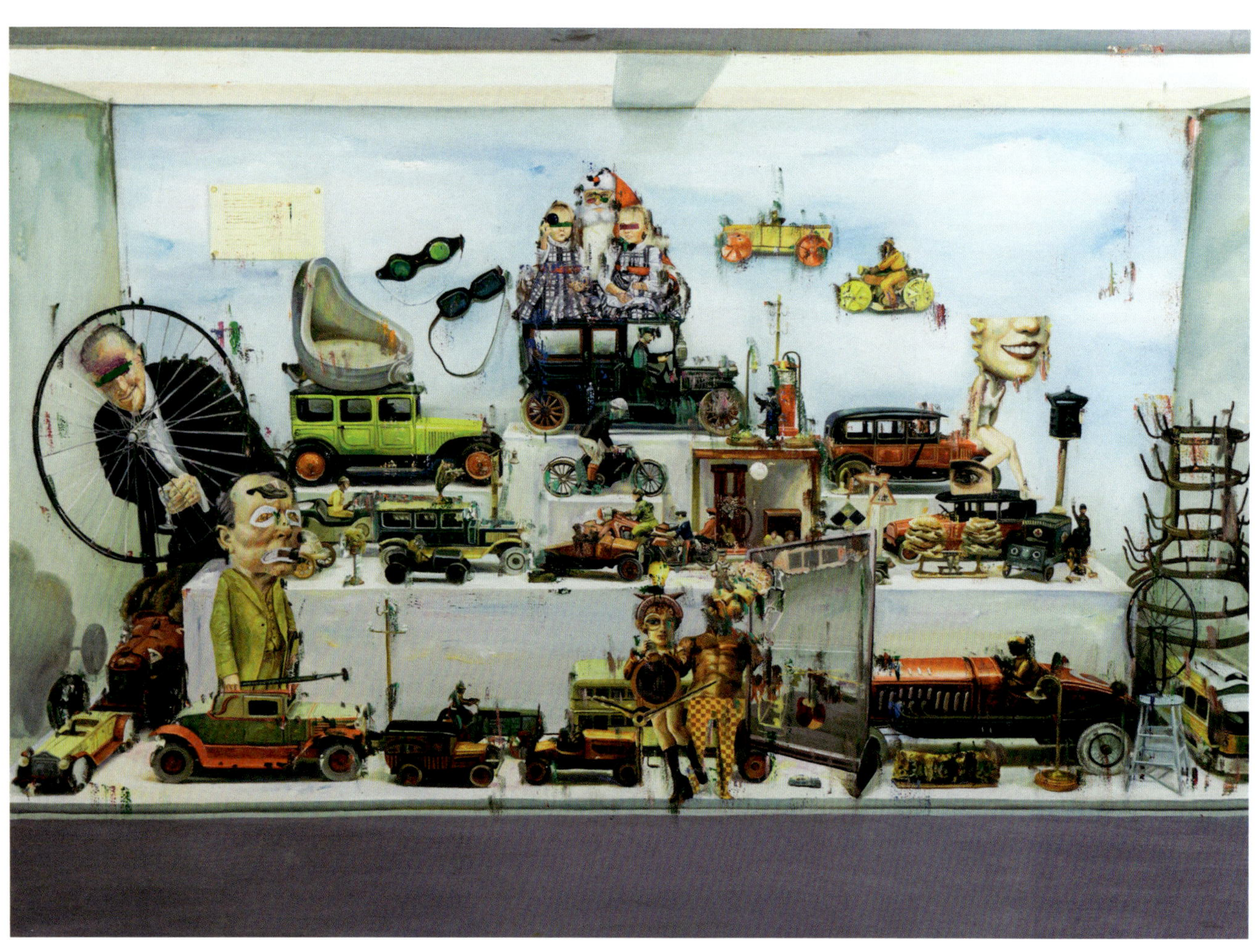

Lifelong Learning - Duchamp's Secret, 2019–20
oil on canvas, 133 × 180 cm

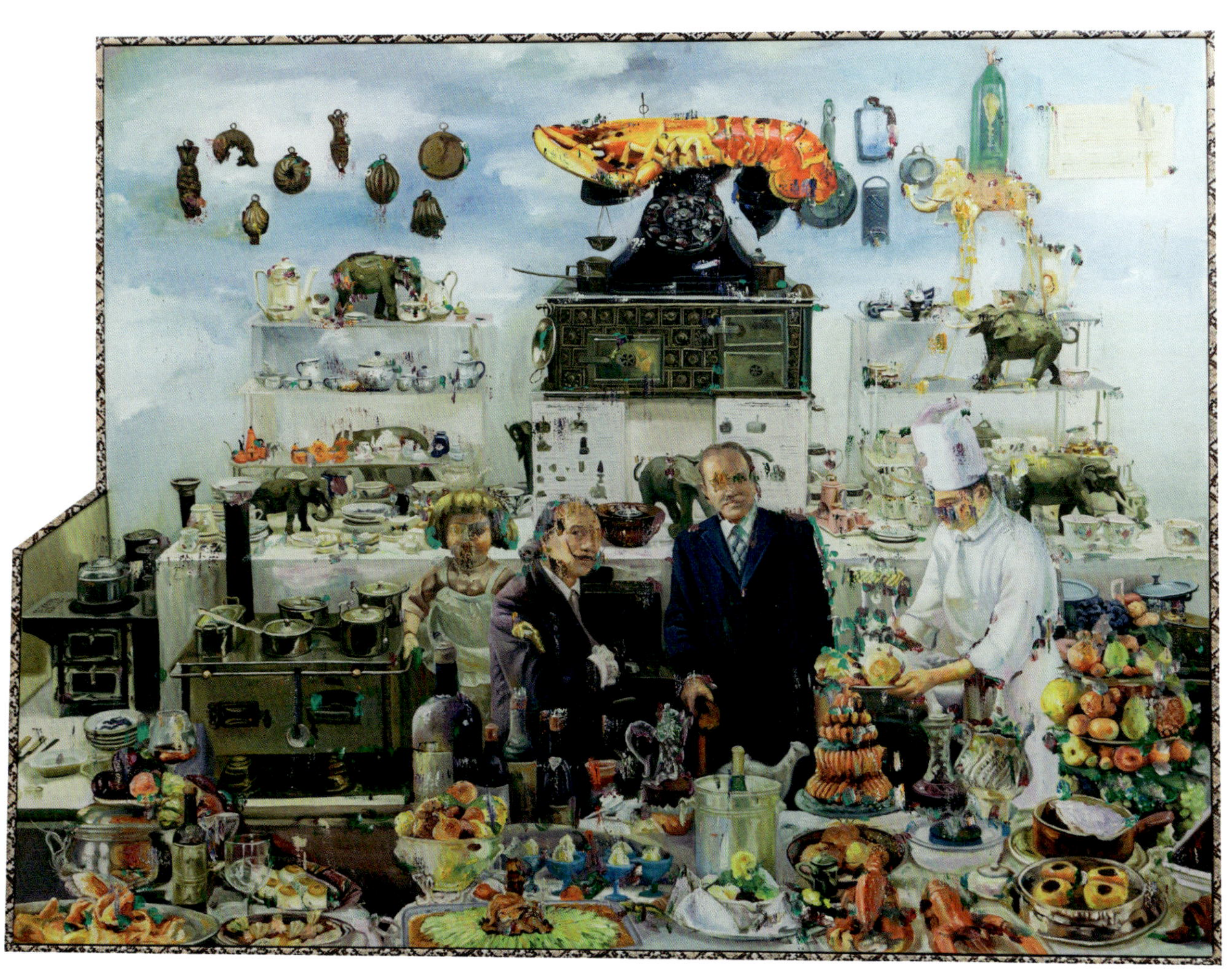

Lifelong Learning - Dalí's Feast, 2019–20
oil on canvas, 140 × 180 cm

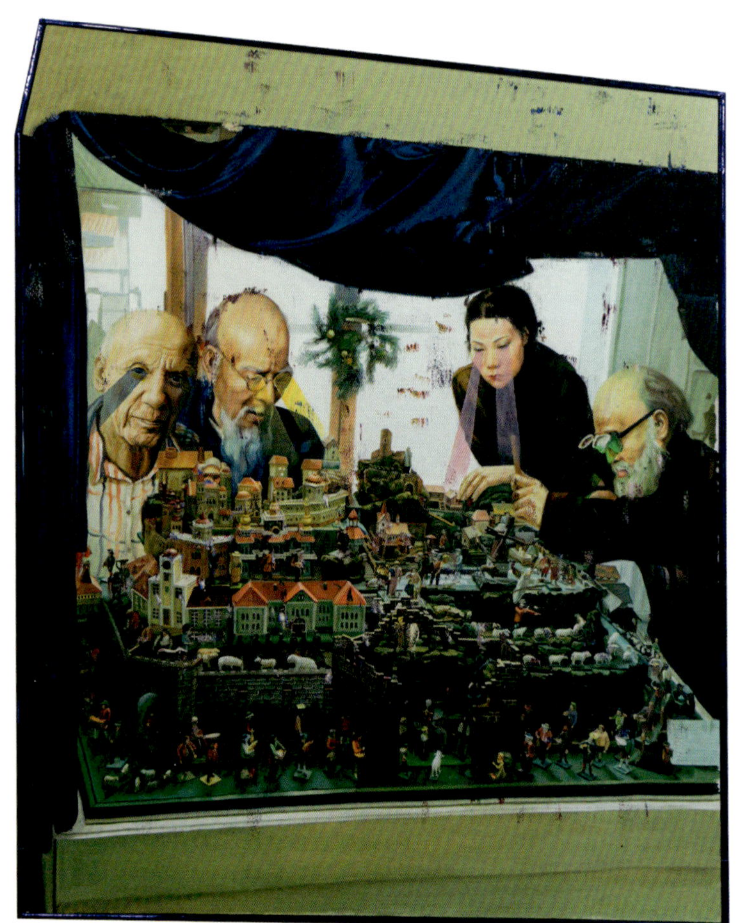

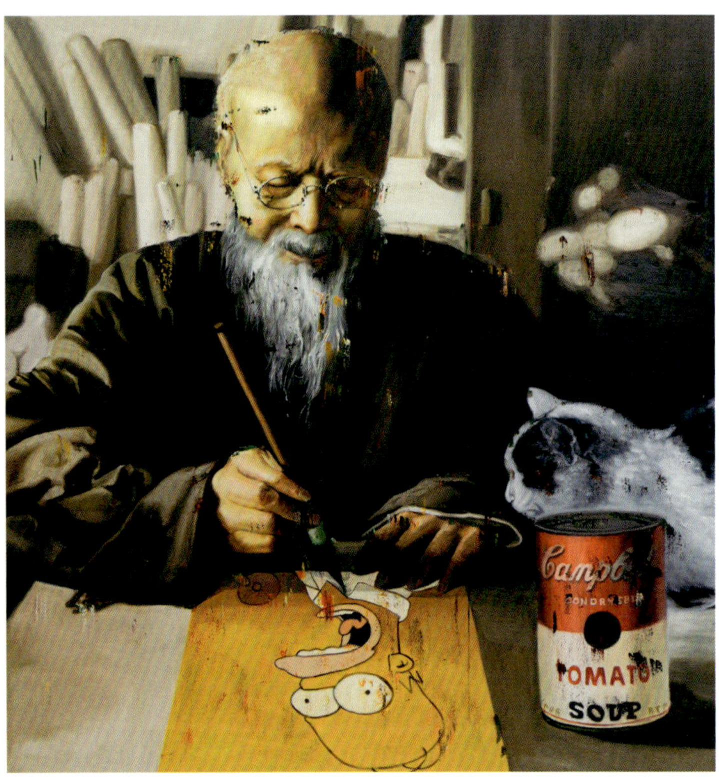

Lifelong Learning - Such a Beautiful Country,
2019–20   oil on canvas, 160 × 100 cm
Lifelong Learning - Qi Baishi's Atlas, 2019–20
oil on canvas, 160 × 150 cm

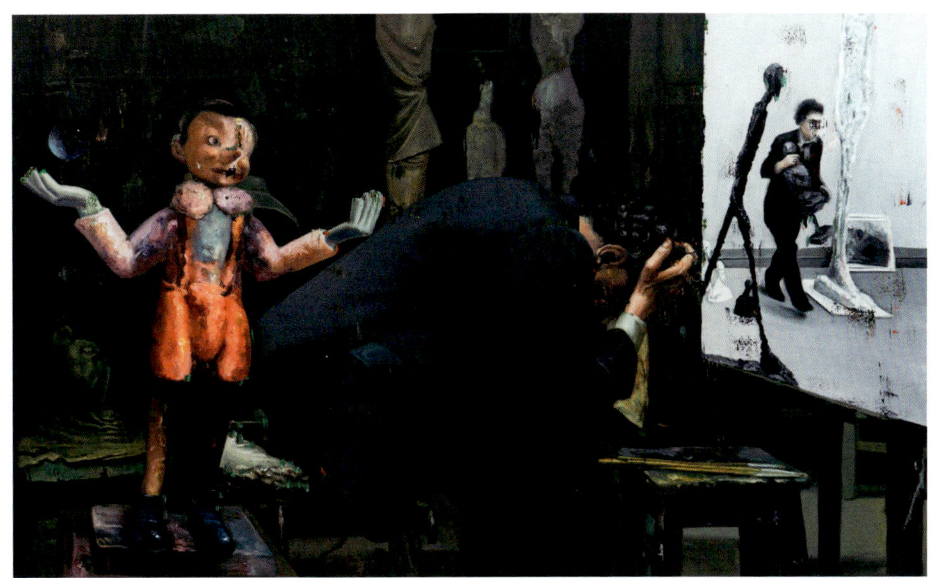

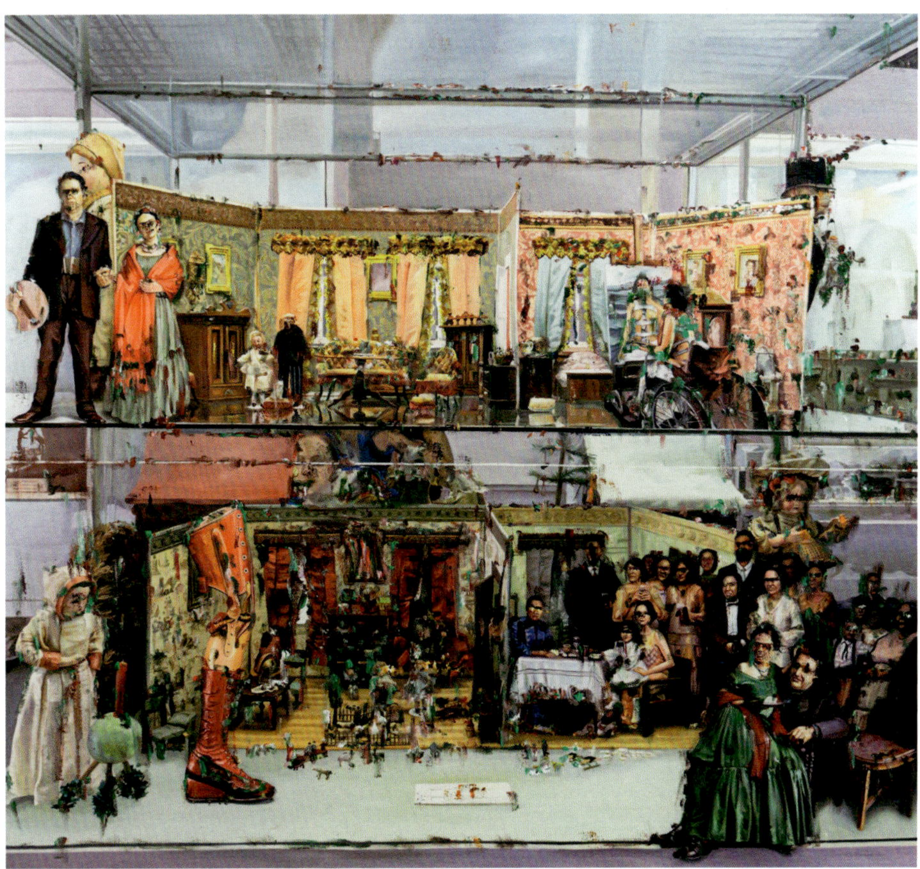

Lifelong Learning - The Plan of Giacometti, 2019–20
oil on canvas, 125 × 200 cm
Lifelong Learning - Frida's Wedding, 2019–20
oil on canvas, 169 × 180 cm

Lifelong Learning – World Amusement Park, Rousseau's Mysterious Forest, 2020–21
oil and spray acrylic on canvas, 195 × 160 cm

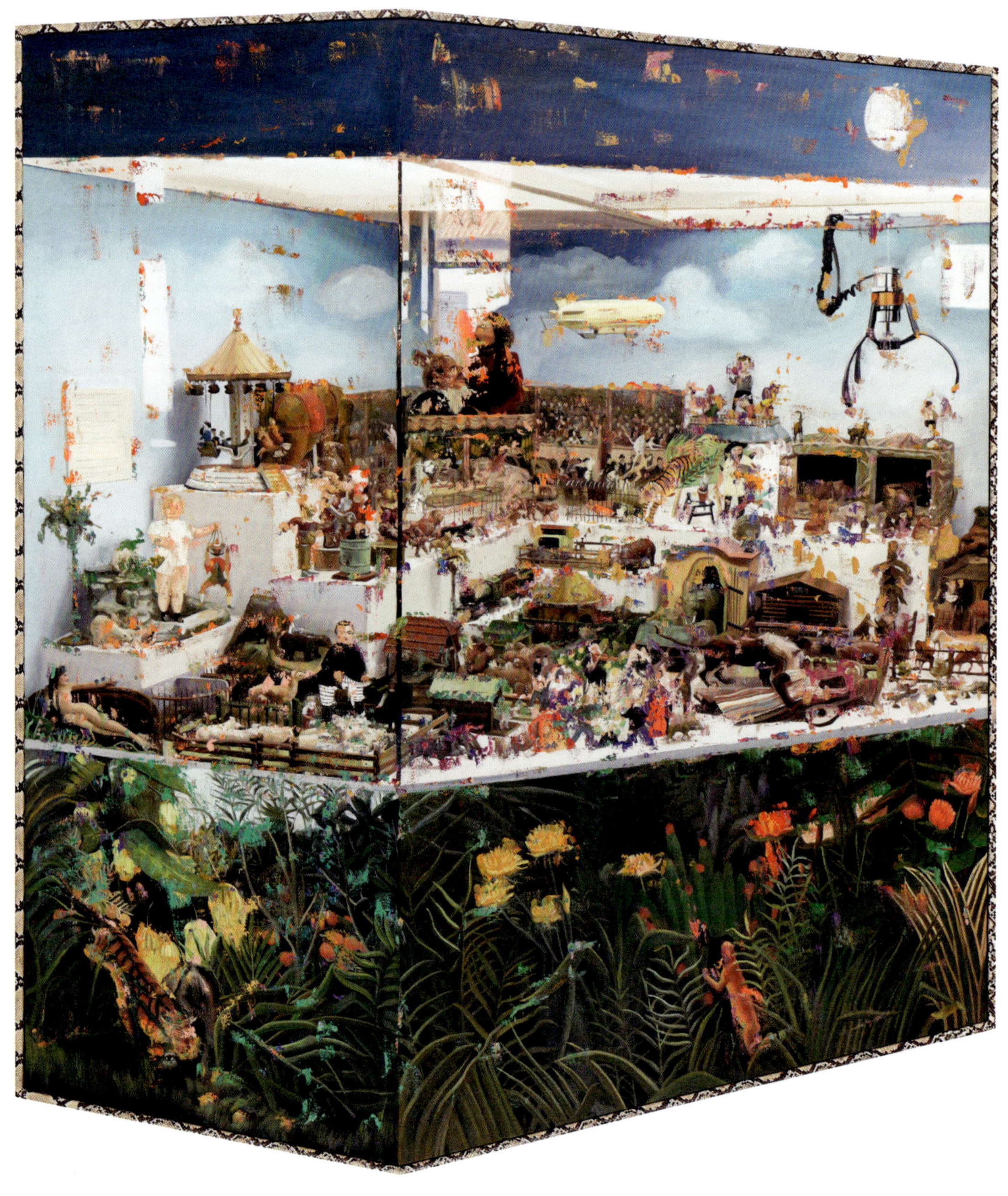

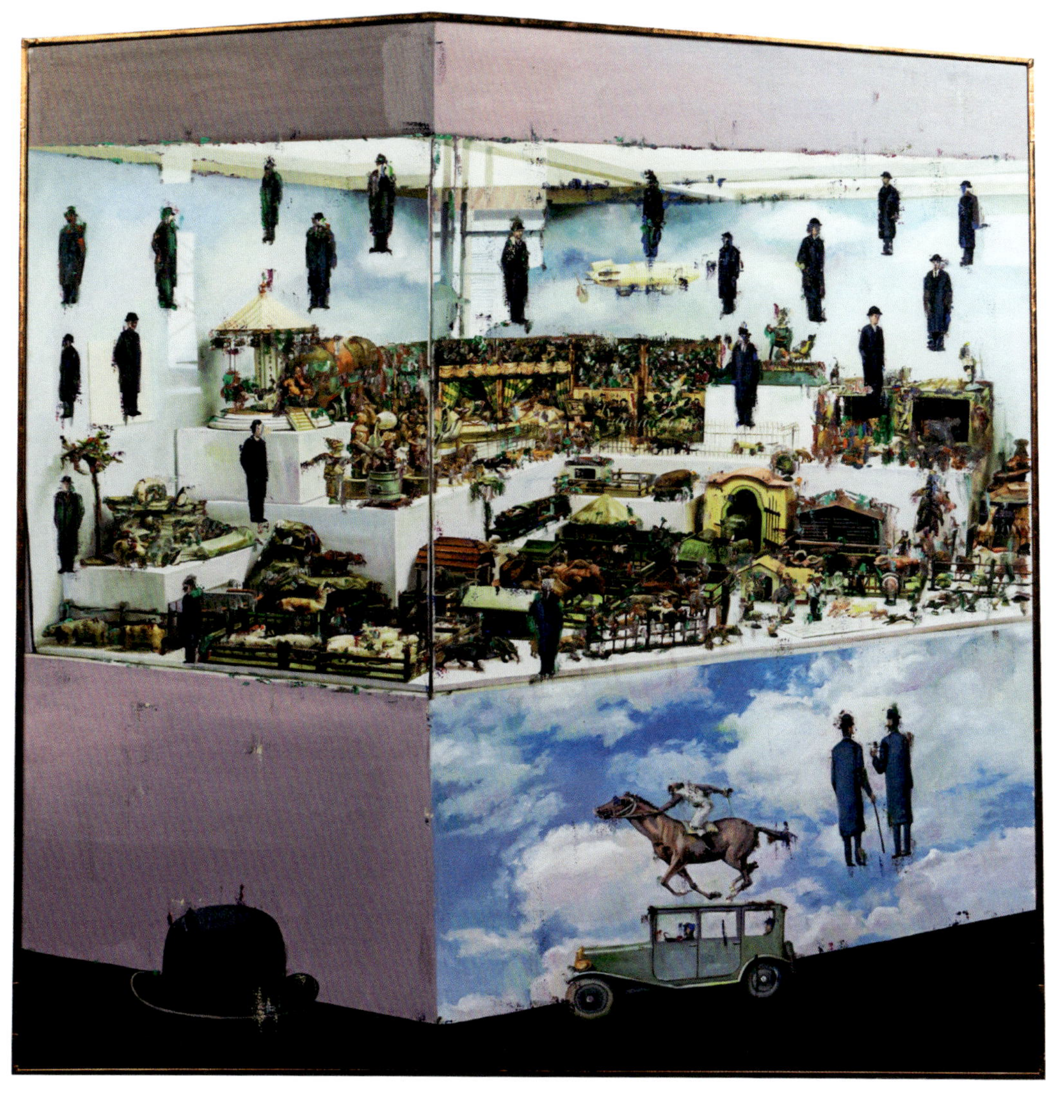

Lifelong Learning - Magritte after the Rain, 2019–20
oil on canvas, 180 × 168 cm

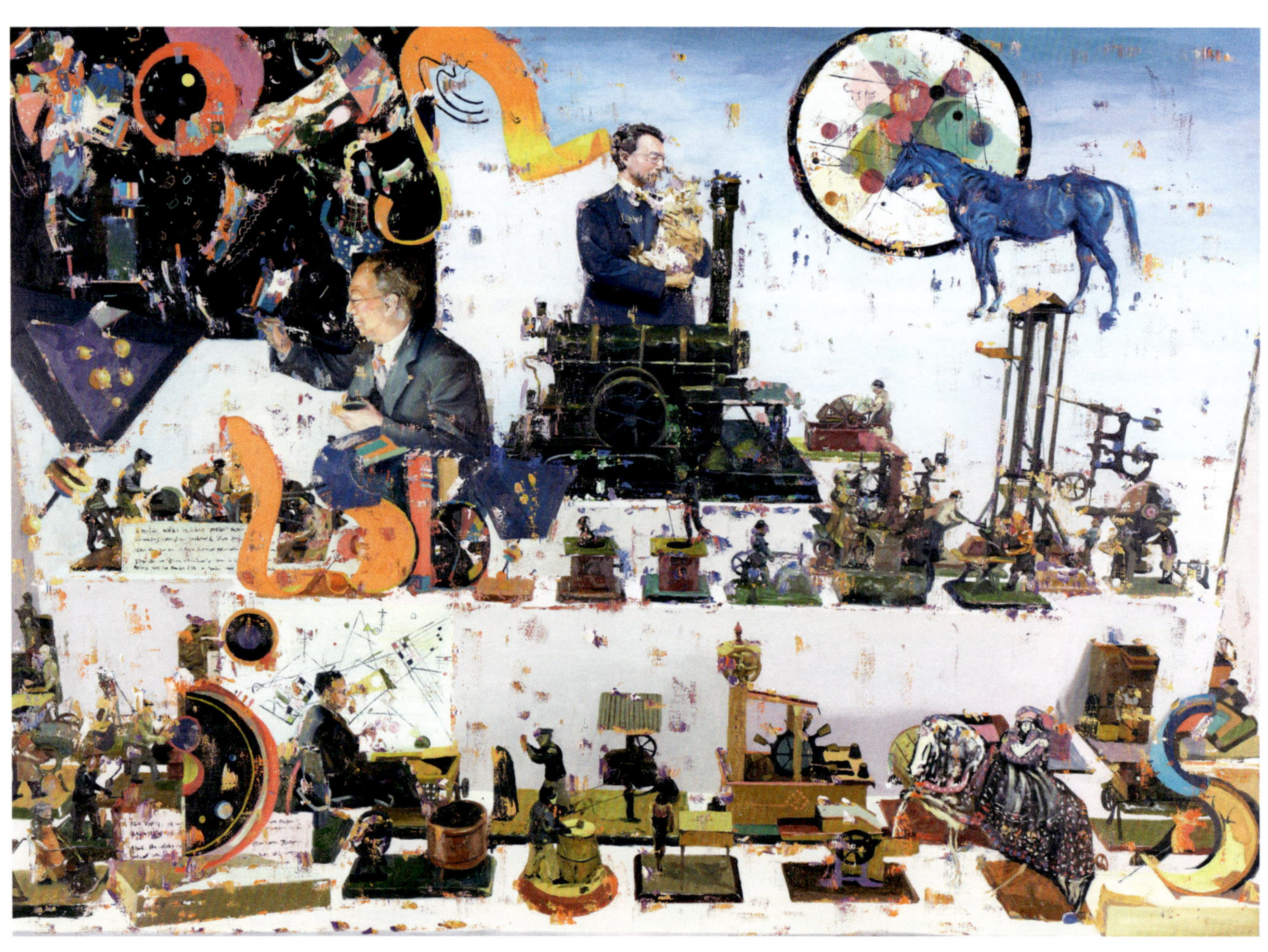

Lifelong Learning – World Amusement Park, Blue Rider Kandinsky, 2020–21
oil and spray acrylic on canvas, 143 × 190 cm

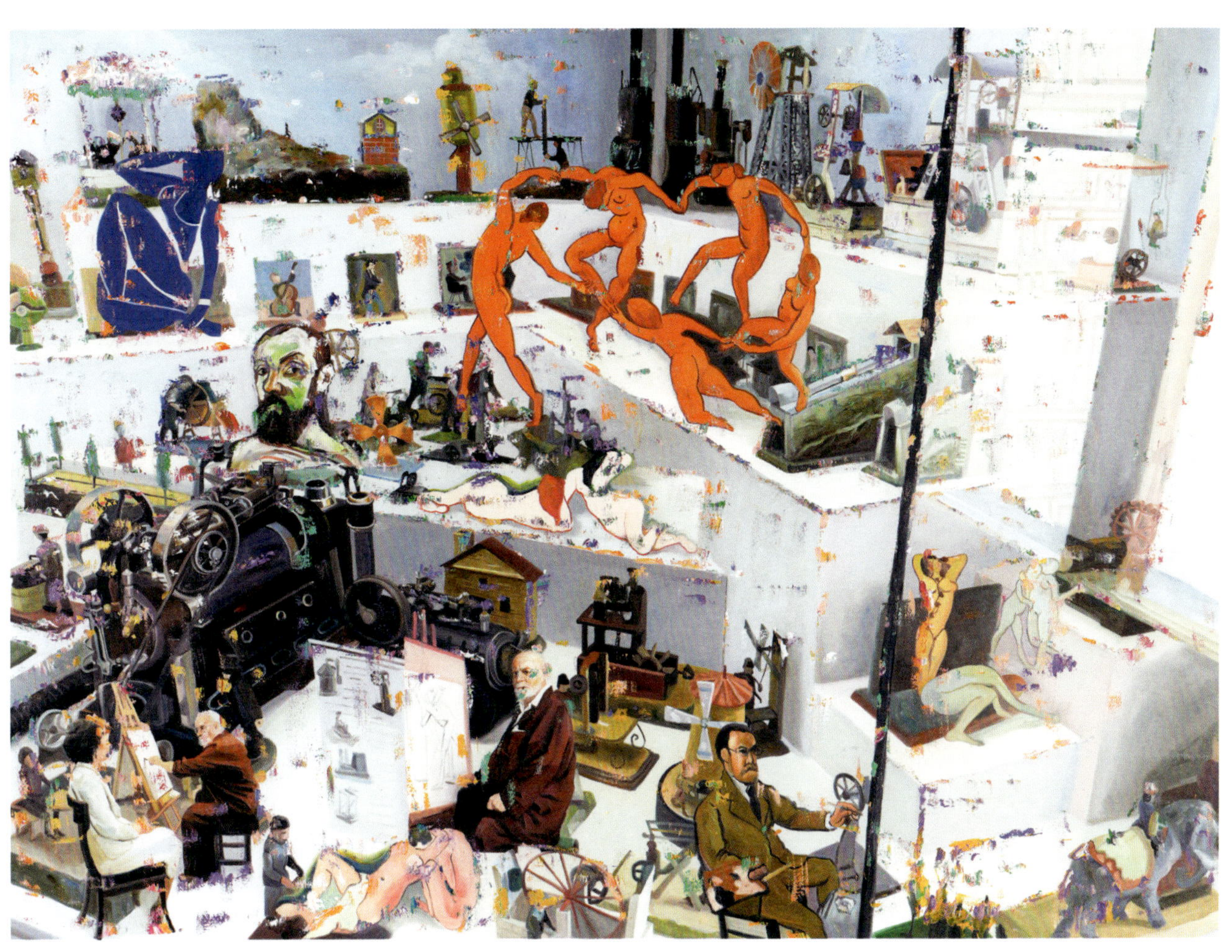

Lifelong Learning – World Amusement Park, Matisse's Waltz, 2020–21
oil and spray acrylic on canvas, 145 × 190 cm

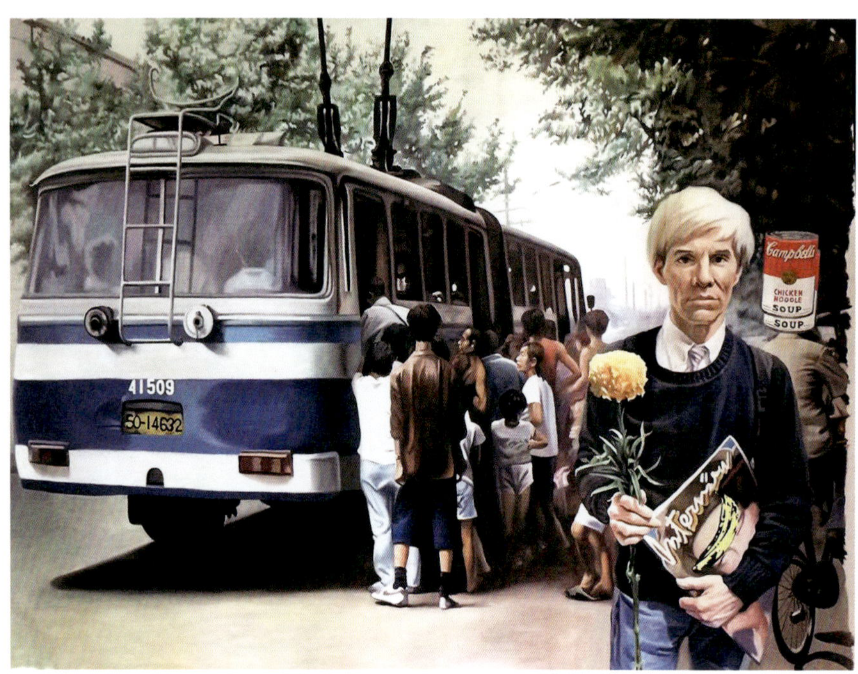
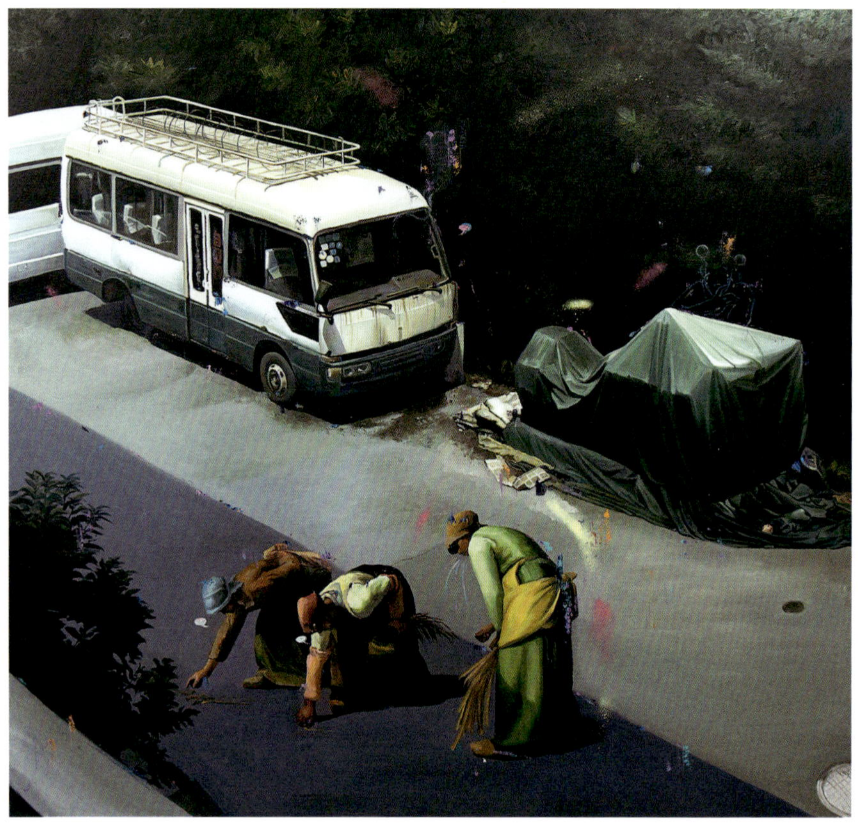

Going to Work, 2022   oil on canvas, 140 × 190 cm
Life Props – Gleaning after Work, 2021–22   oil on canvas, 200 × 200 cm

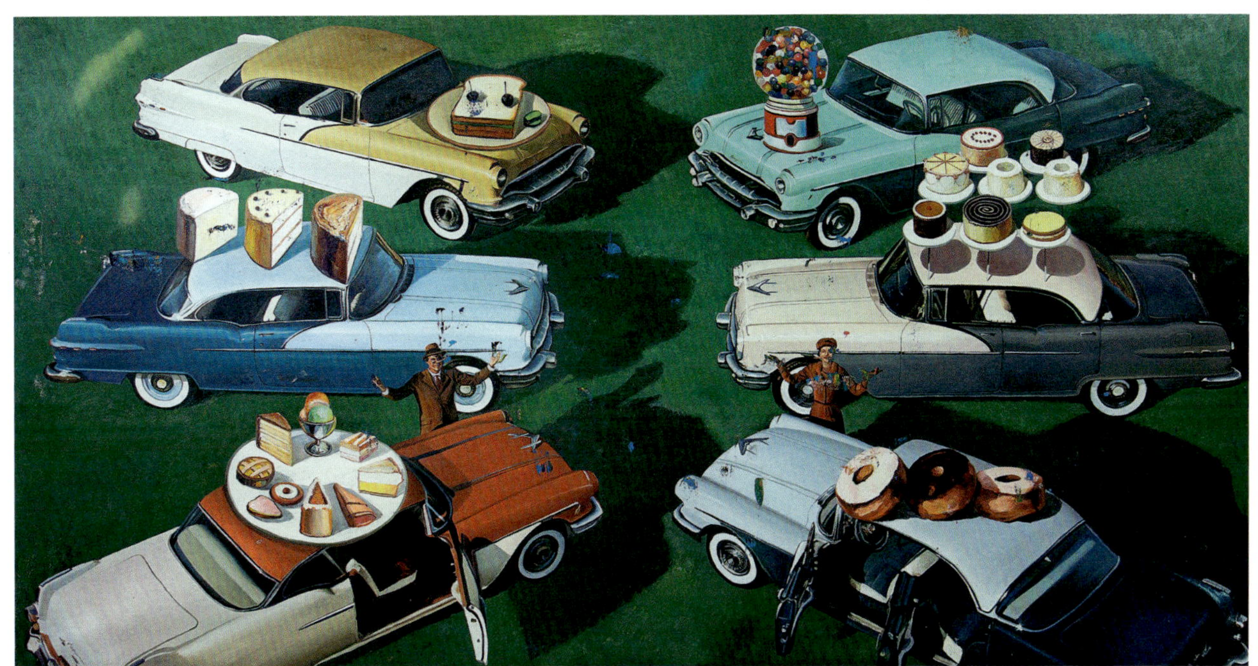

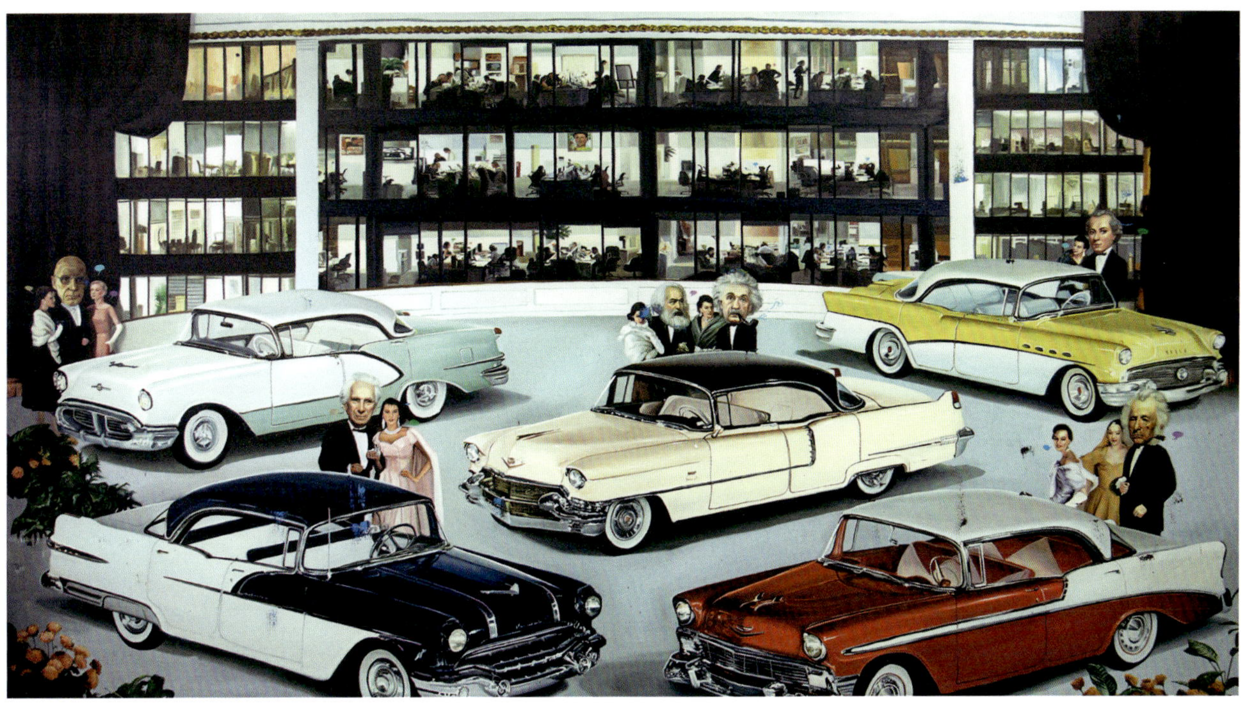

Life Props – We Have Beautiful Friendships, 2021–22
oil on canvas, 150 × 290 cm
Life Props – Overtime and the City That Never Sleeps, 2021–22
oil on canvas, 180 × 328 cm

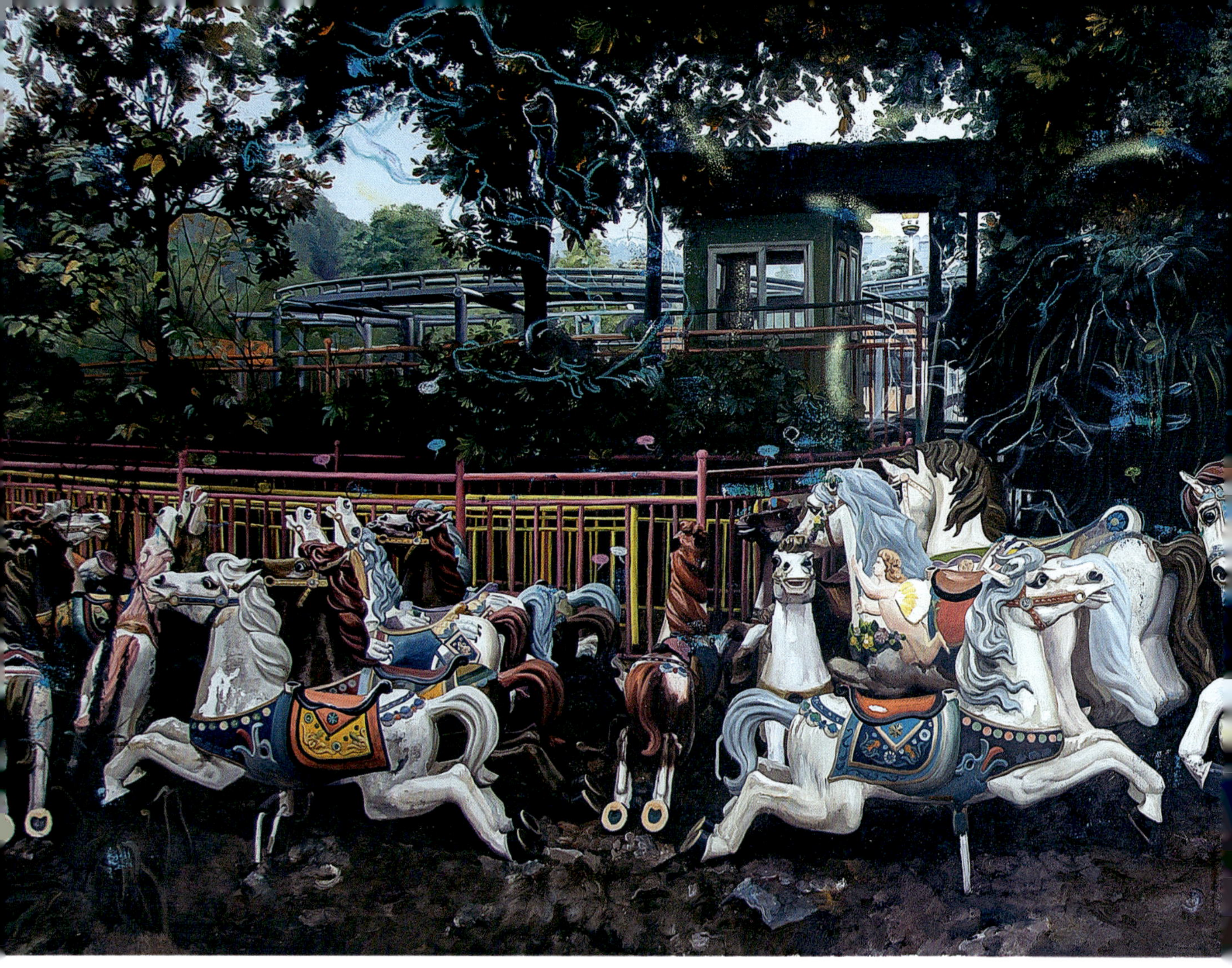

Life Props – Galloping Horses, 2021–22   oil on canvas, 150 × 400 cm

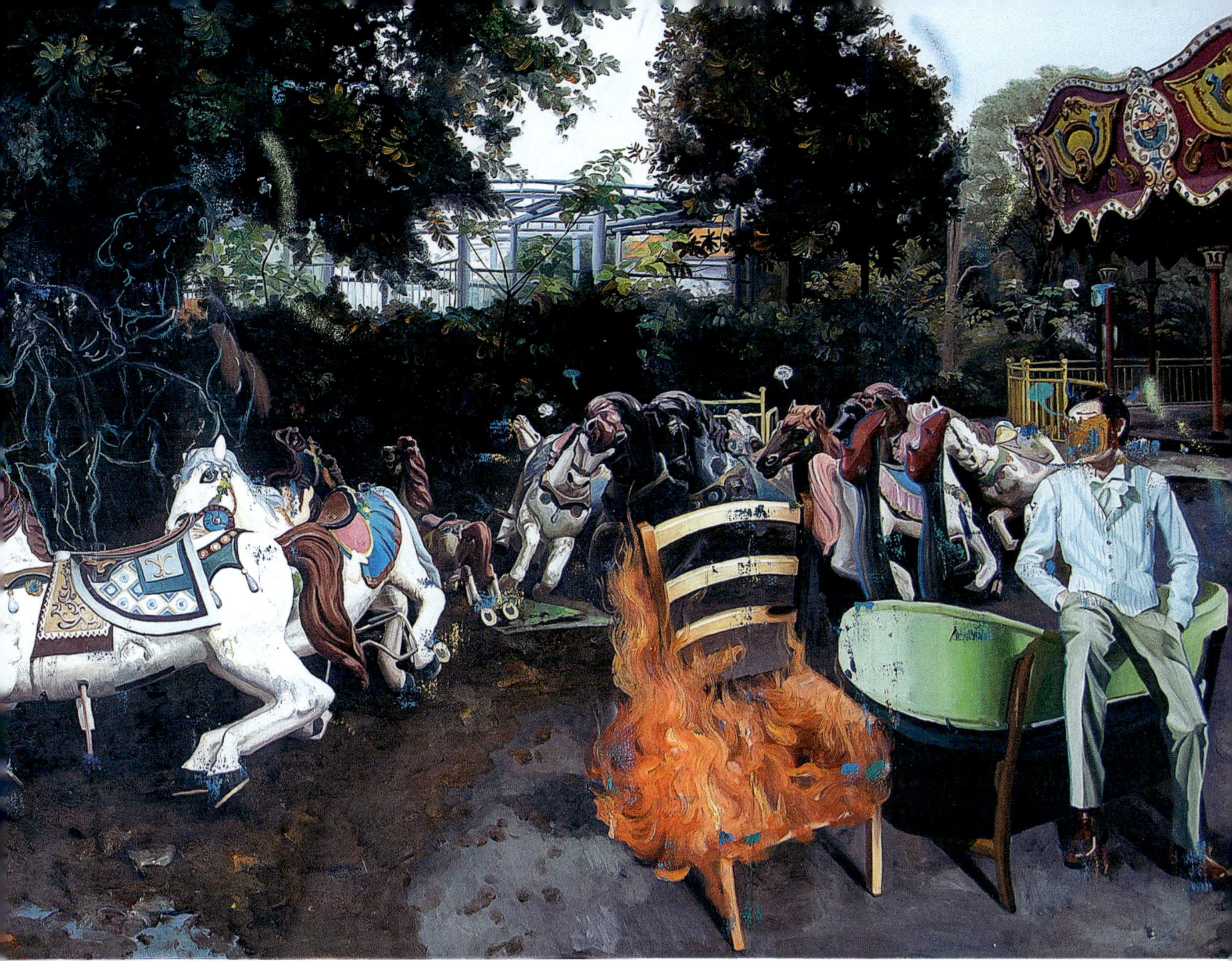

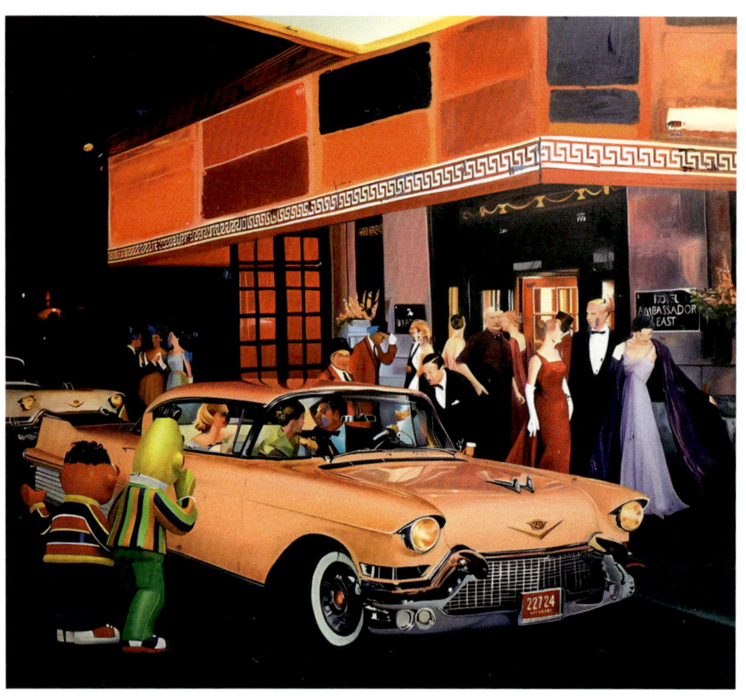

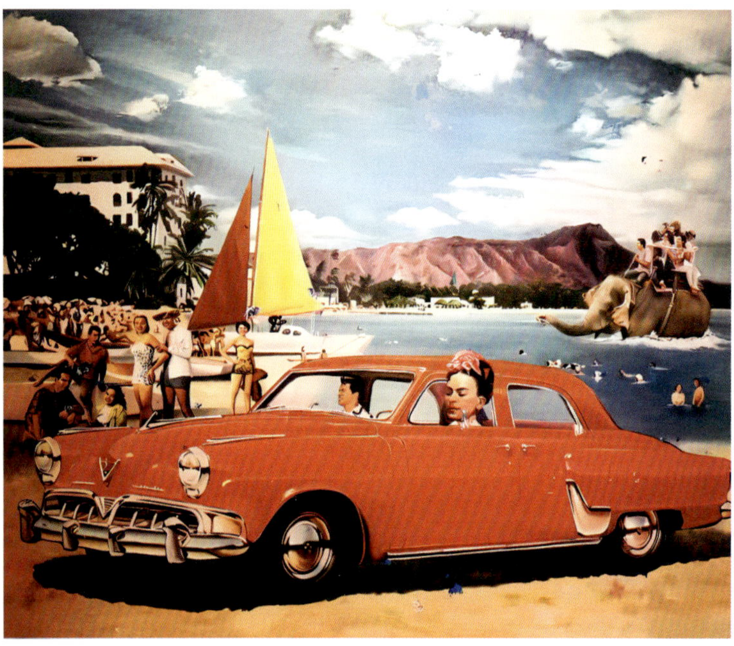

Life Props – Heading to an Exhibition of Resplendent
Colour Fields, 2021–22   oil on canvas, 200 × 220 cm
Life Props – Cao Chong Weighs the Elephant, Frida, Sunshine,
Beach, 2021–22   oil on canvas, 178 × 200 cm

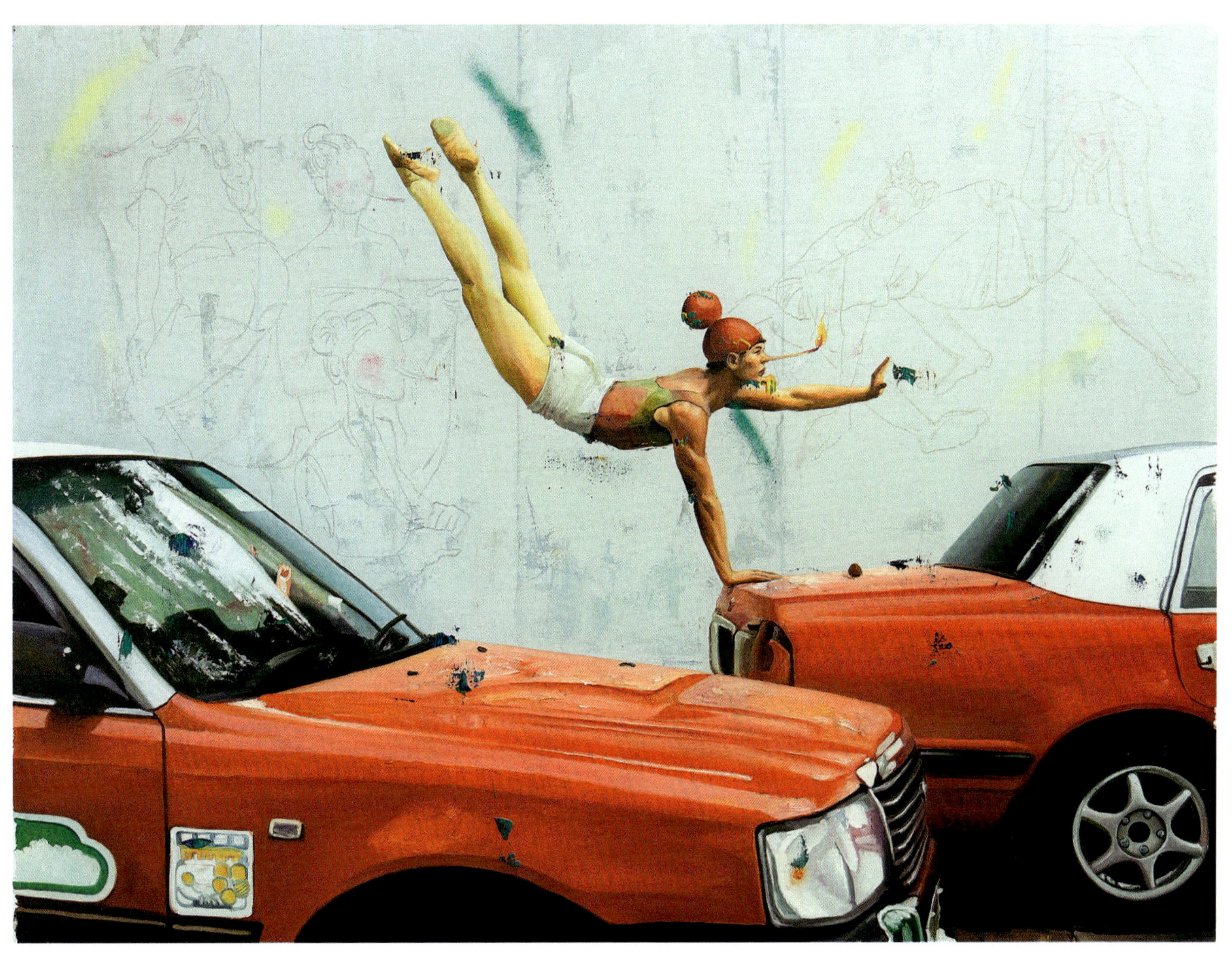

Life Props – Acrobatics, Taxi, Pinocchio, 2021–22
oil on canvas, 130 × 165 cm

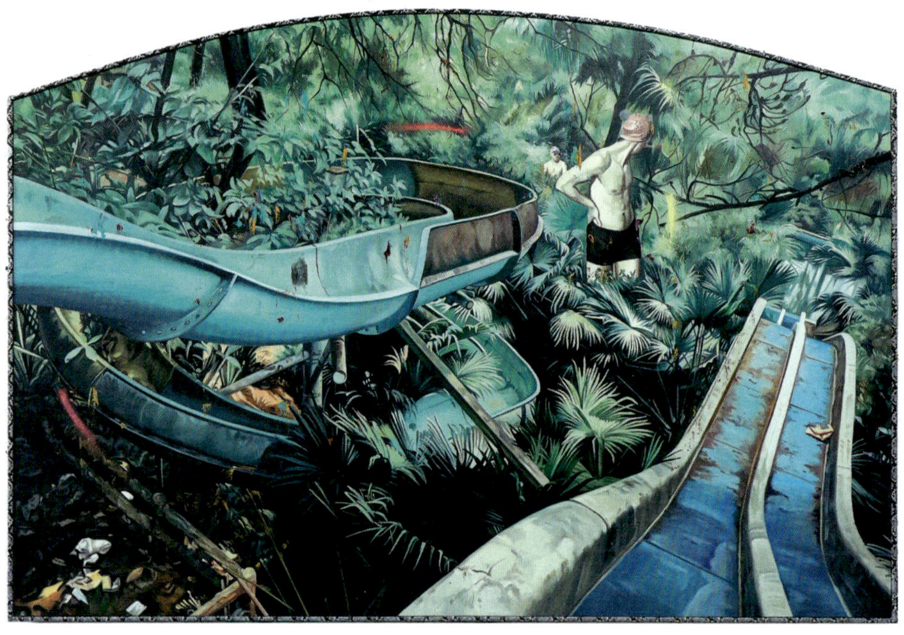

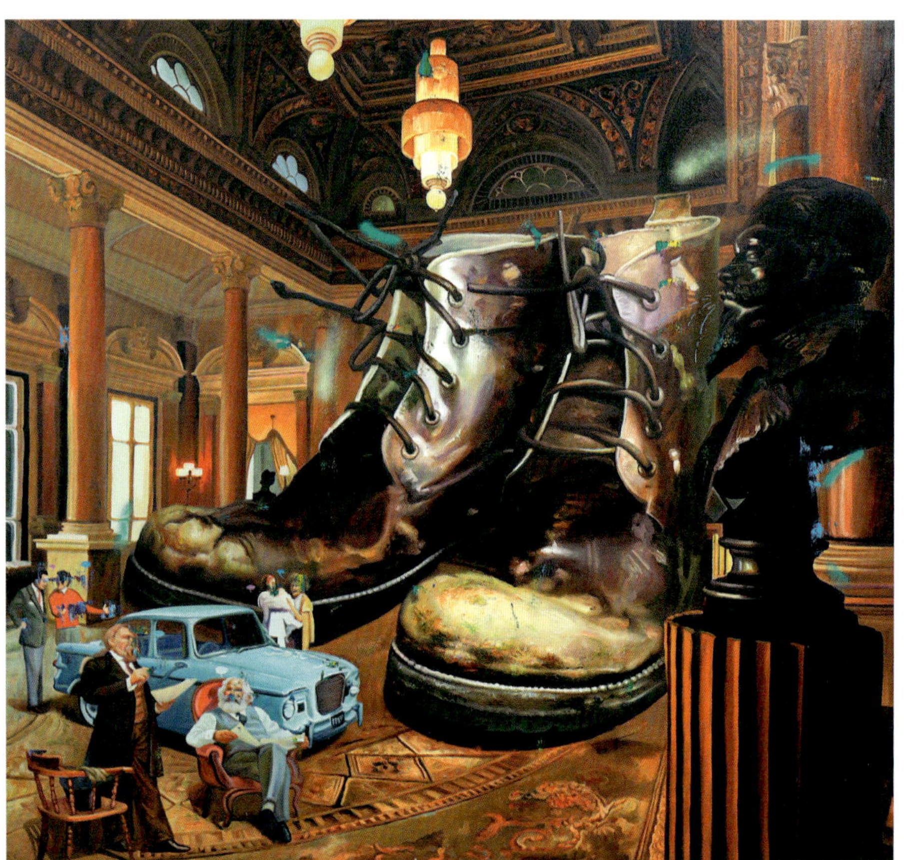

Life Props - Art Jungle, 2021–22   oil on canvas, 160 × 233 cm
Life Props - Journey of a Thousand Miles, 2021–22
oil on canvas, 200 × 200 cm

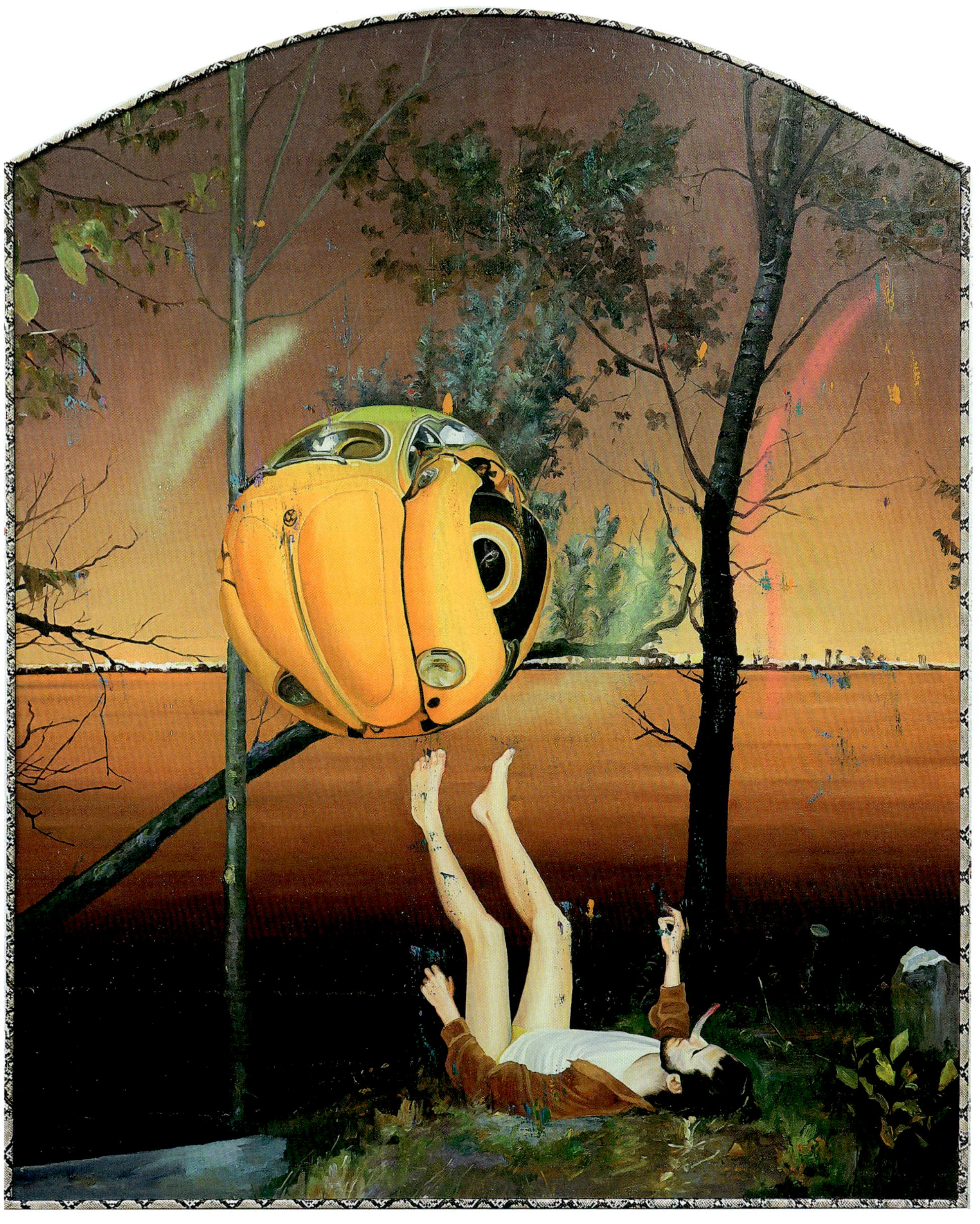

Life Props - Art Island, 2021–22   oil on canvas, 200 × 160 cm

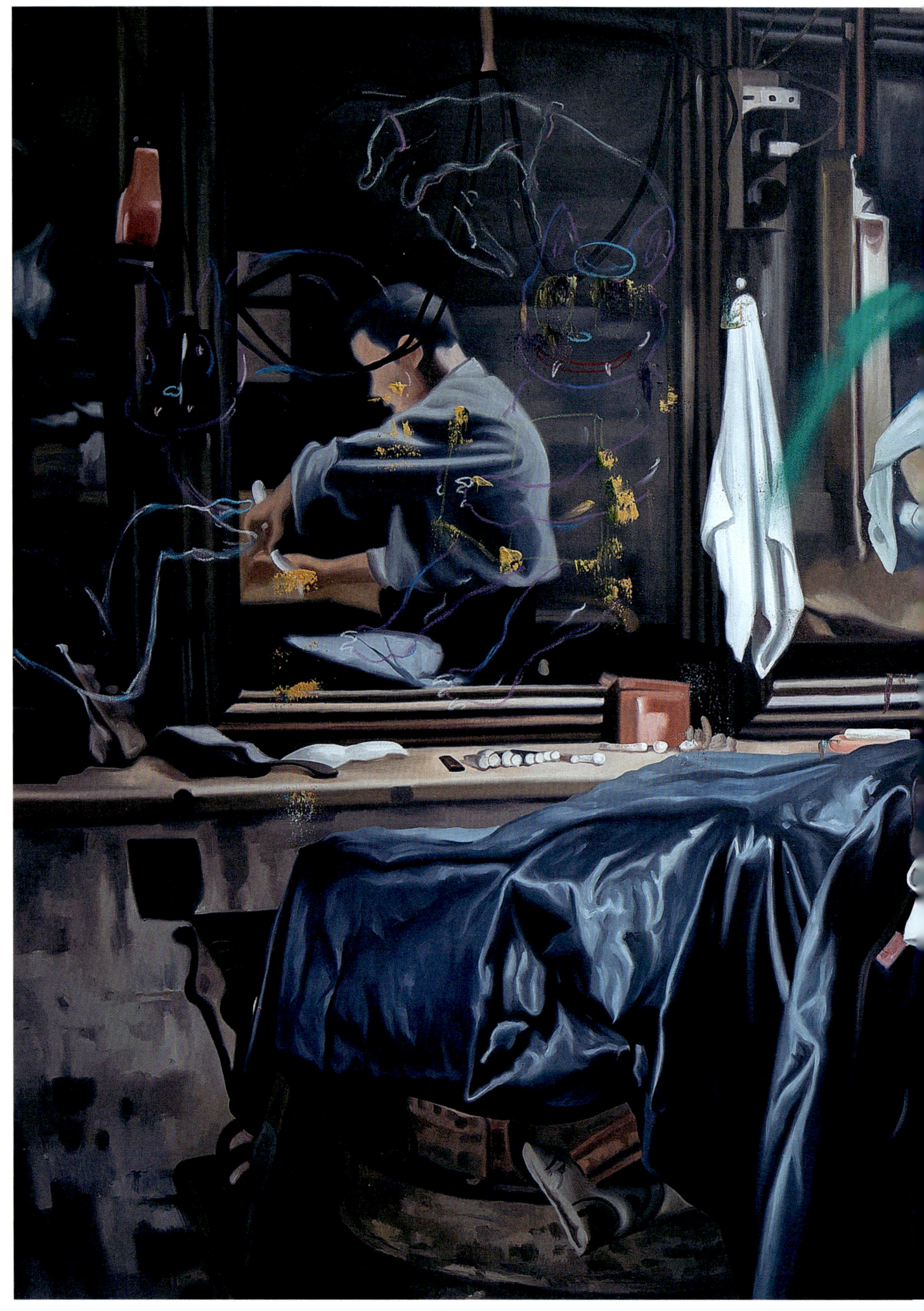

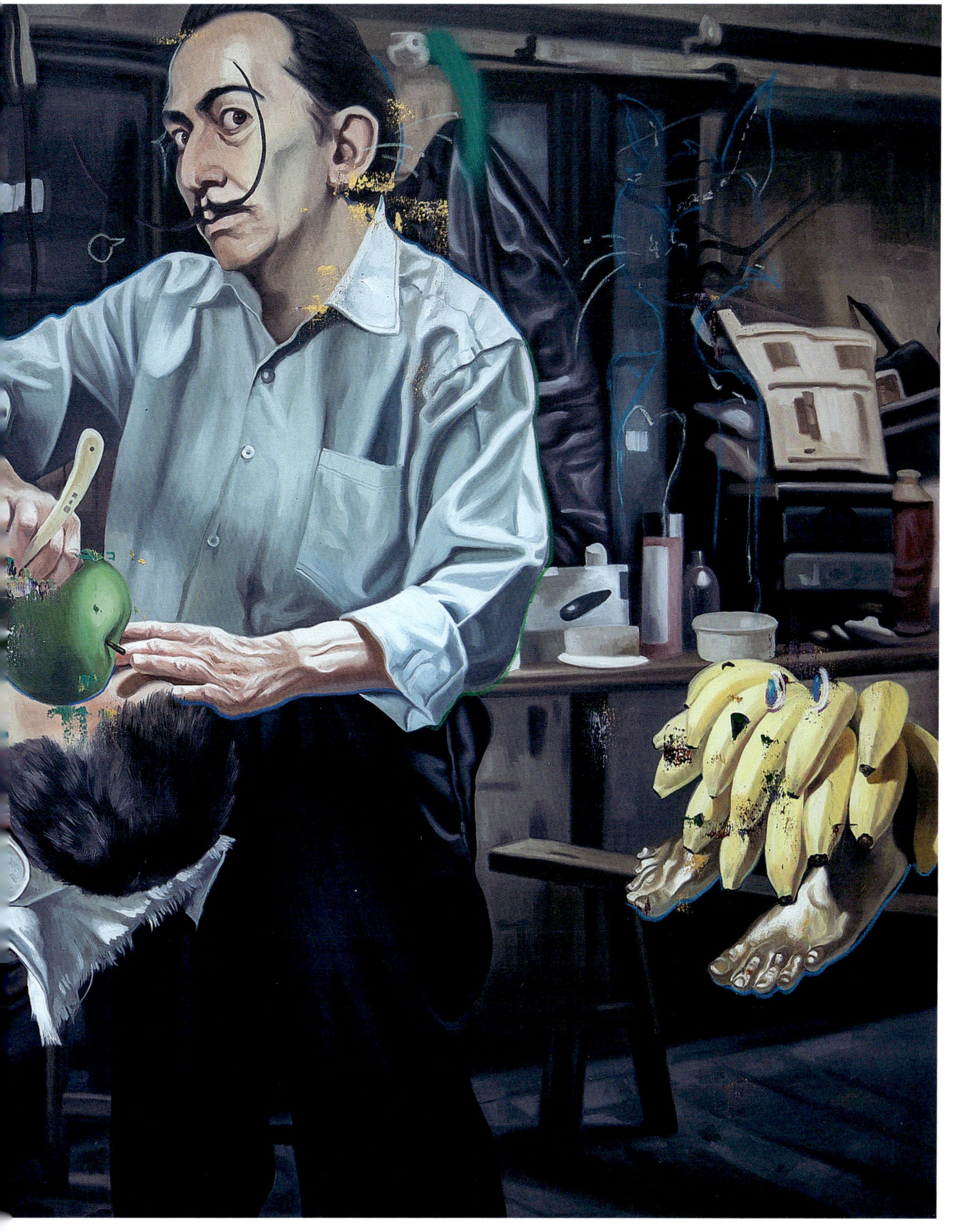

Life Props - Surrealist Barber Shop, 2021–22   oil on canvas, 133 × 200 cm

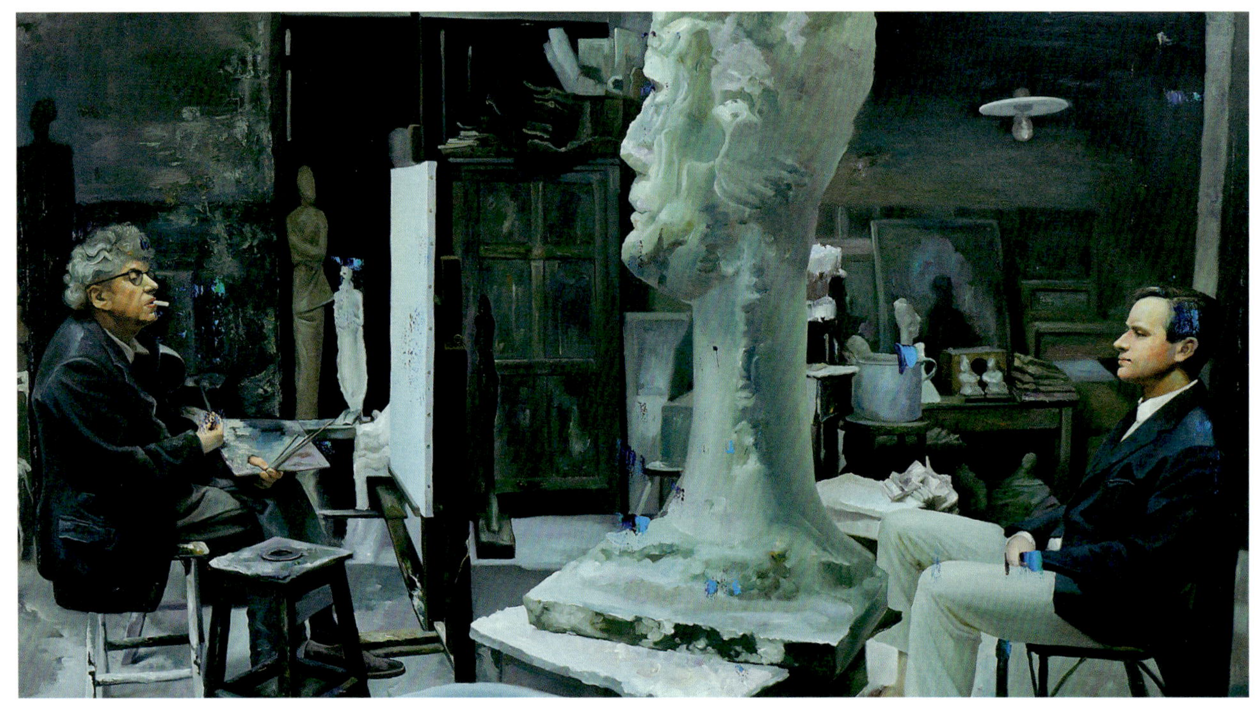

Life Props – Giacometti and the Model, 2021–22
oil on canvas, 120 × 213 cm

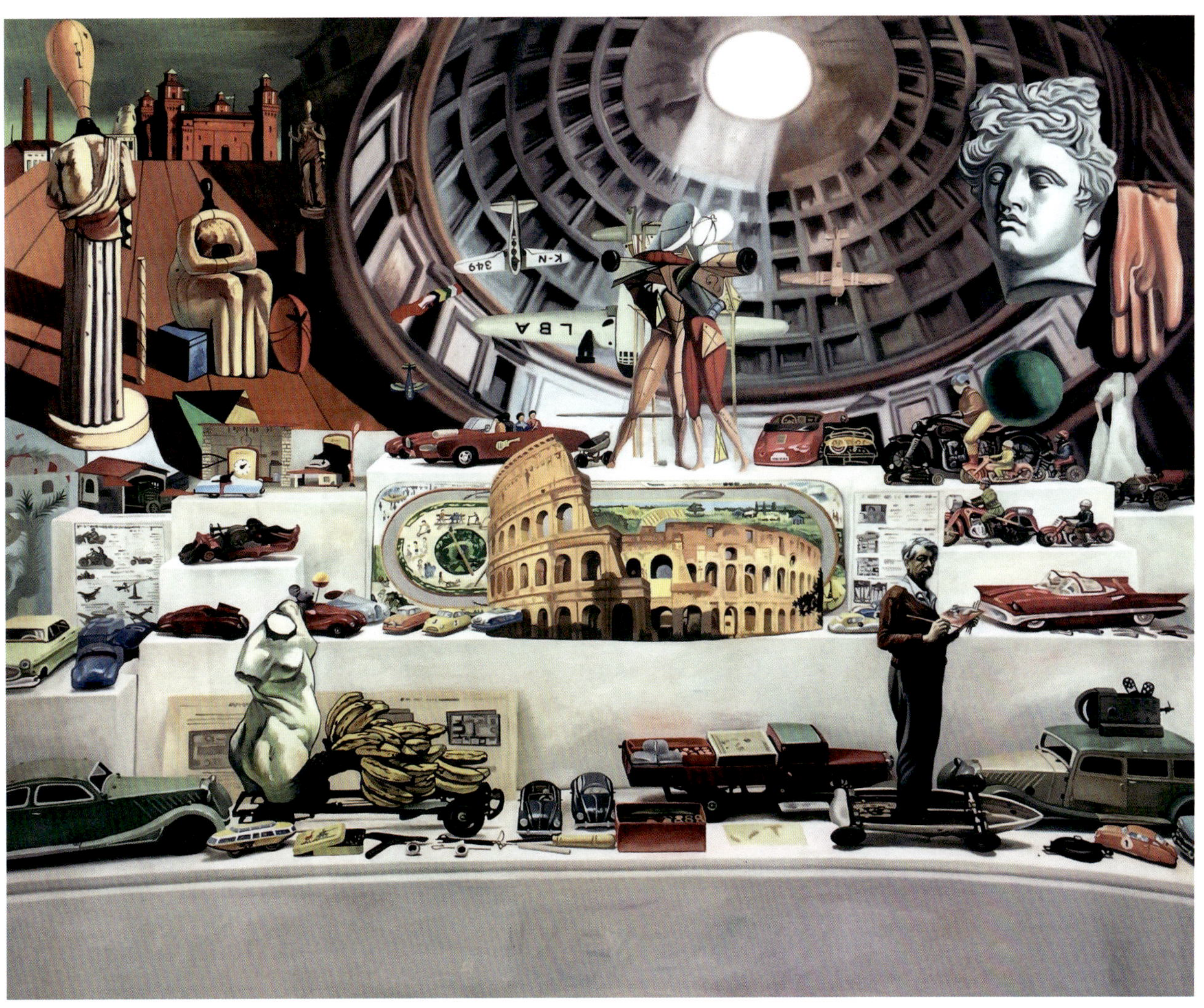

65   *Life Props – Giorgio de Chirico*, 2022   oil on canvas, 130 × 150 cm

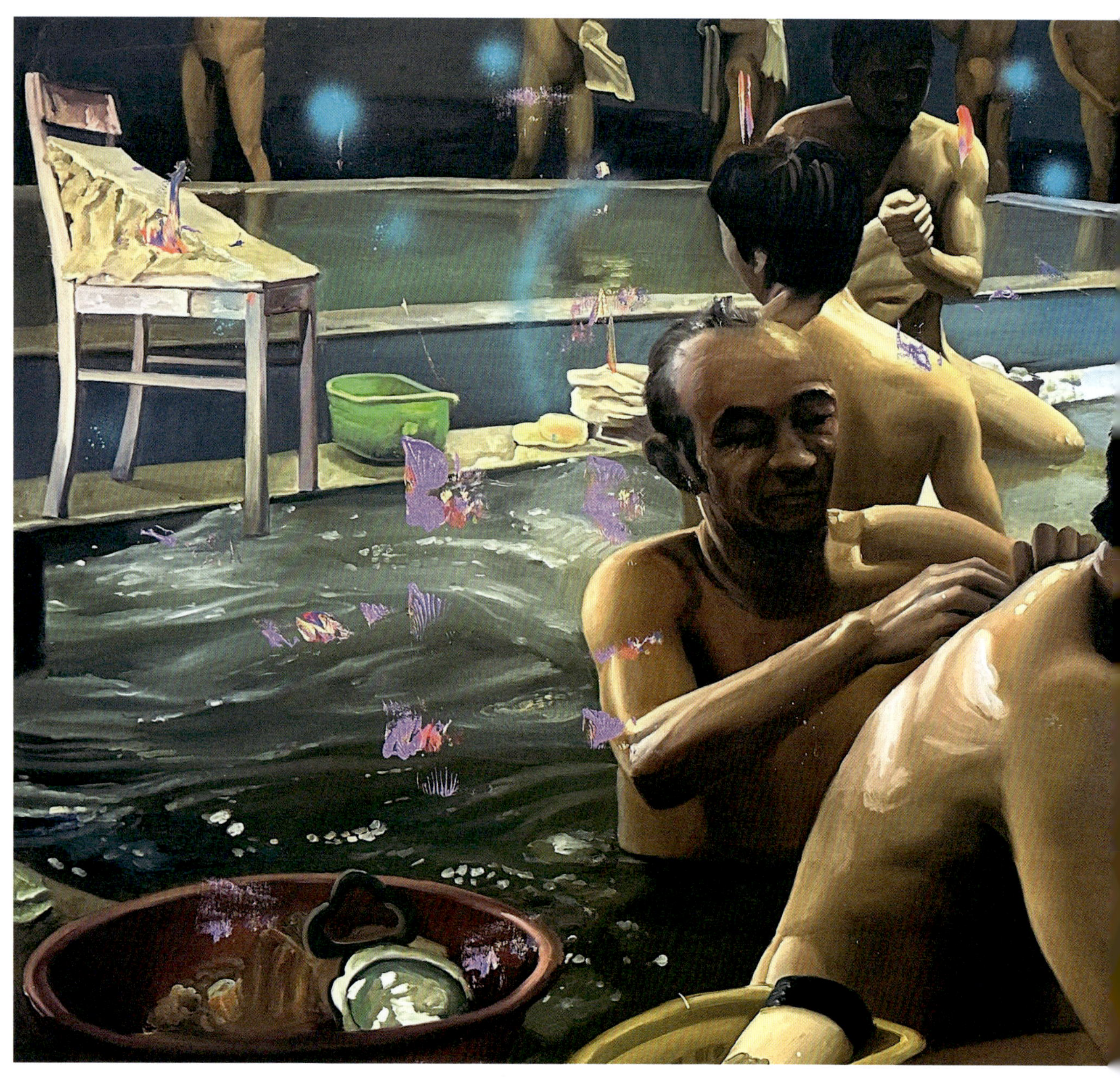

Hare, Bathhouse, Art History, 2021–22   oil on canvas, 100 × 200 cm

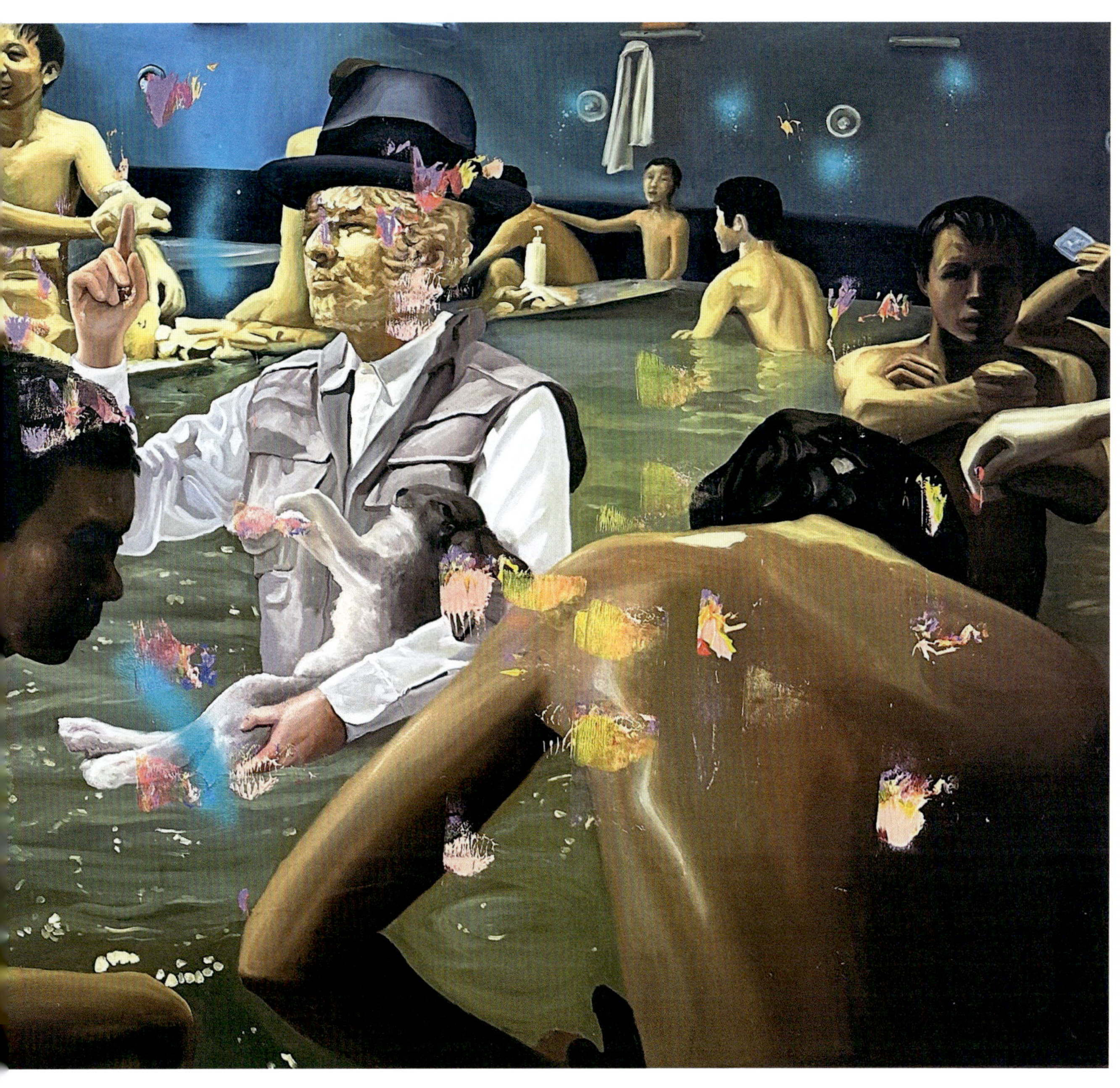

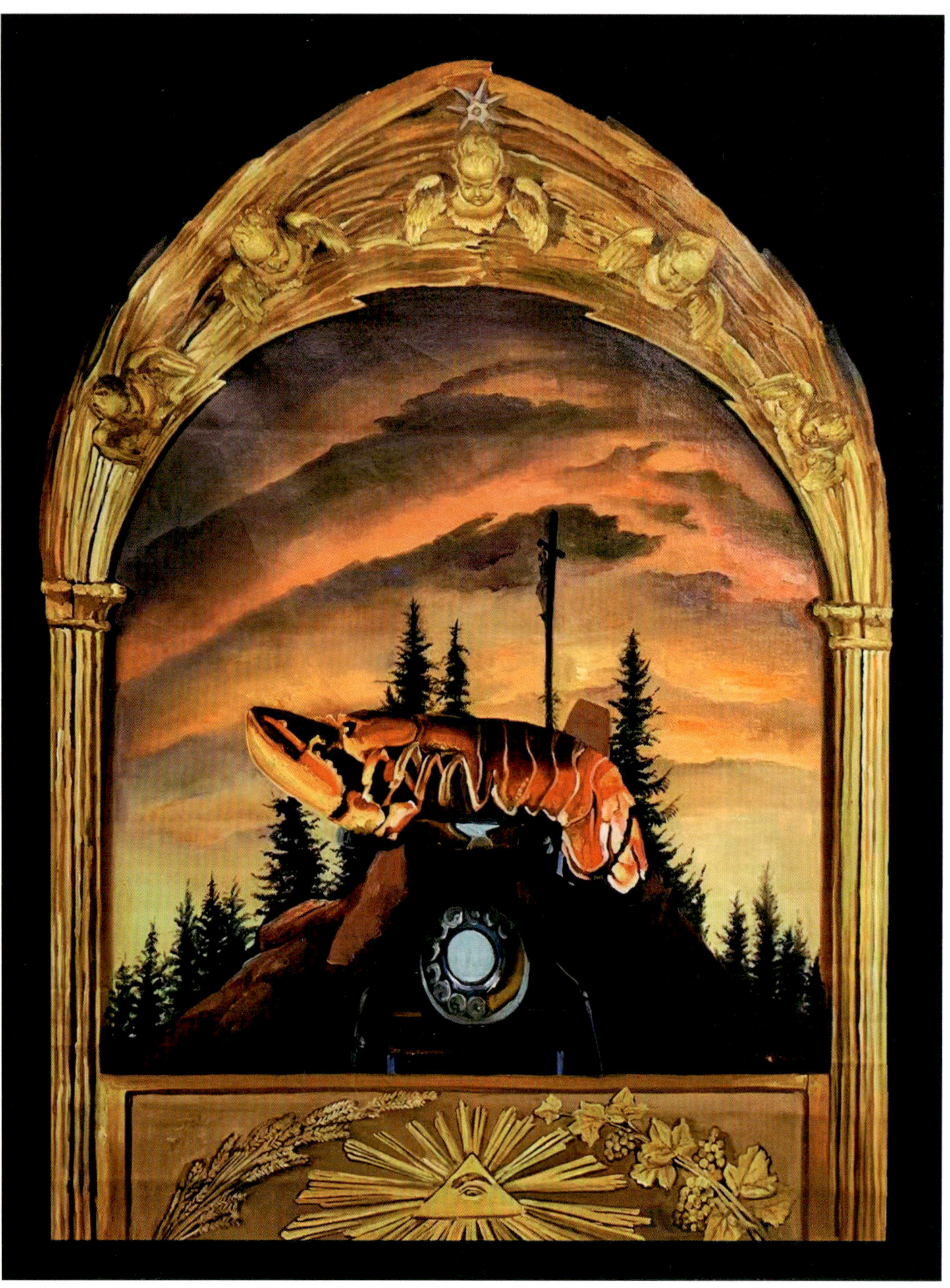

Calling the Distant Land, 2022   oil on canvas, 120 × 88 cm   **68**

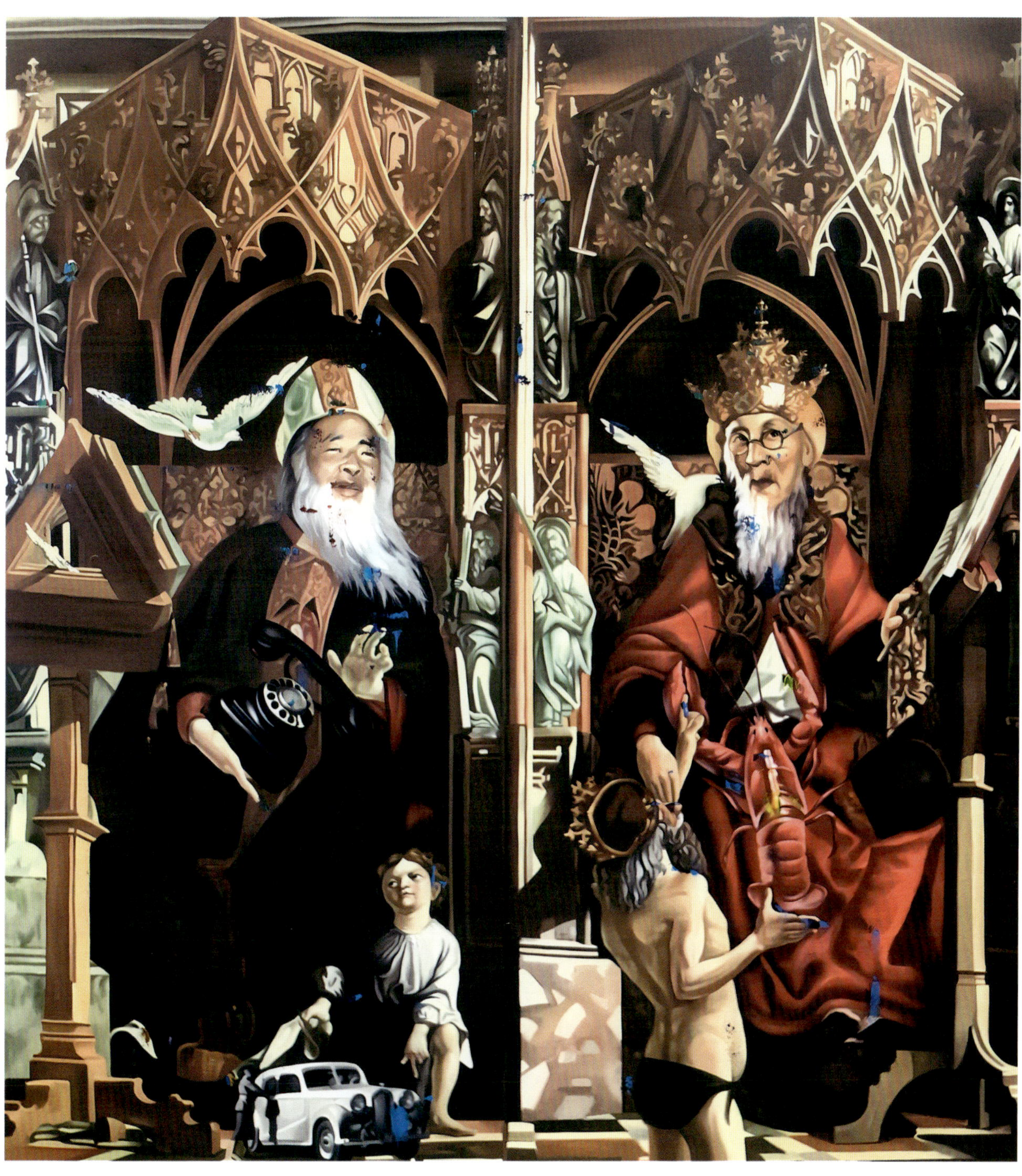

Qi Baishi and Zhang Daqian's Joyful Talk, 2022
oil on canvas, 200 × 180 cm

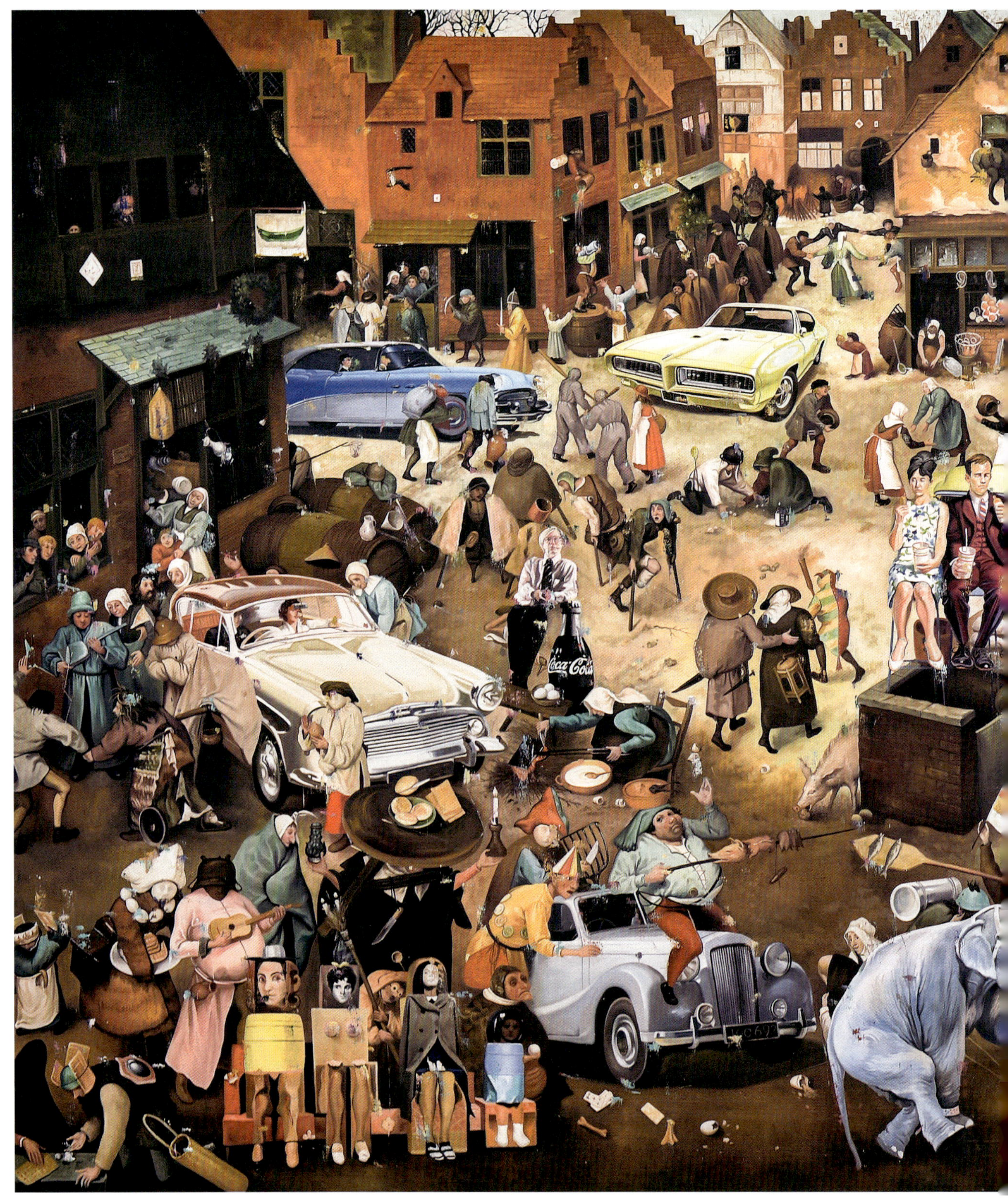

Fables of the Netherlands – Art Makes Tomorrow Better, 2023
oil on canvas, 295 × 500 cm

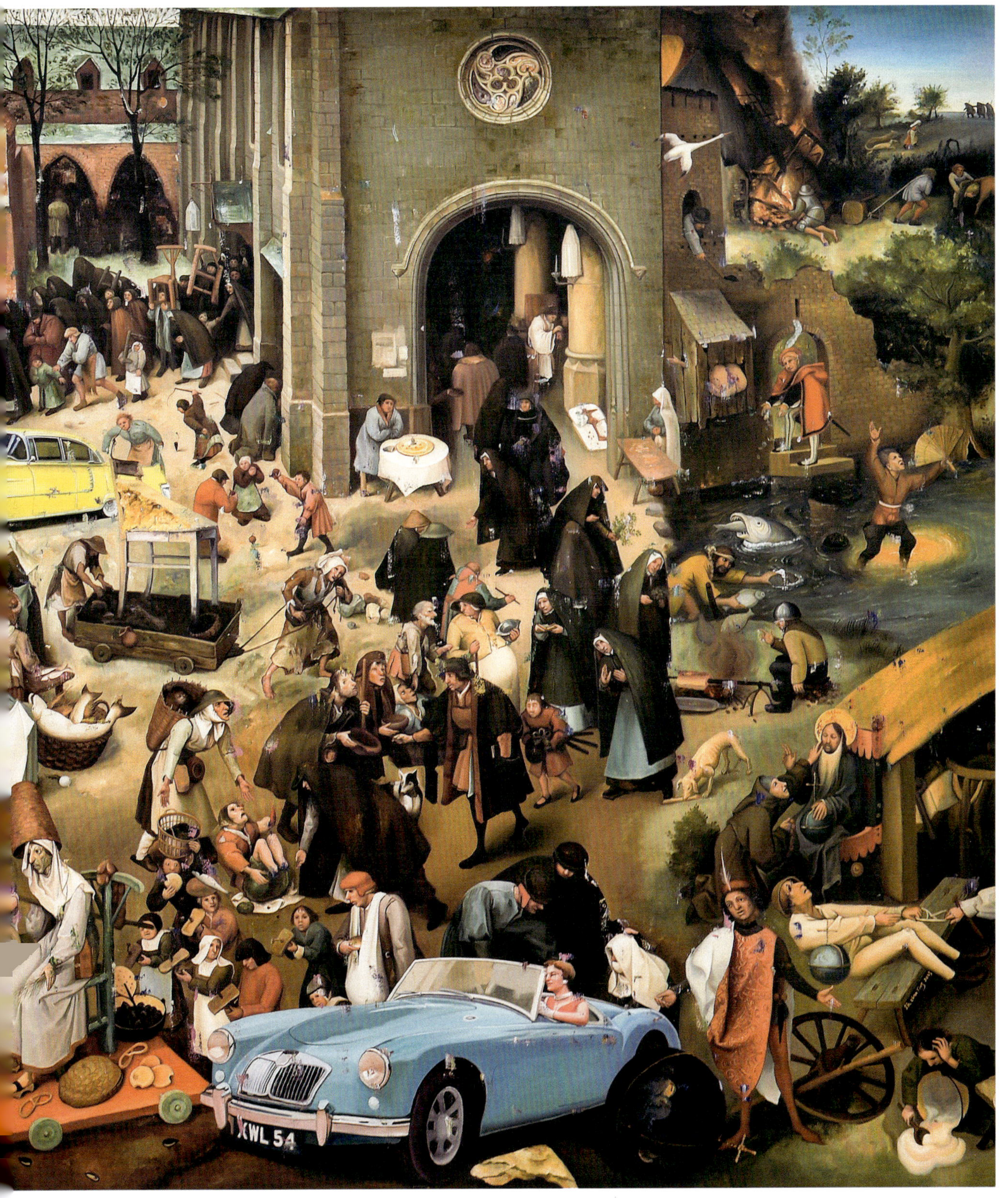

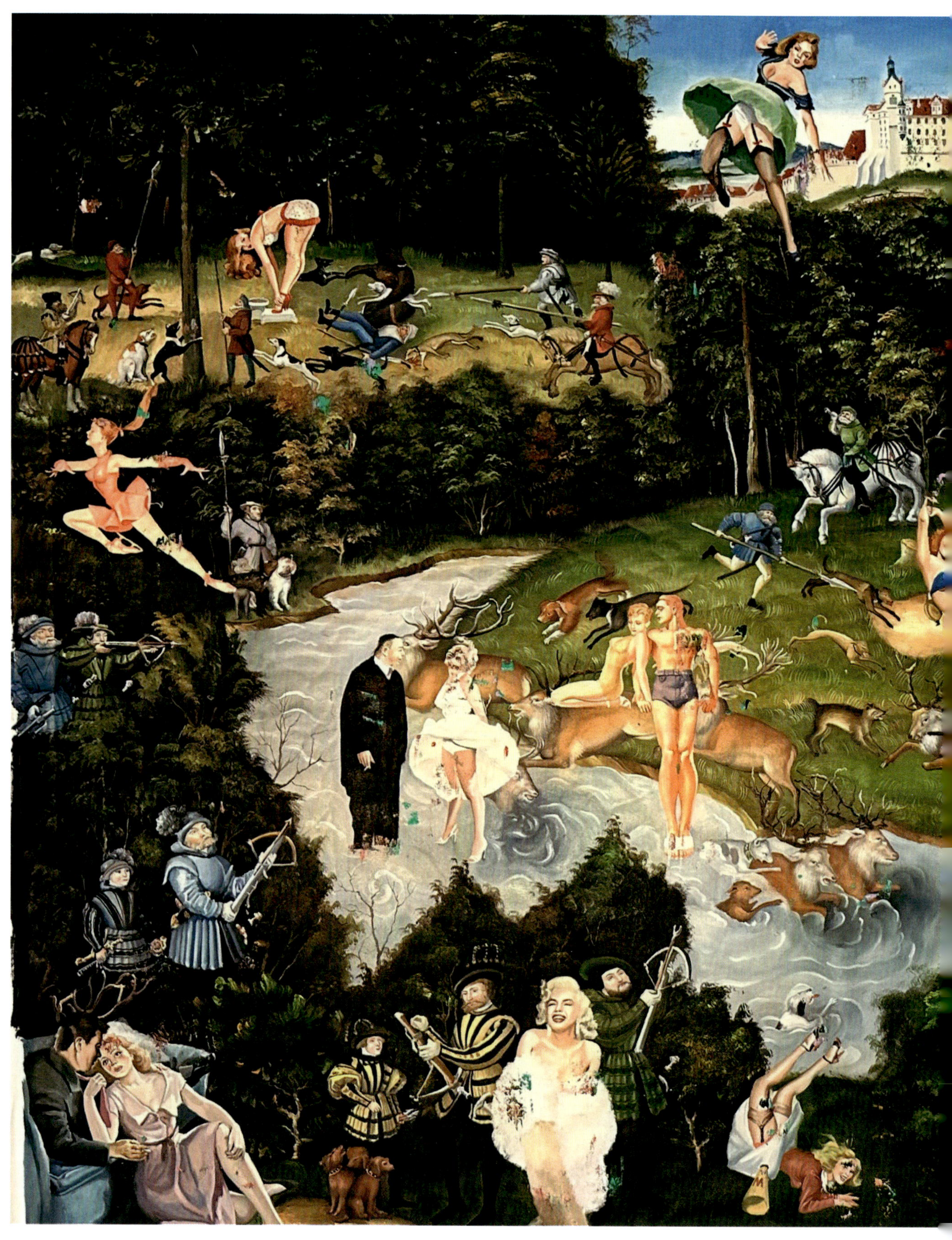

Appropriation and Use – The Valley of Beauties in the Castle, 2023
oil on canvas, 150 × 200 cm

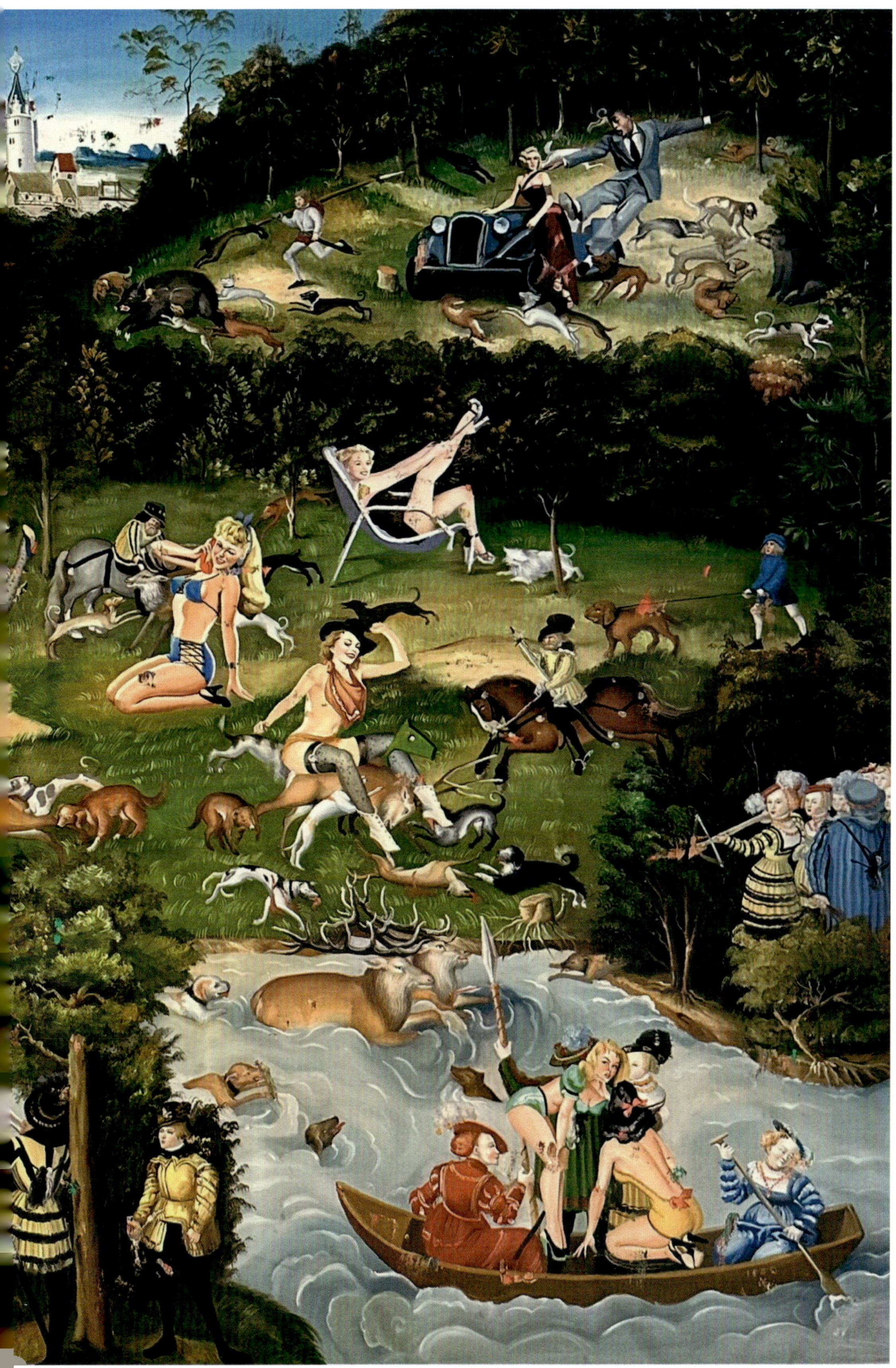

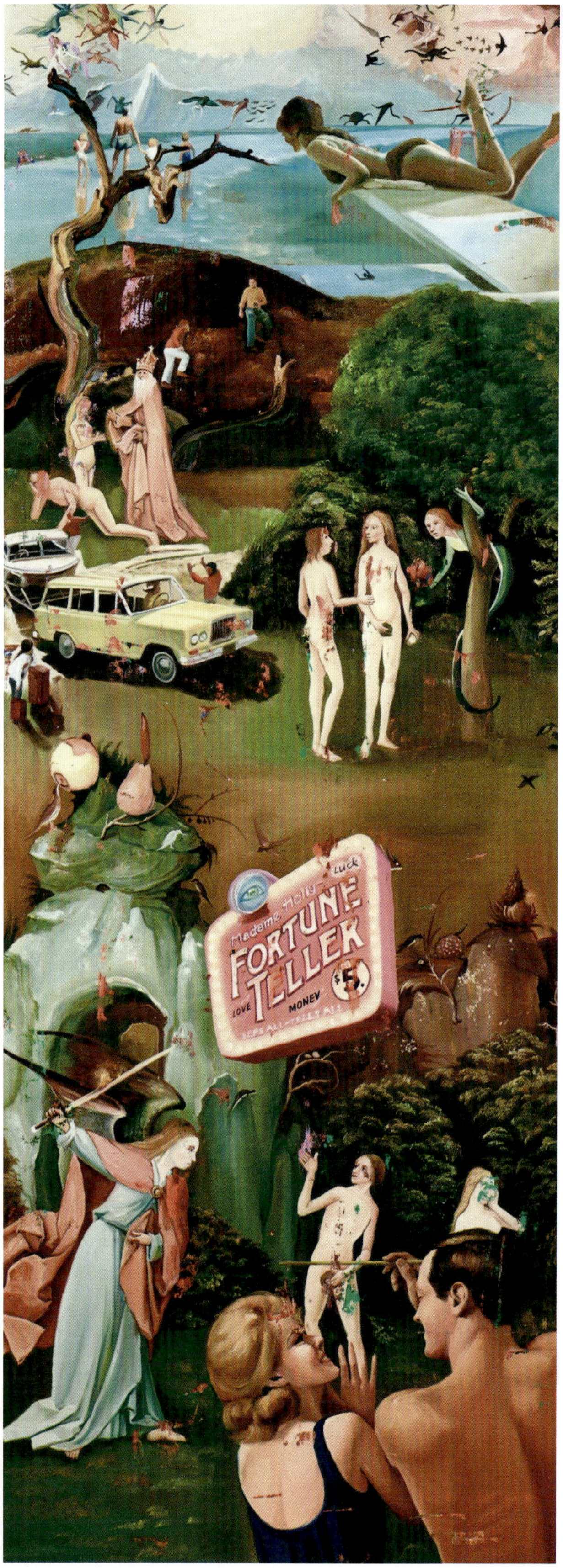

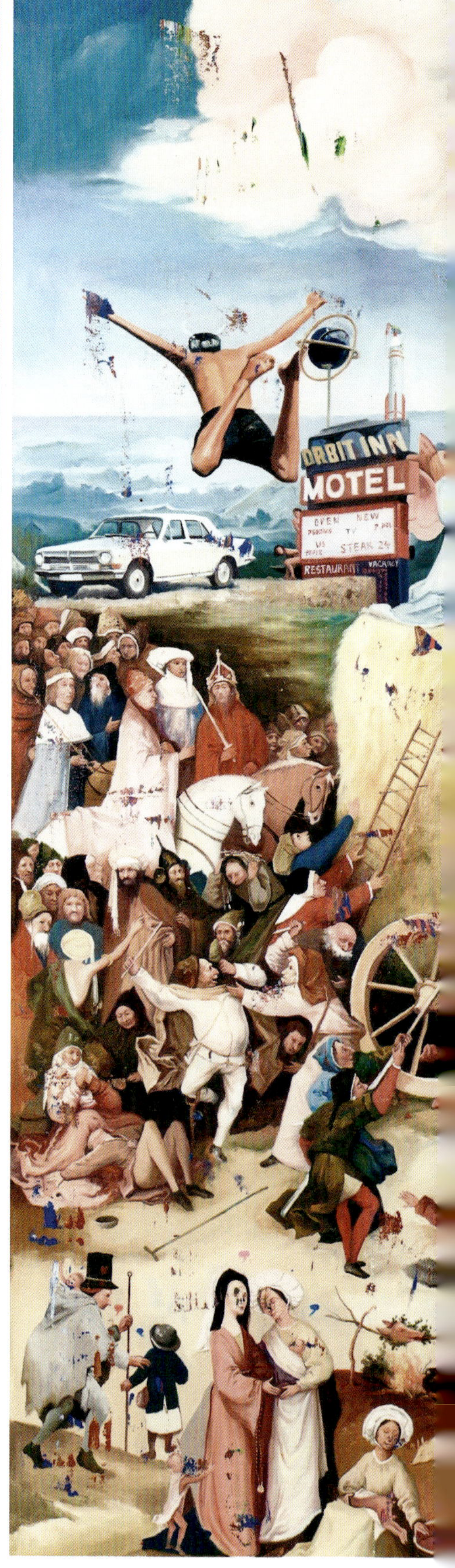

Madame Holly Luck
FORTUNE TELLER
$5.
LOVE   MONEY

ORBIT INN
MOTEL
OPEN   NEW
7 PM
STEAK 24
RESTAURANT   VACANCY

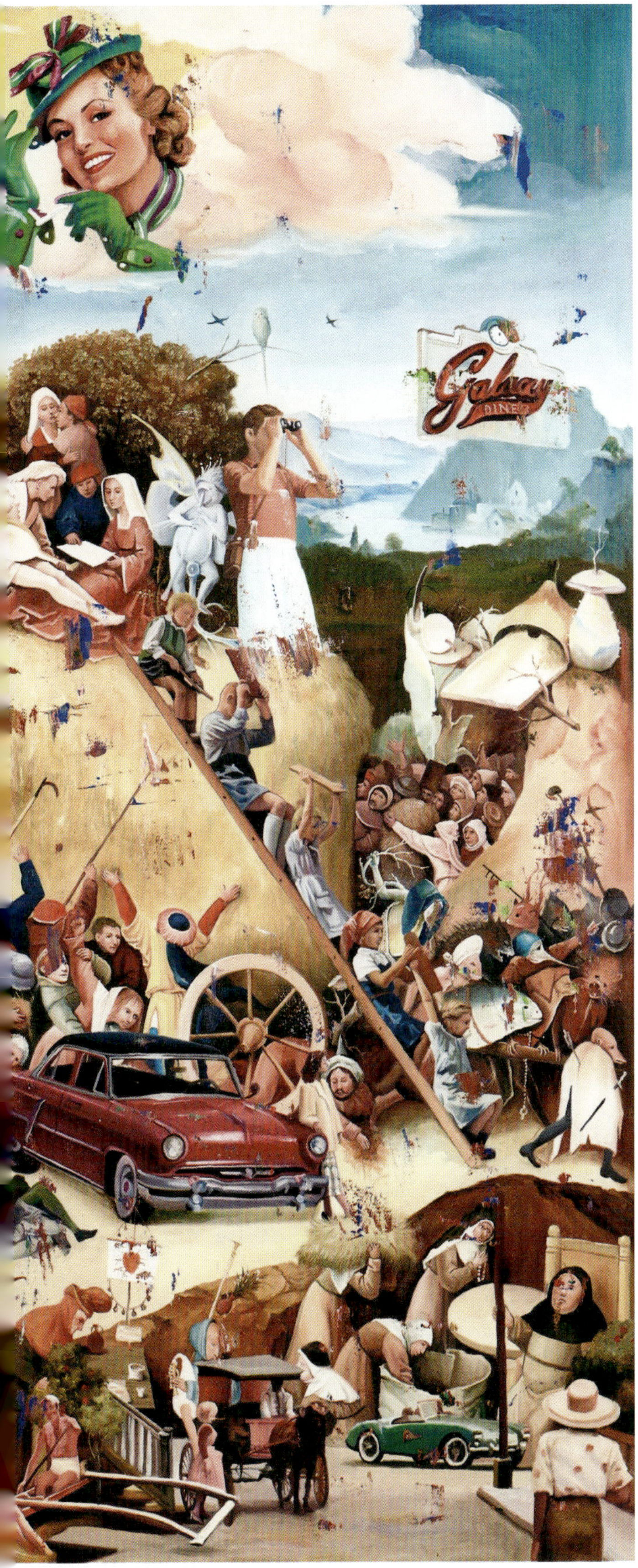

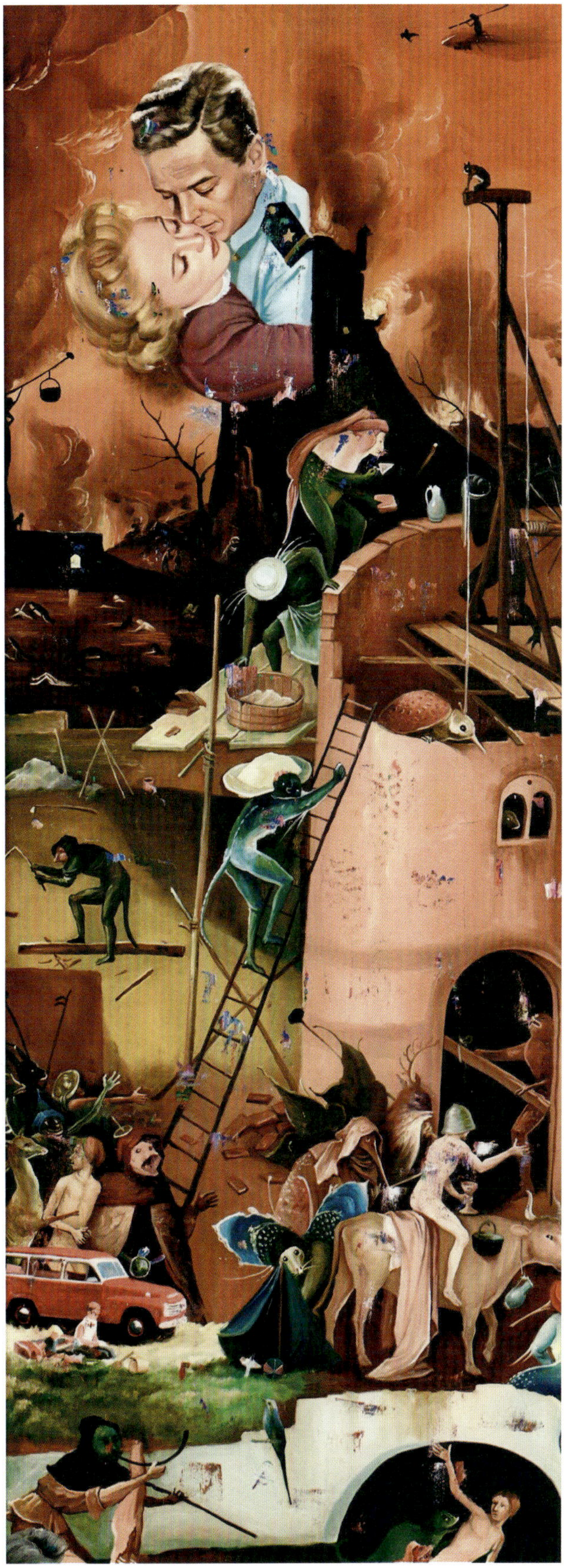

Appropriation and Use - Hay Wagon and Happy Life, 2023
oil on canvas, triptych, 200 × 150 cm (central panel), 200 × 75 cm (side panels)

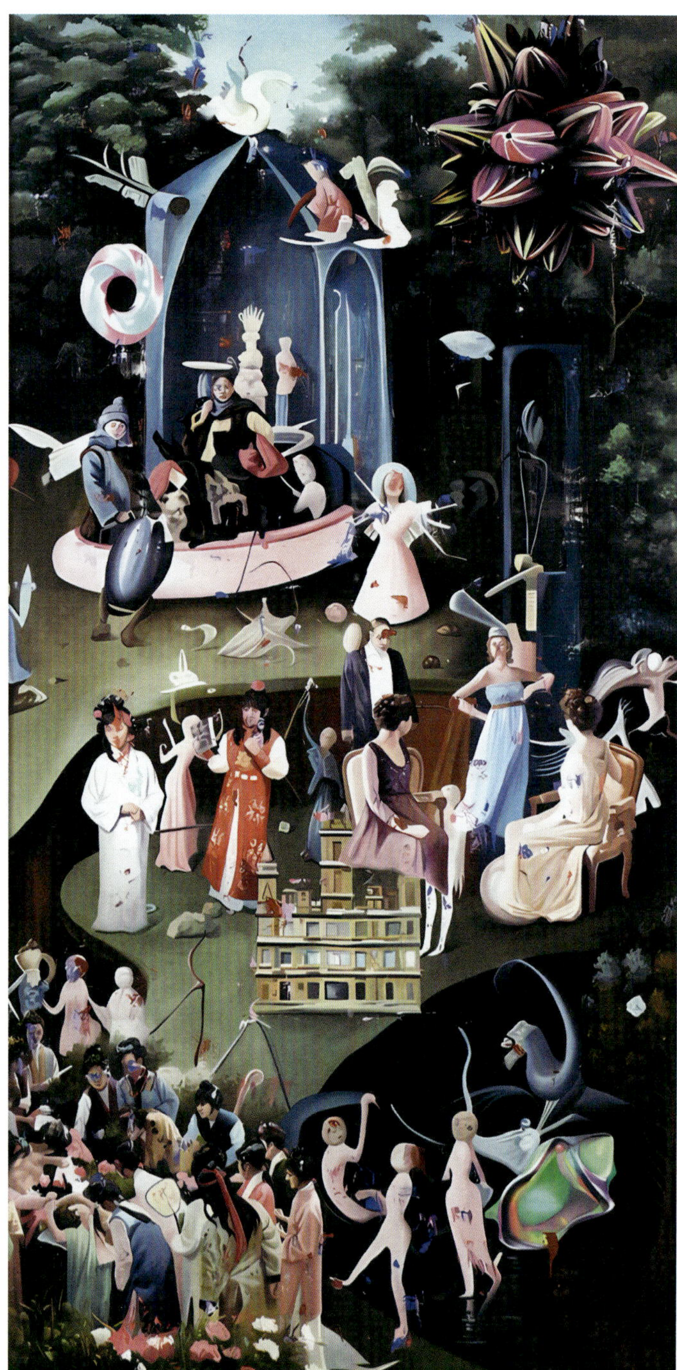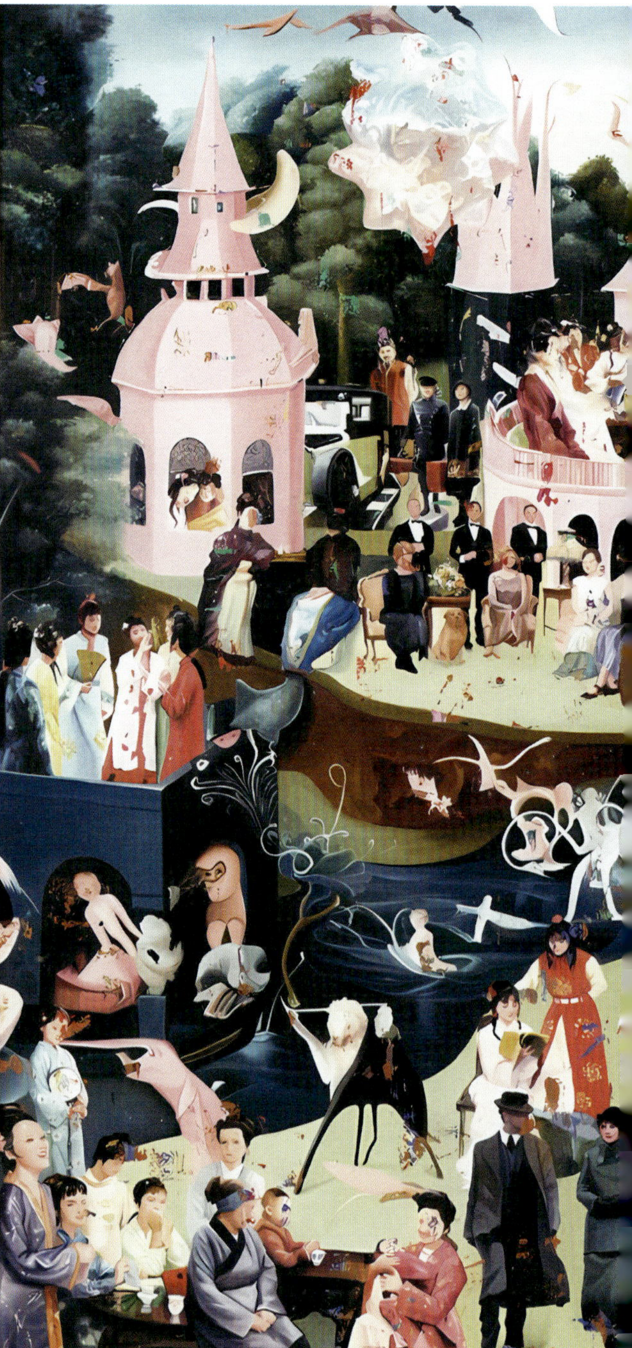

Appropriation and Use – Red Chamber, Downton, One Dream, 2023
oil on canvas, triptych, 200 × 200 cm (central panel), 200 × 100 cm (side panels)

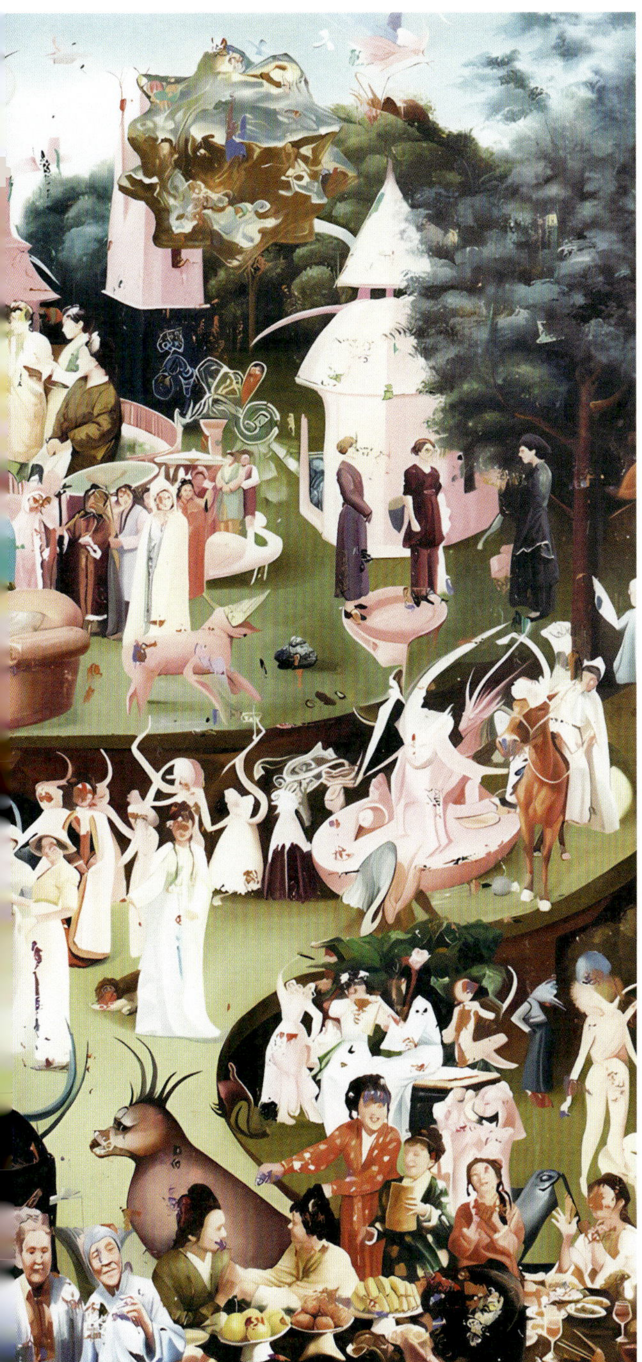
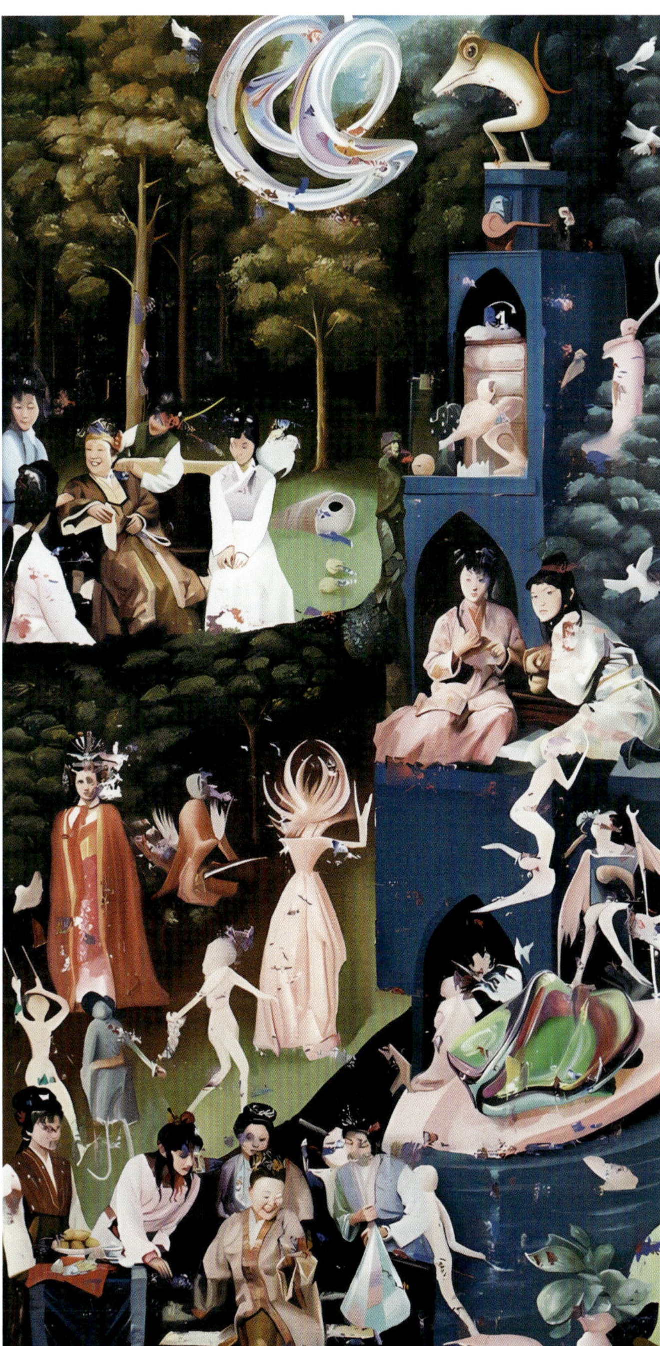

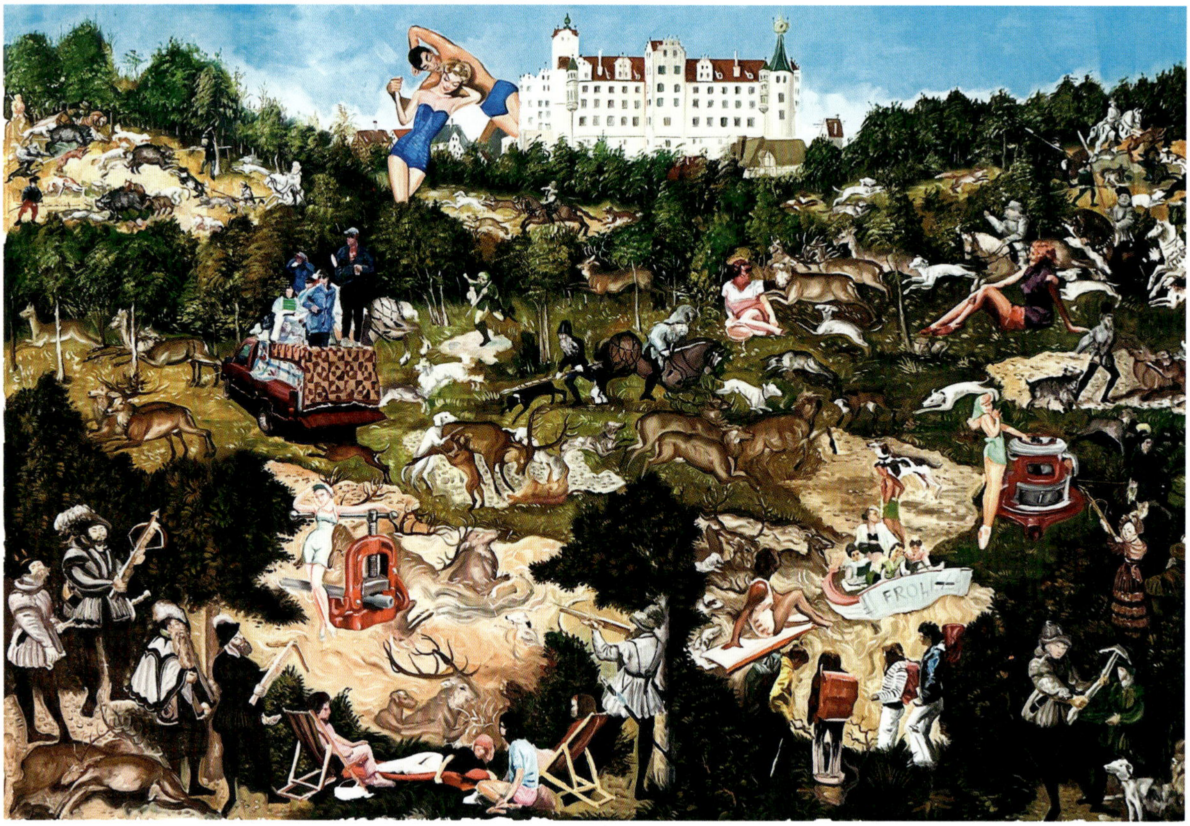

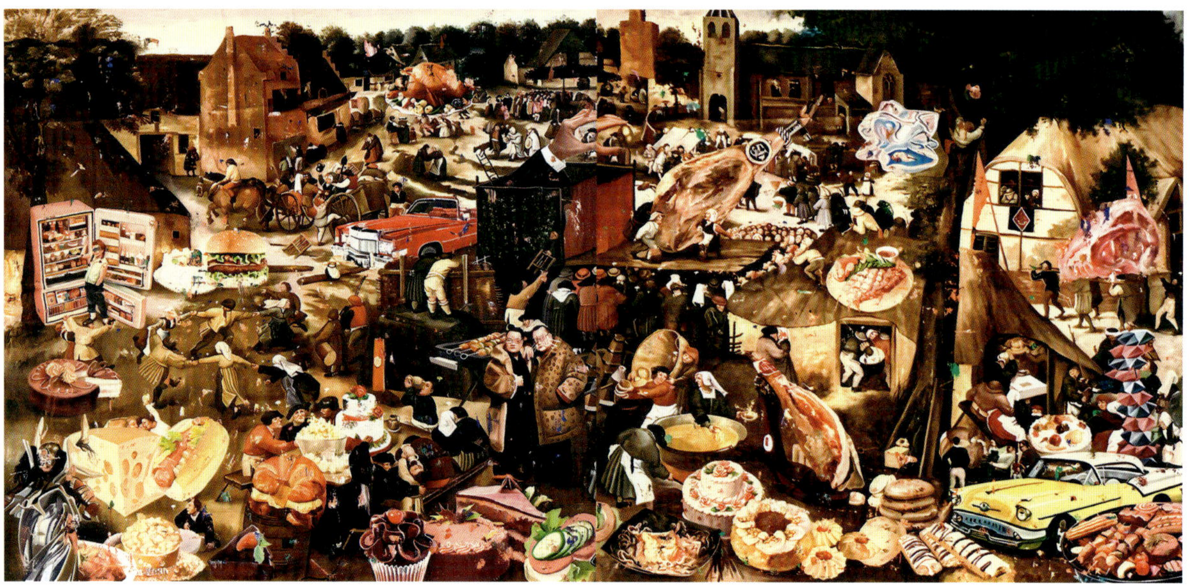

Appropriation and Use – Hunting Scene (unfinished), 2023
oil on canvas, 150 × 200 cm
Appropriation and Use – Brueghel's Picnic on the Grass
and *The Great Wealth of the Netherlands*, 2023
oil on canvas, 200 × 400 cm

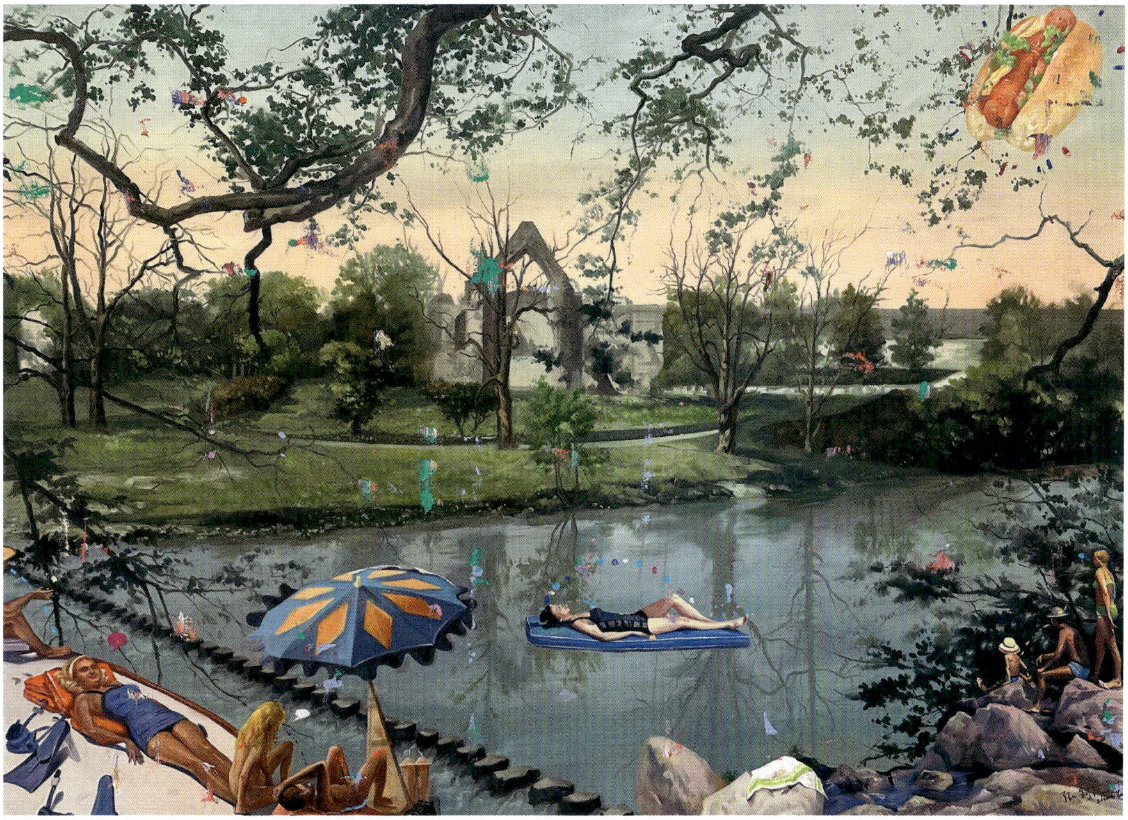

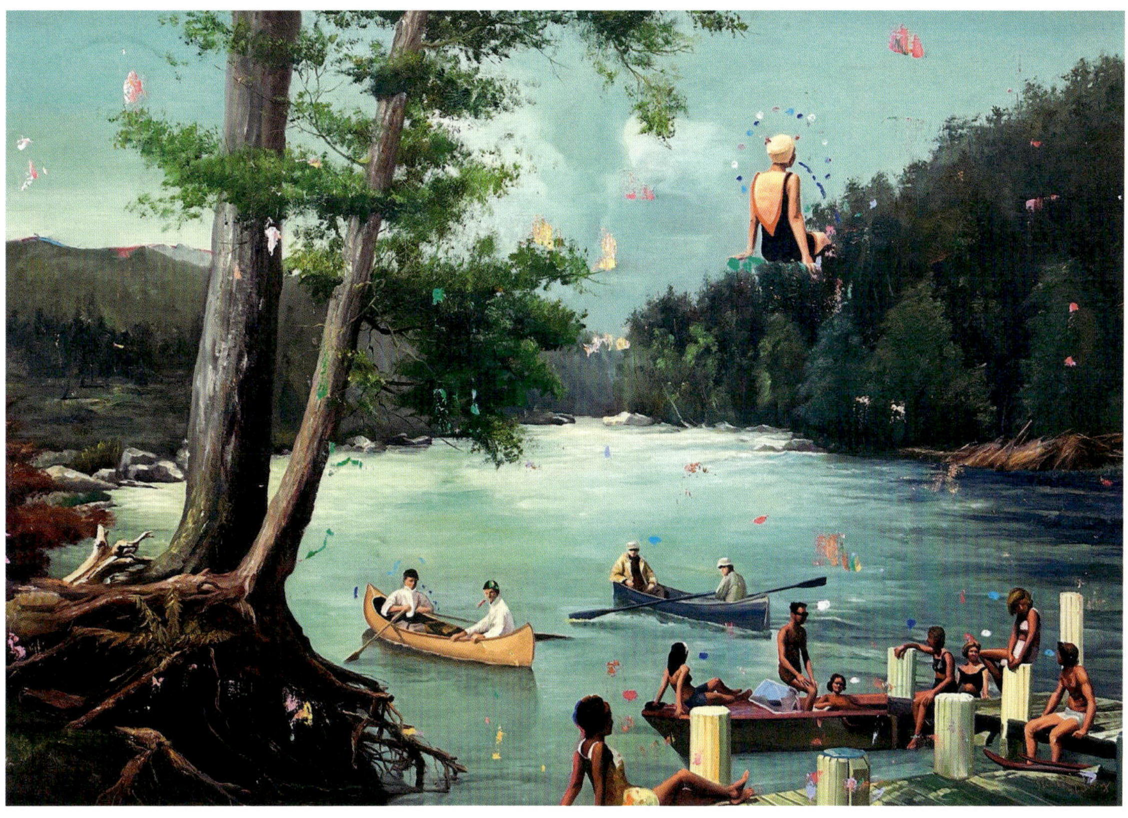

Lifelong Beauty - Vacation, 2022   oil on canvas, 100 × 140 cm
Lifelong Beauty - A Journey of Happiness, 2023–24
oil on canvas, 100 × 140 cm

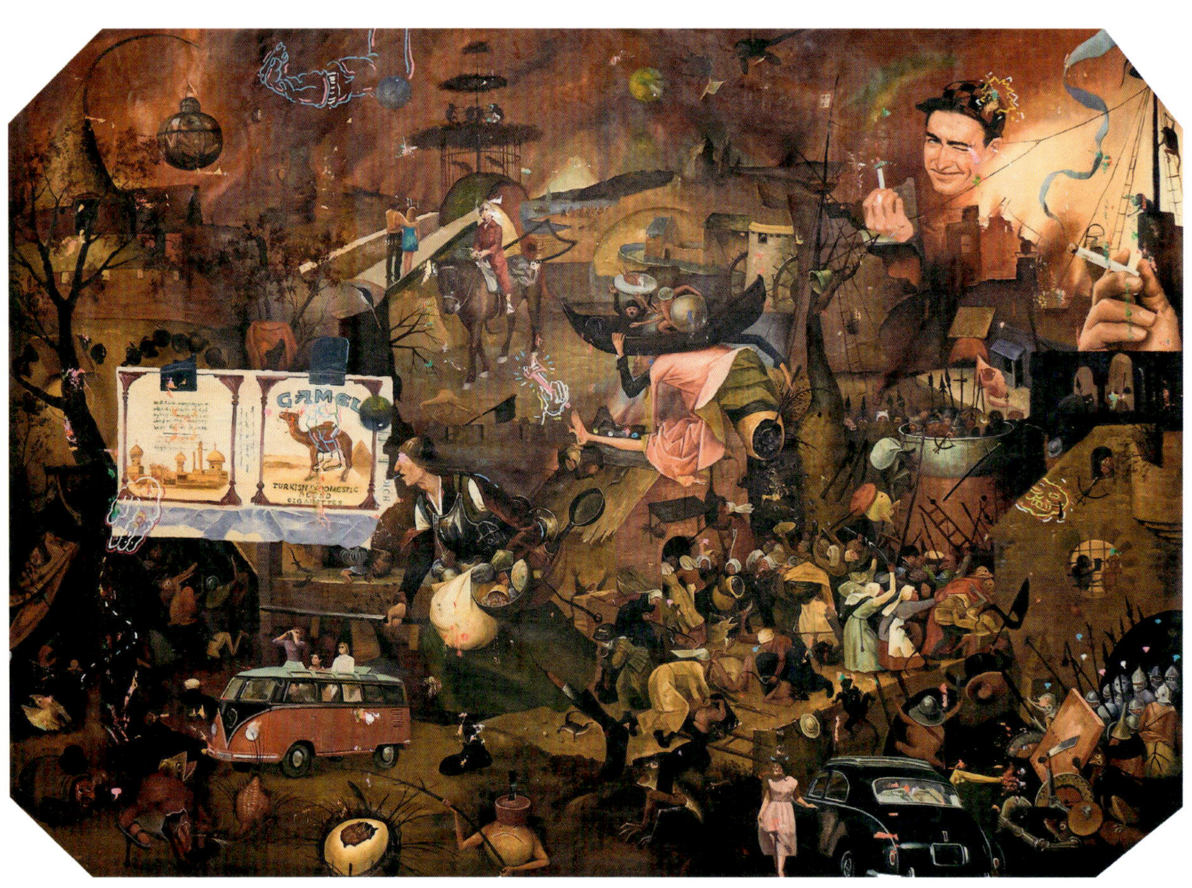

Lifelong Beauty - Bosch's Camel Cigarettes, 2023–24
oil on canvas, 186 × 260 cm

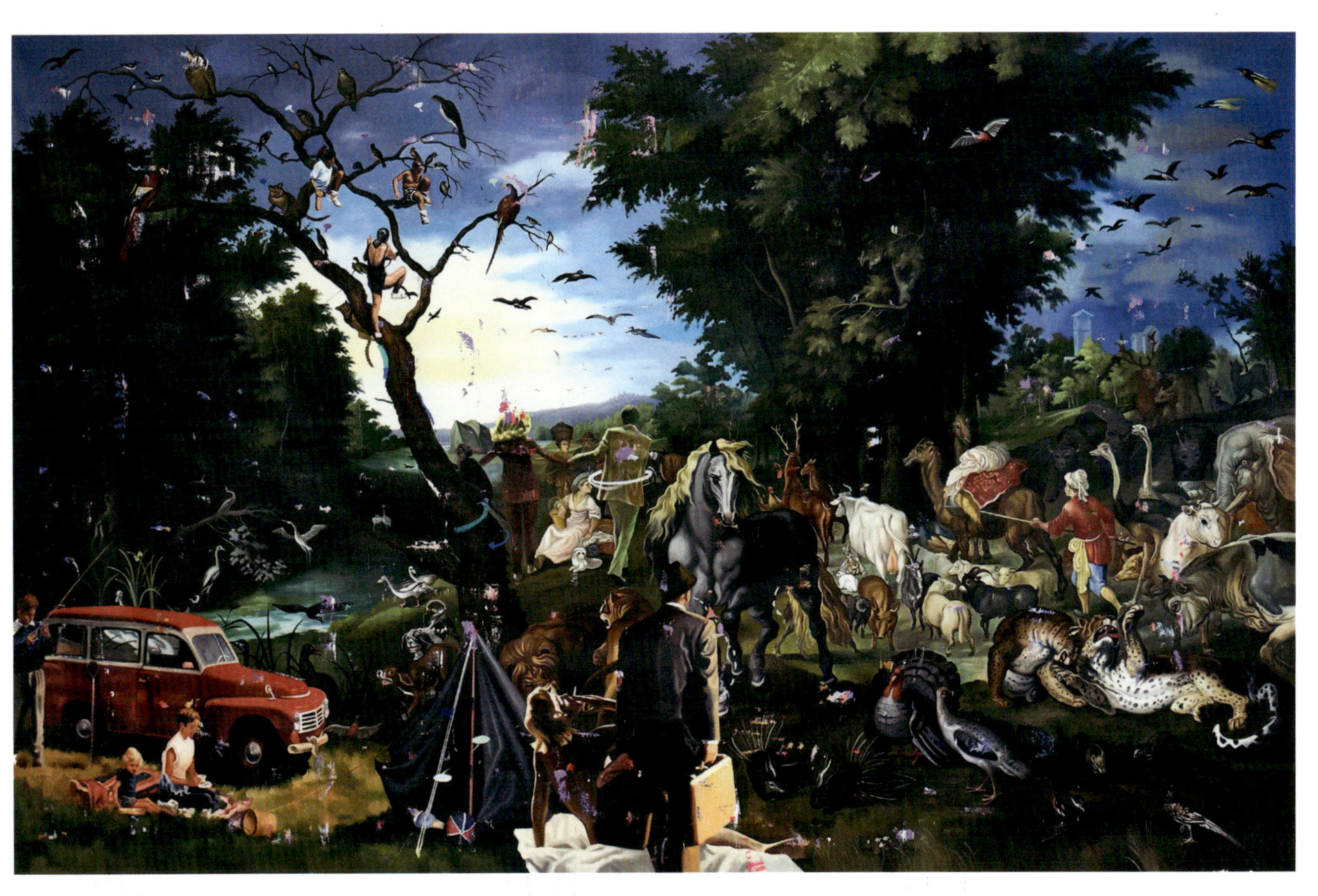

Lifelong Beauty – The Pursuit of Happiness, 2023–24
oil on canvas, 170 × 260 cm

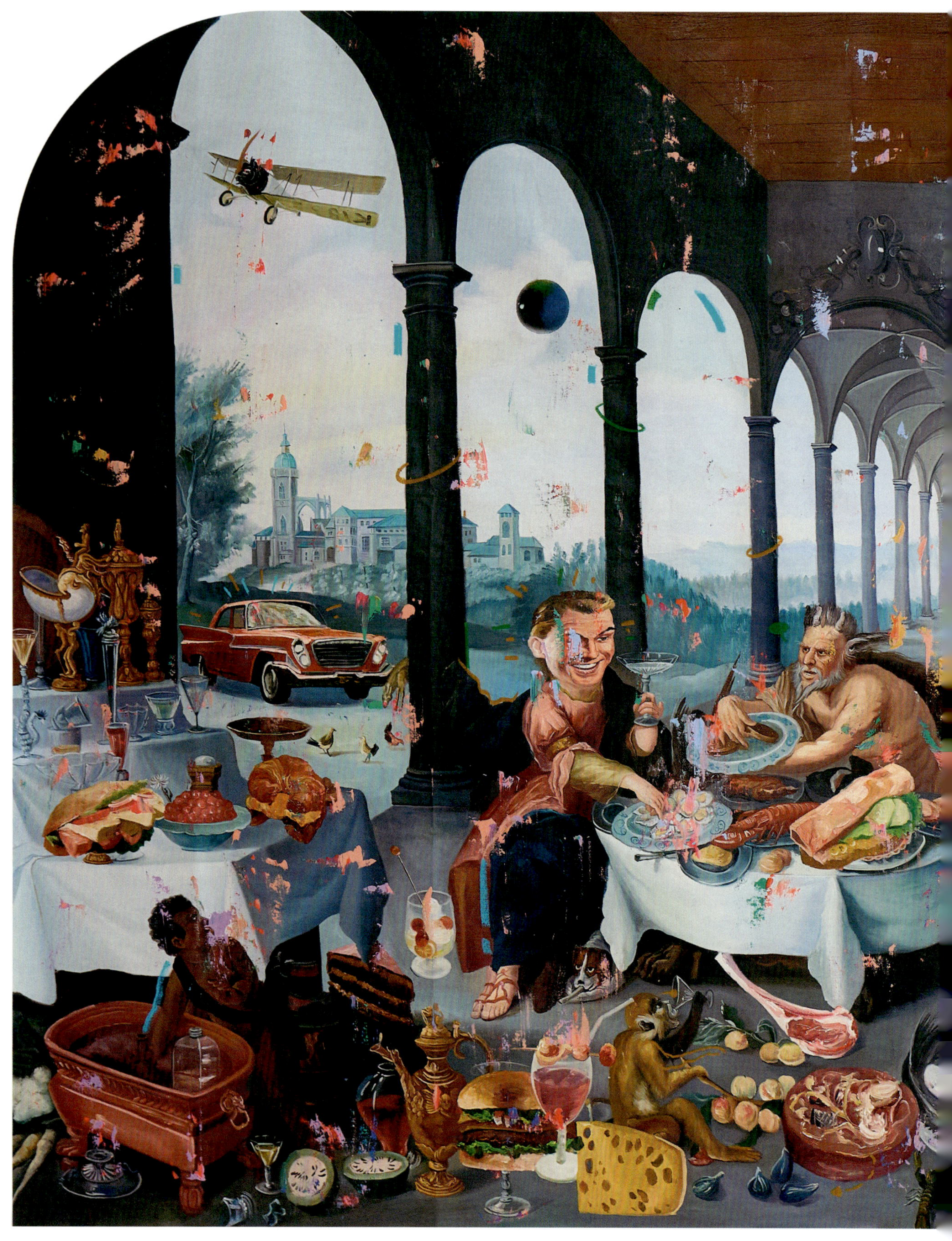

Lifelong Beauty – The Feast of Mr. Pan, 2023–24   oil on canvas, 170 × 260 cm

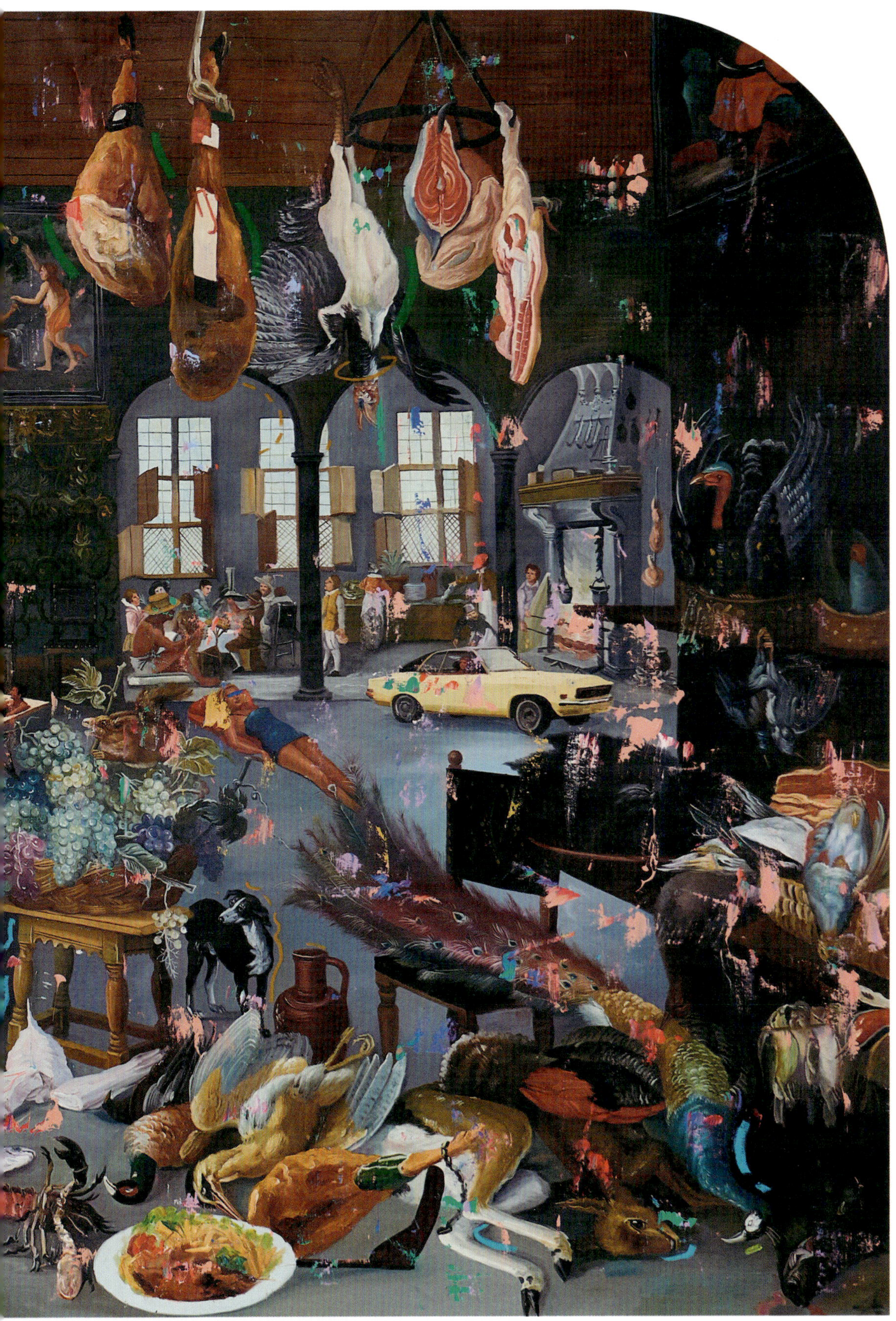

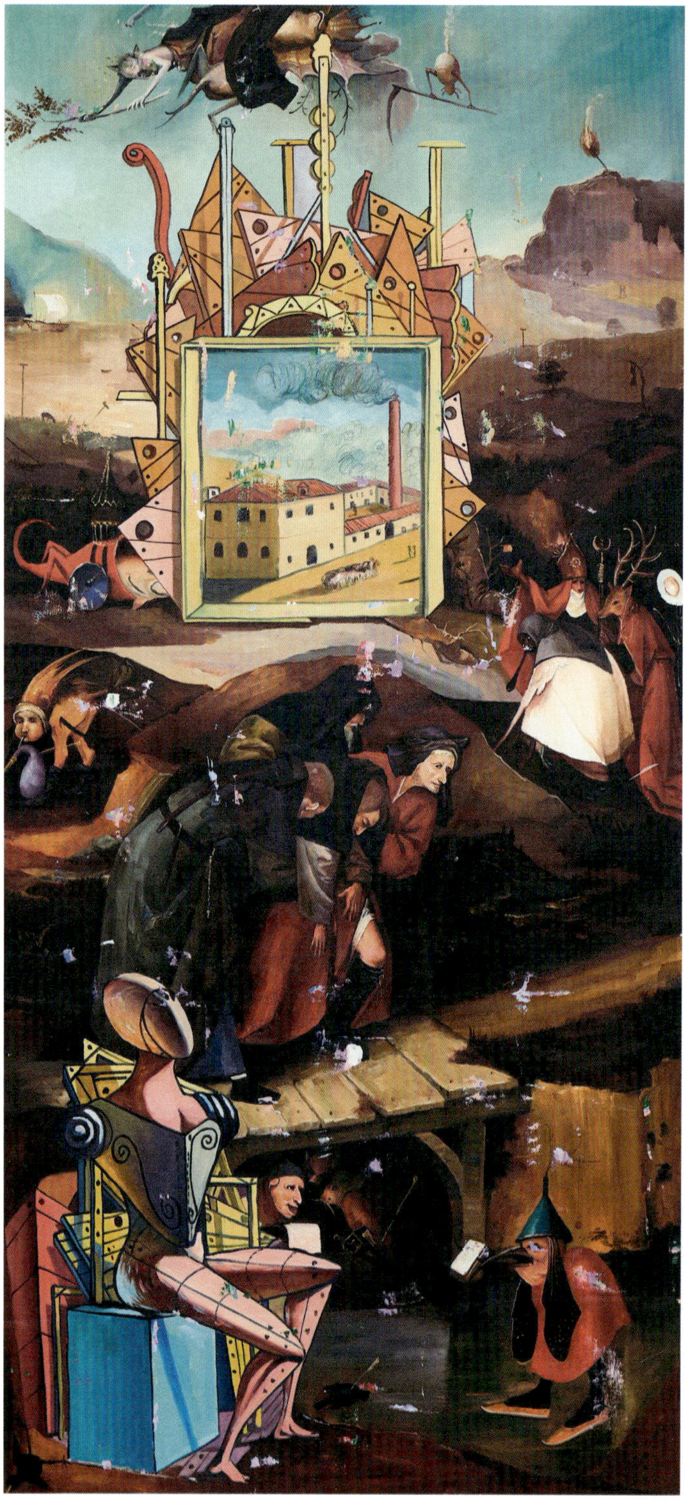

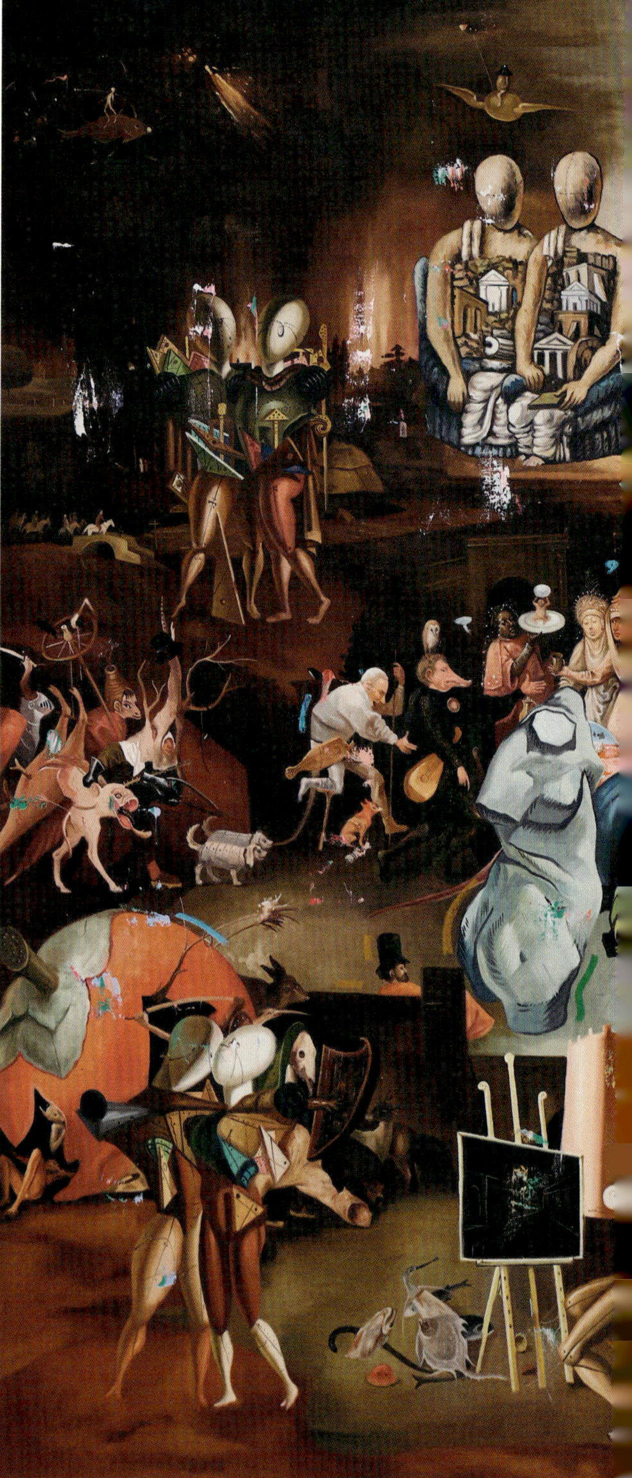

Lifelong Beauty – The Temptation of Giorgio de Chirico, 2023–24
oil on canvas, triptych, 200 × 180 cm (central panel), 200 × 90 cm (side panels)

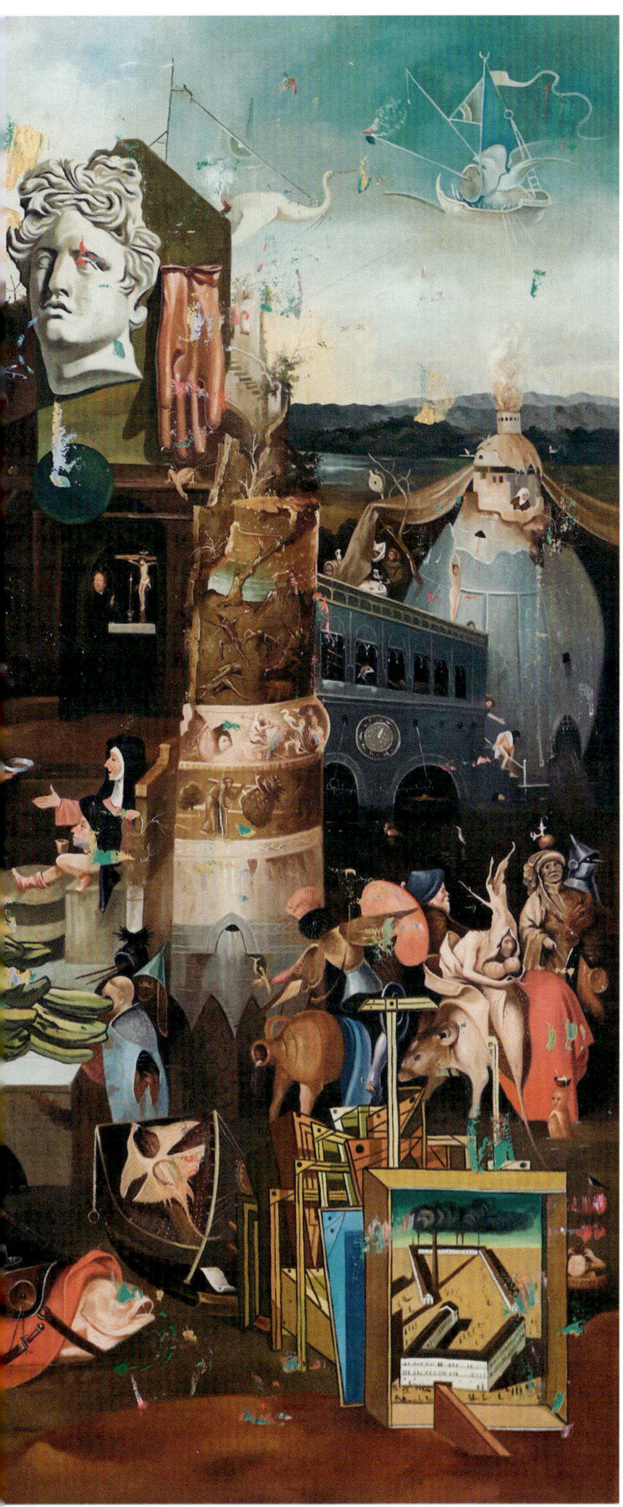

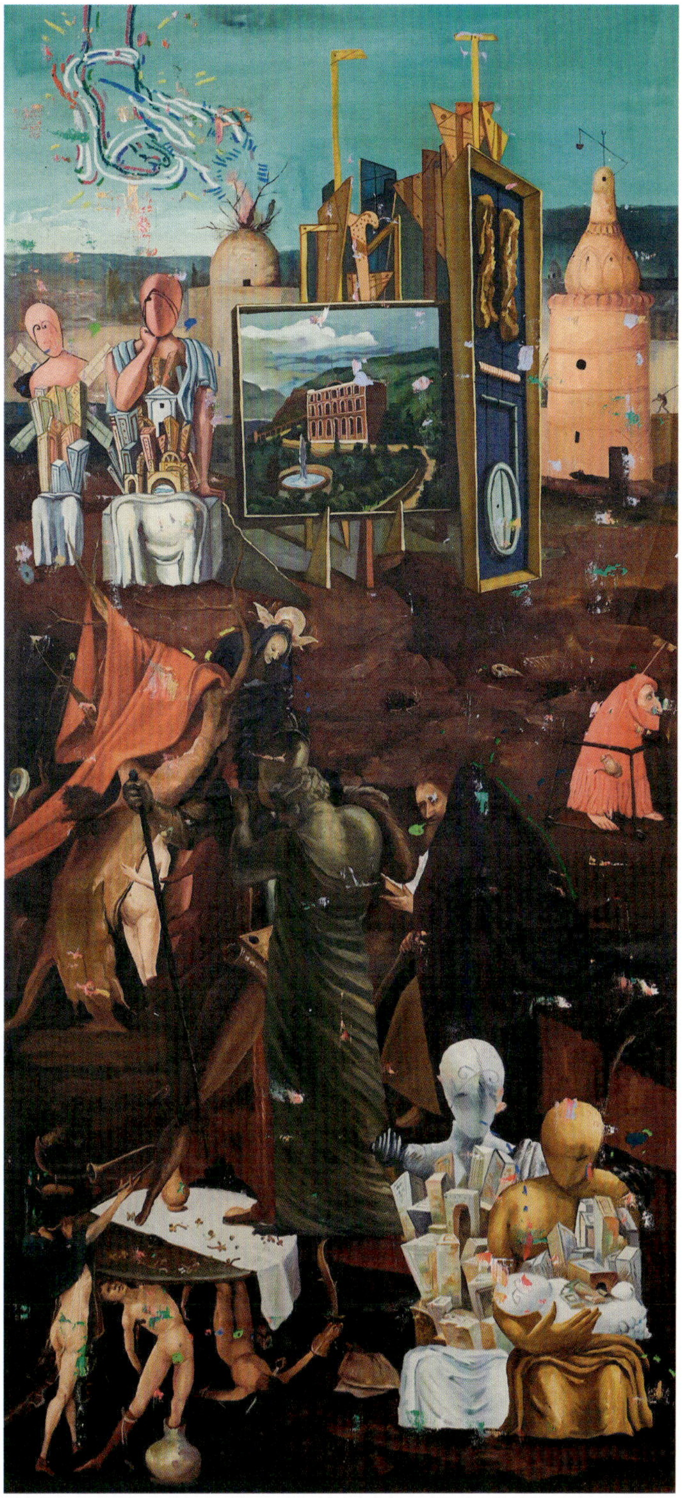

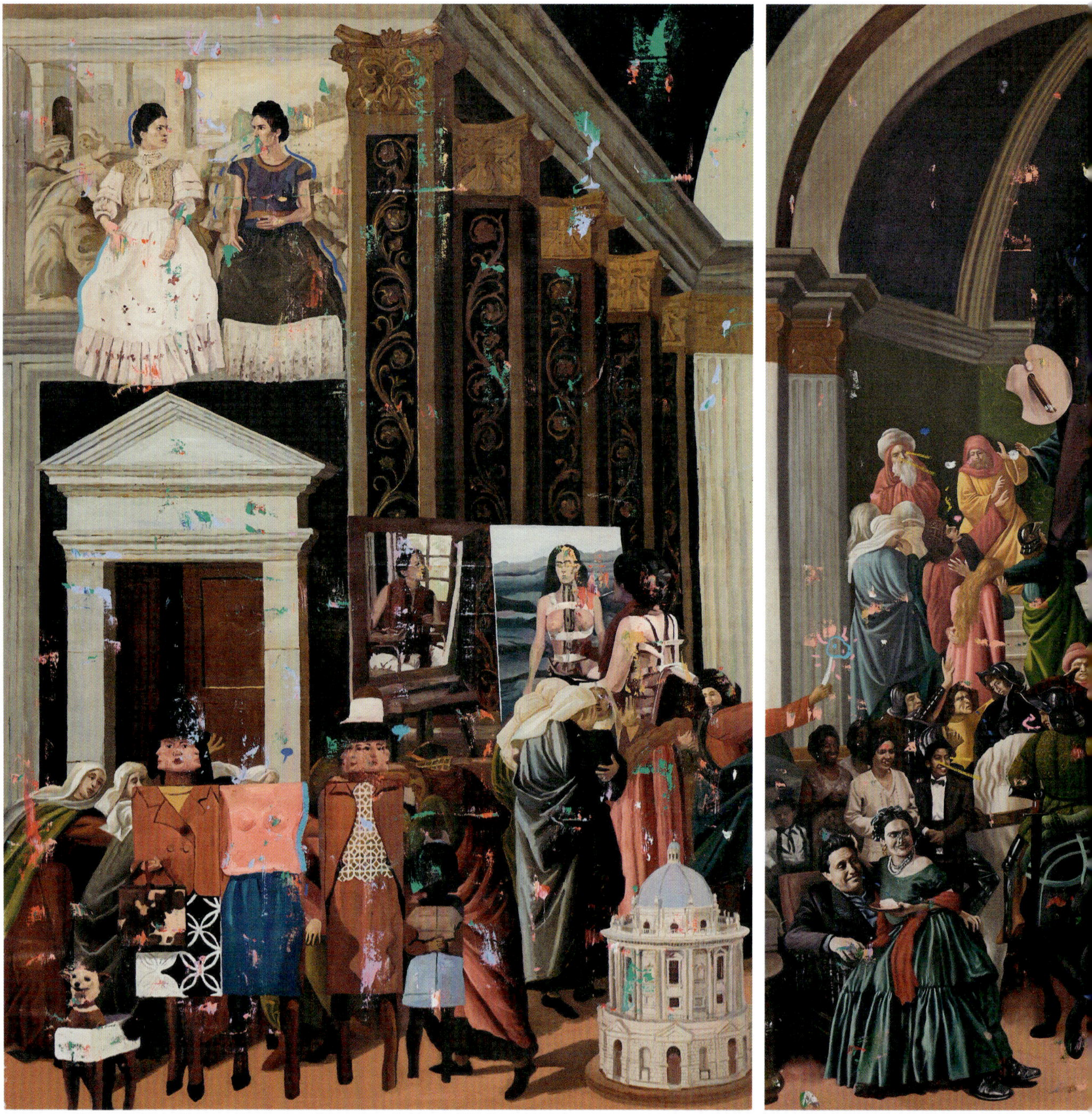

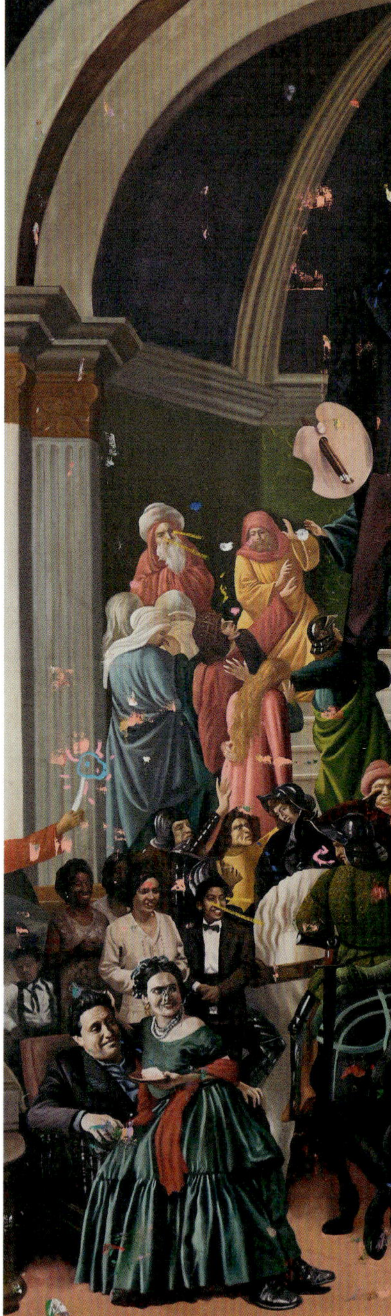

Lifelong Beauty - Frida's Love, Friendship, and Eternity, 2023–24
oil on canvas, triptych, 180 × 120 cm each panel

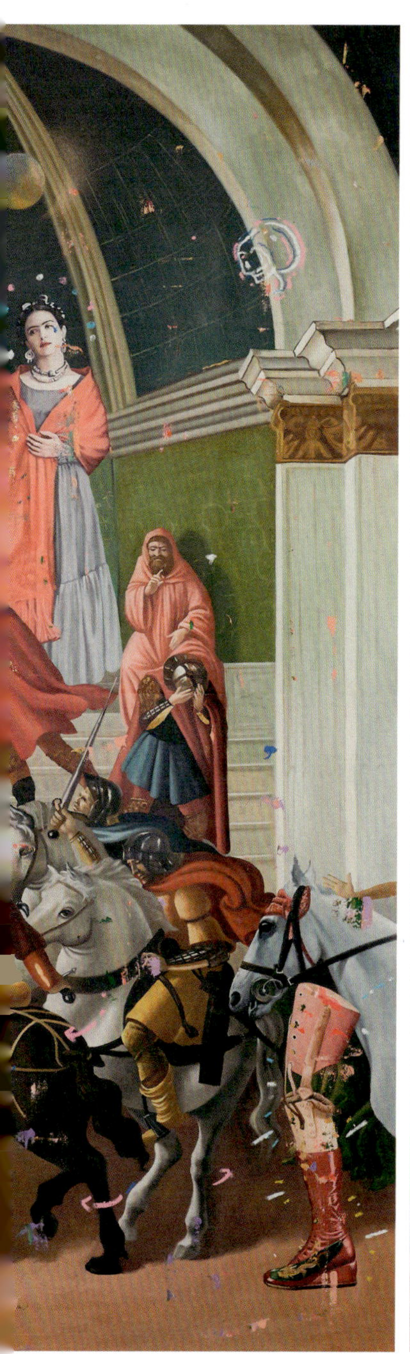

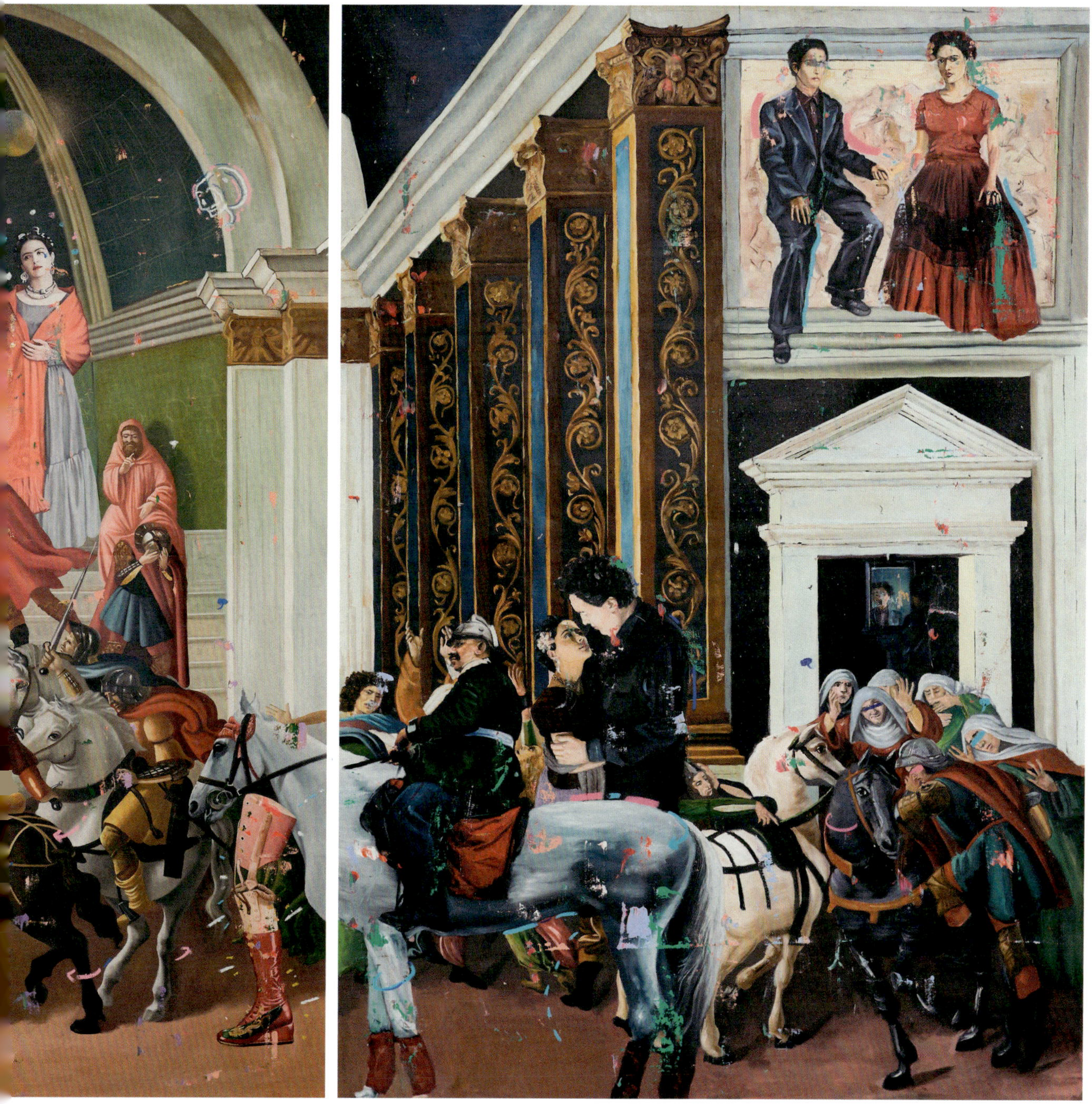

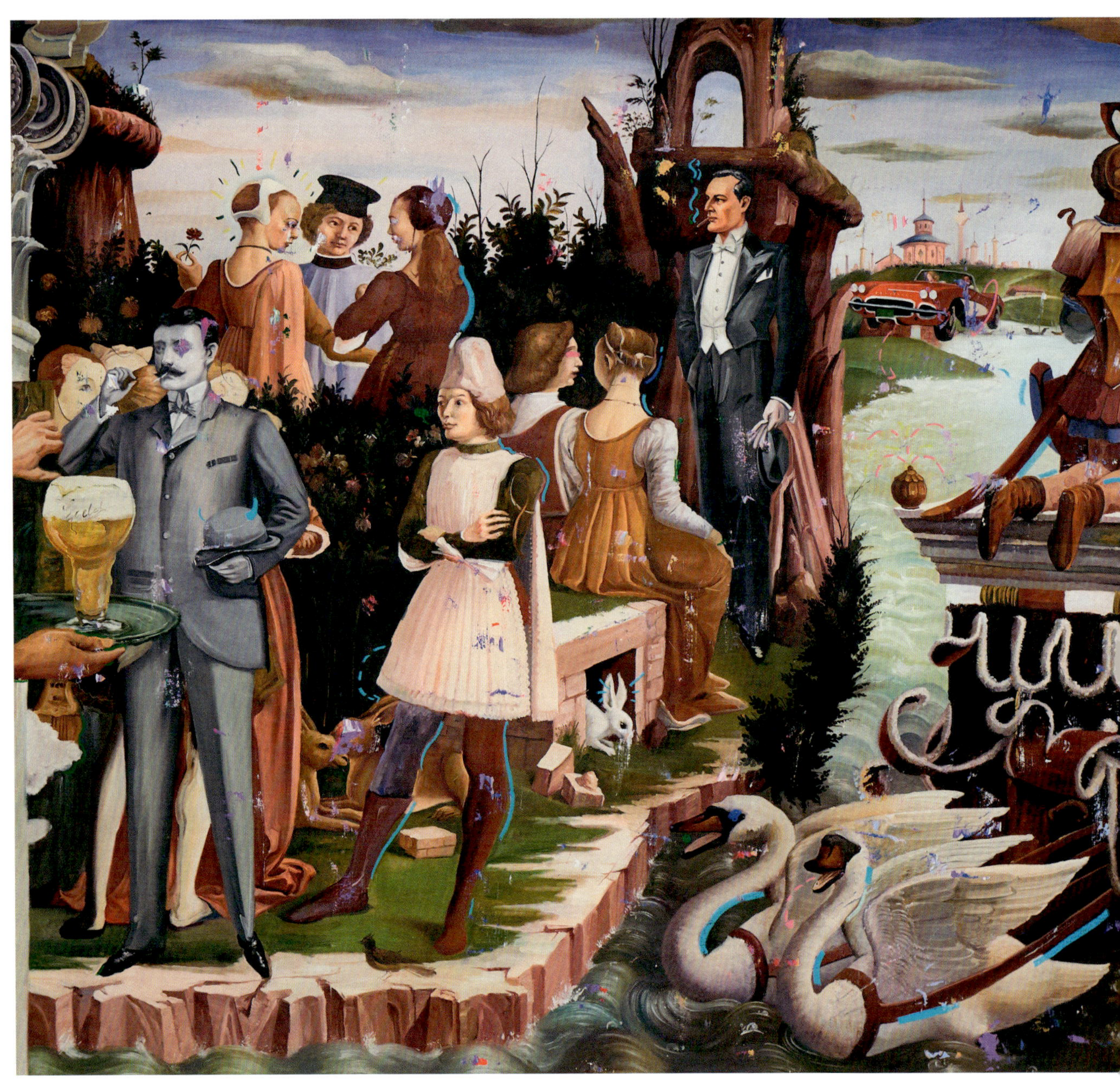

Lifelong Beauty - The Handsome Scholar and the Beautiful Woman, 2023–24
oil on canvas, 185 × 200 cm each panel

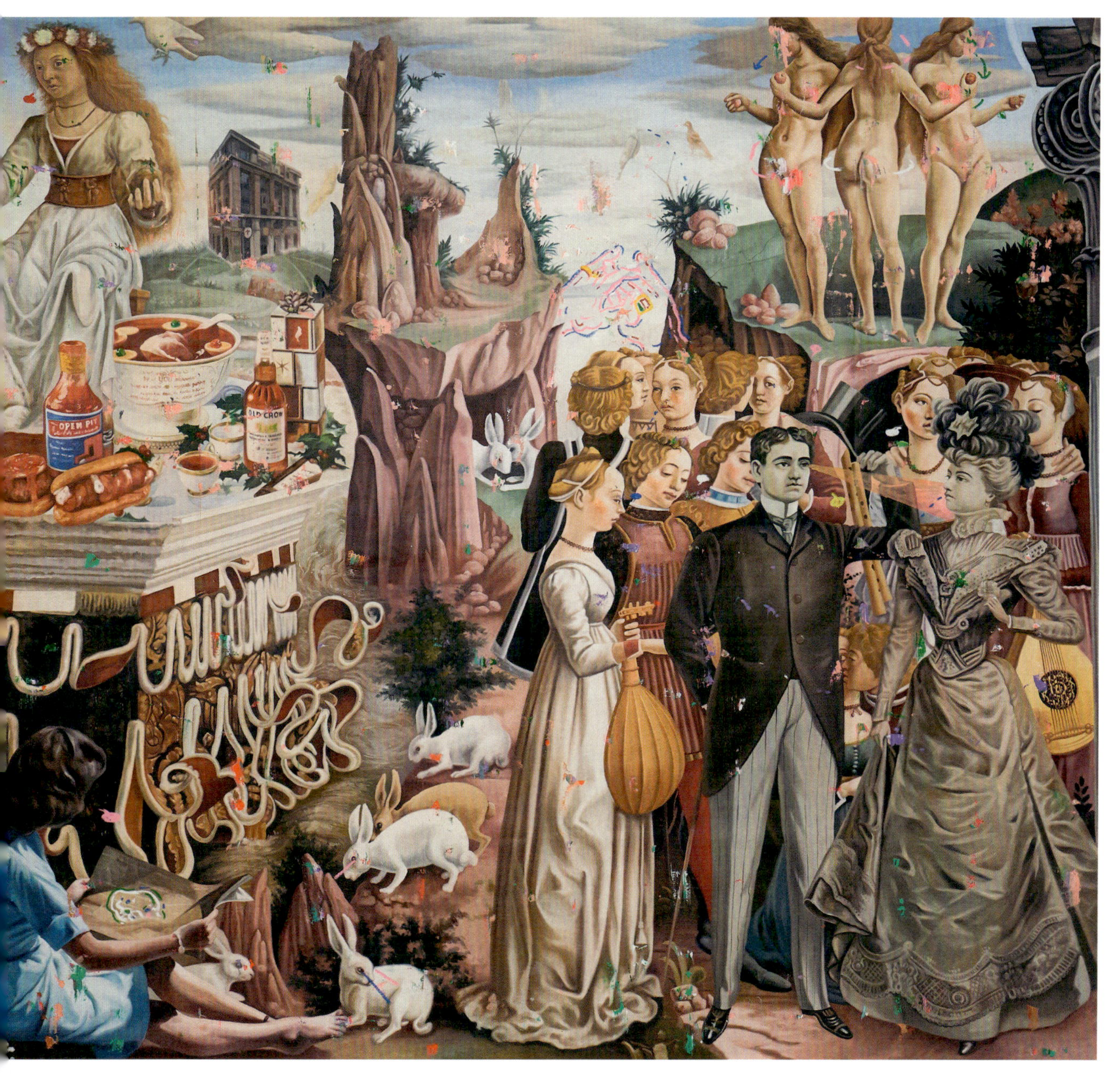

Following pages   *Lifelong Beauty – Blue-Blooded Nobility*, 2023–24
oil on canvas, 100 × 150 cm

89

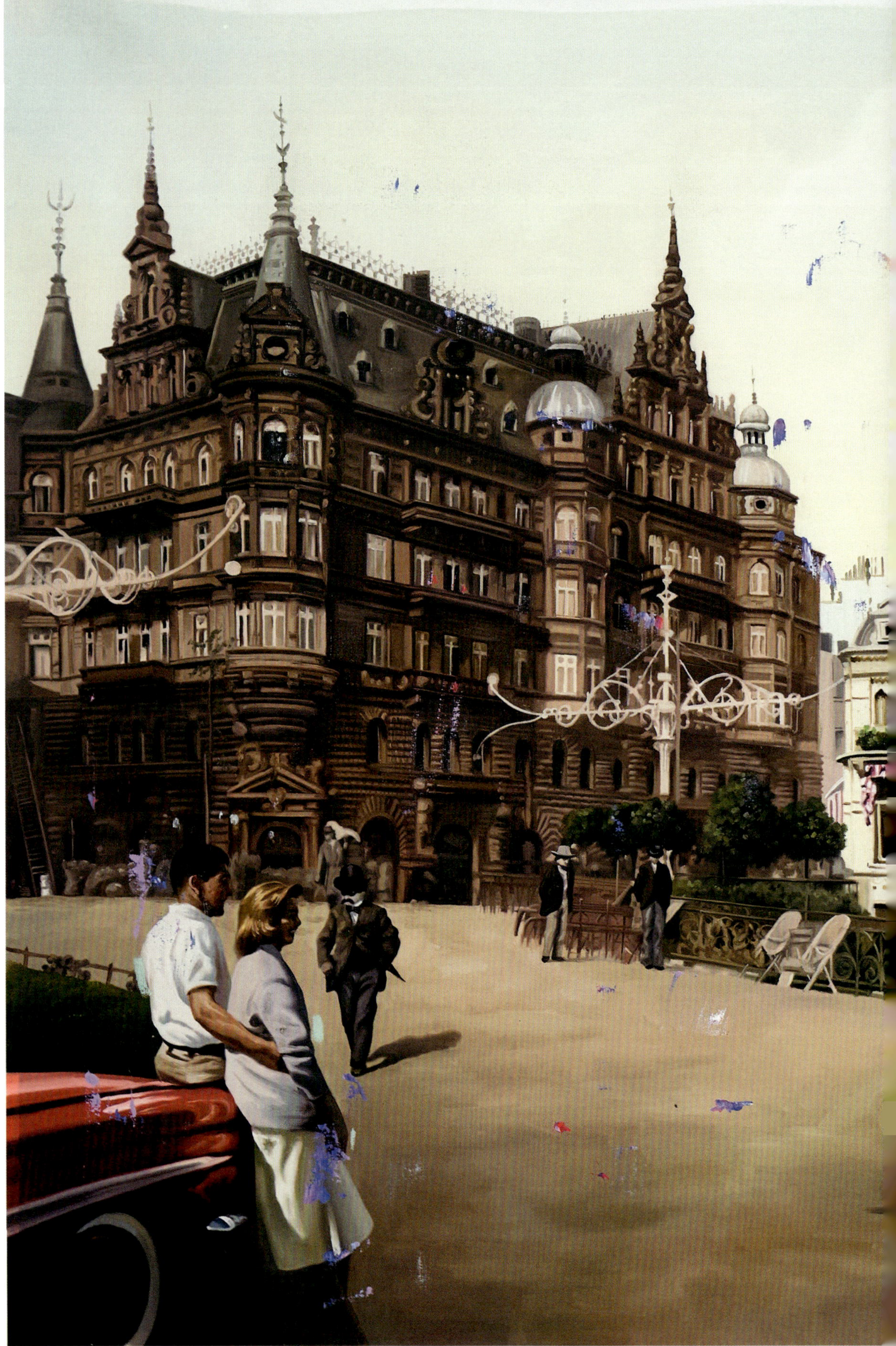

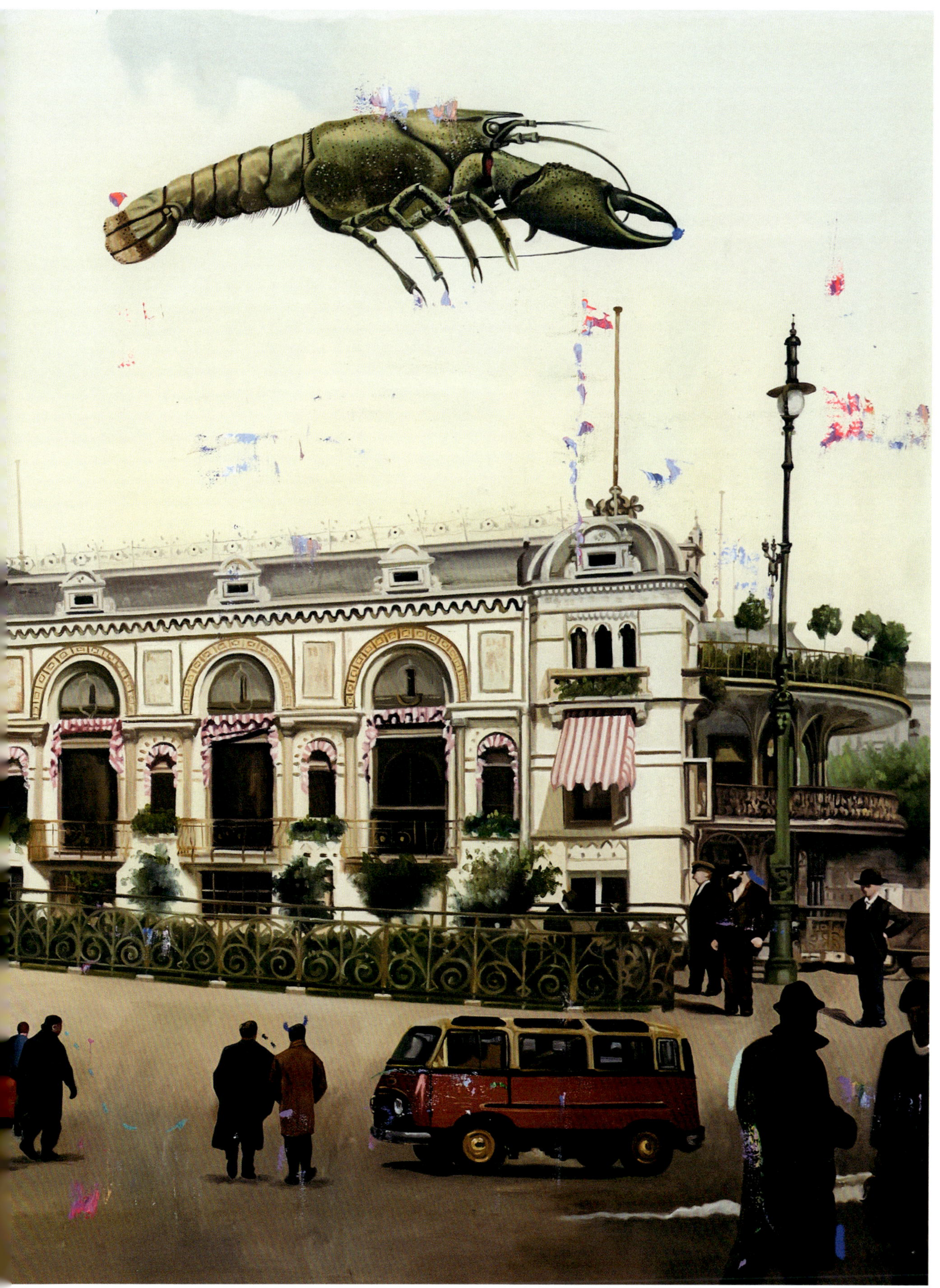

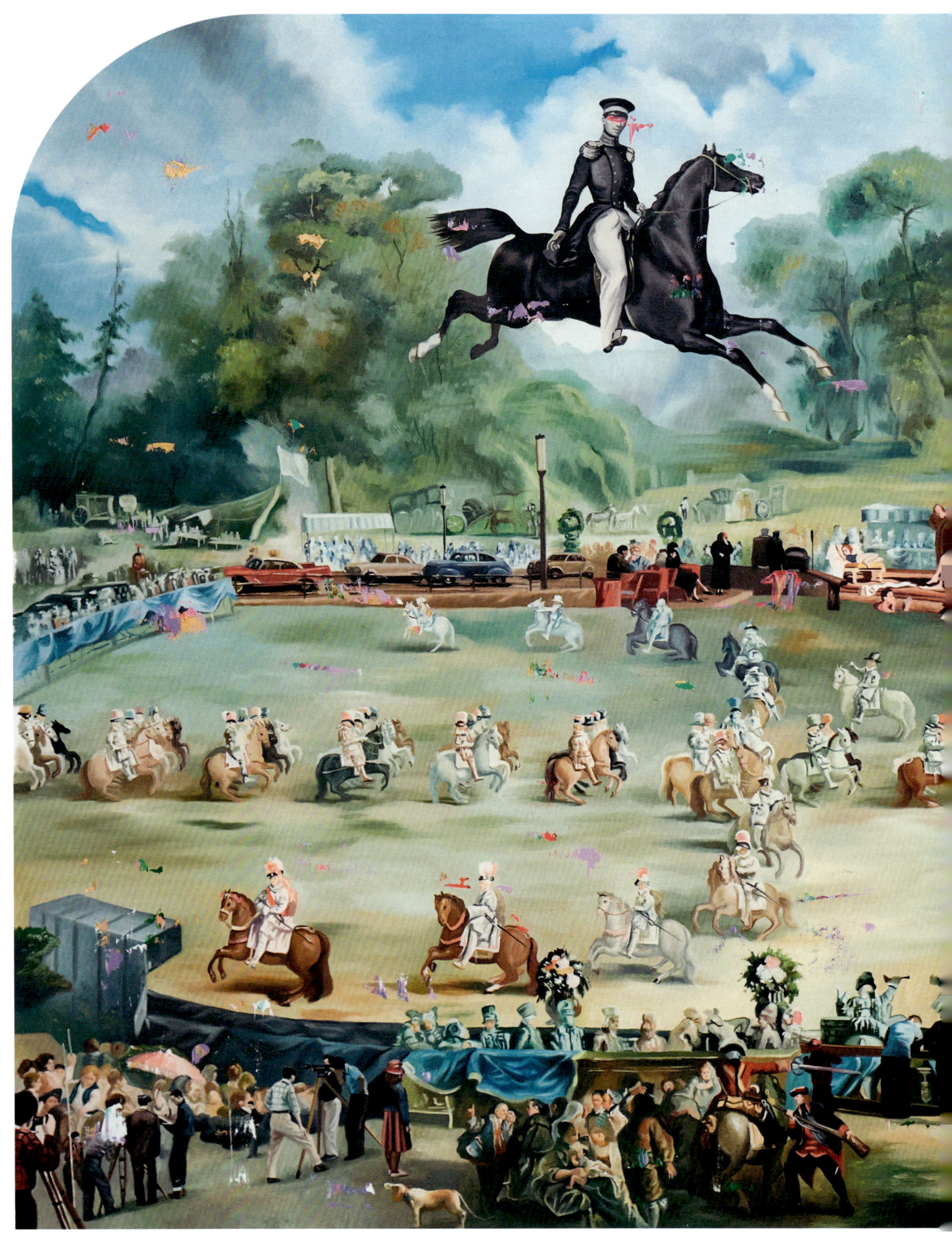

Lifelong Beauty – Seeking a Beautiful Life, 2023–24
oil on canvas, 120 × 180 cm

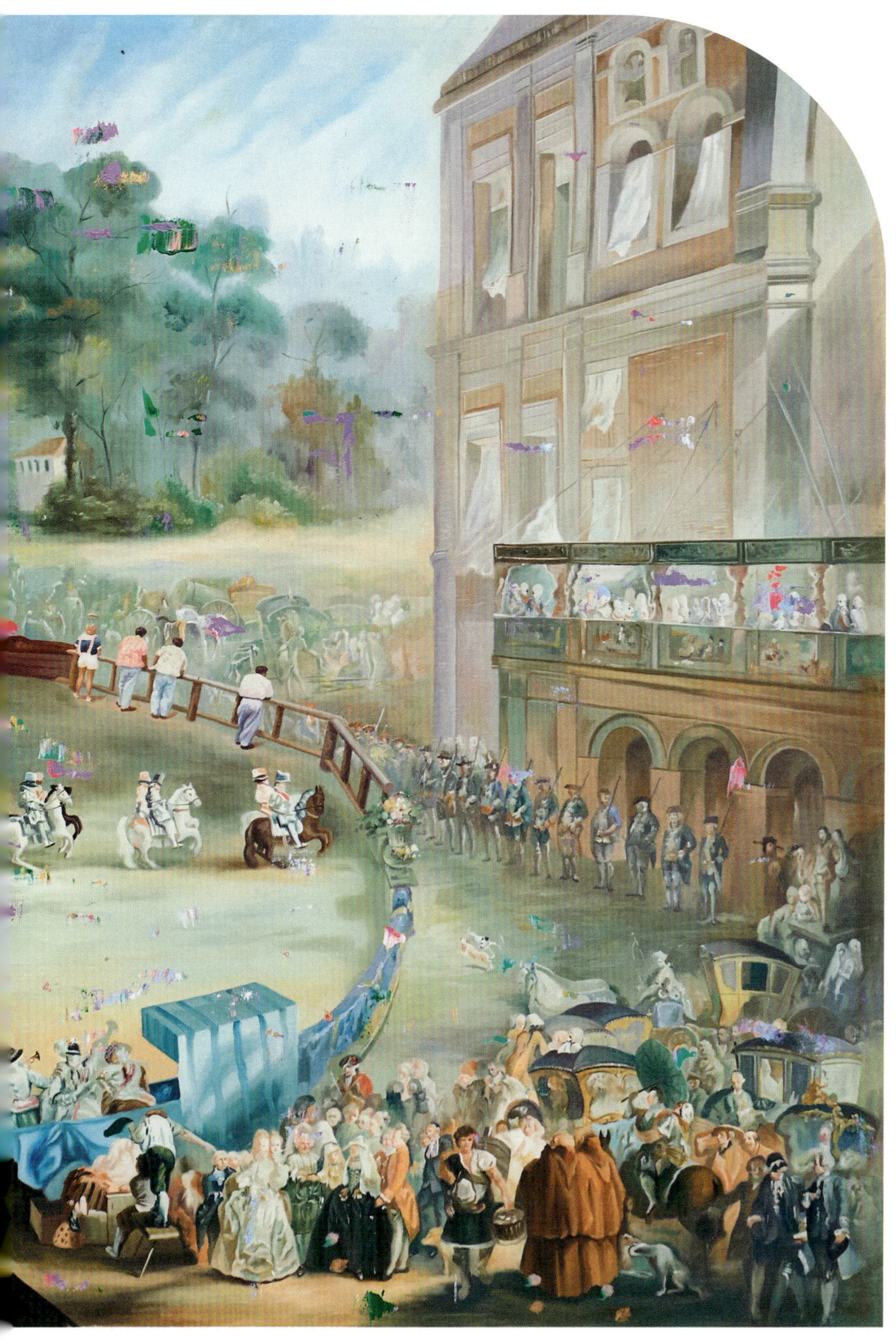

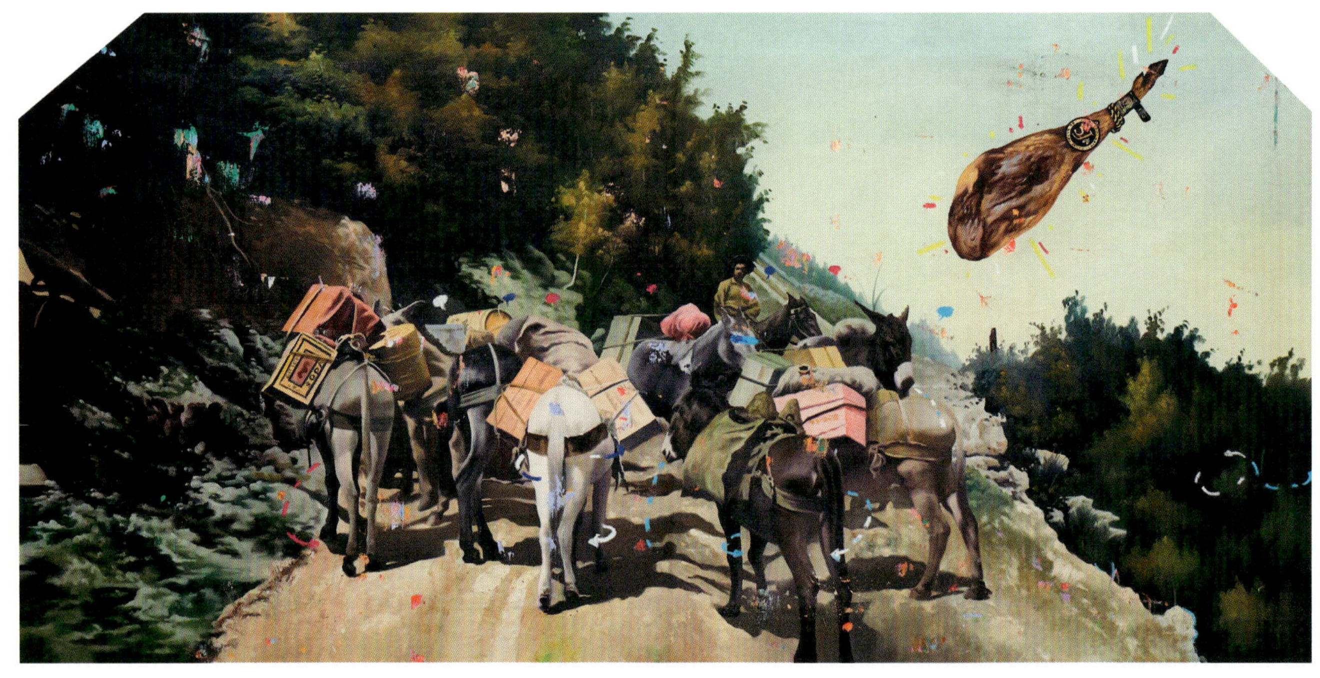

Lifelong Beauty – The Fruit of Victory, 2023–24
oil on canvas, 90 × 180 cm

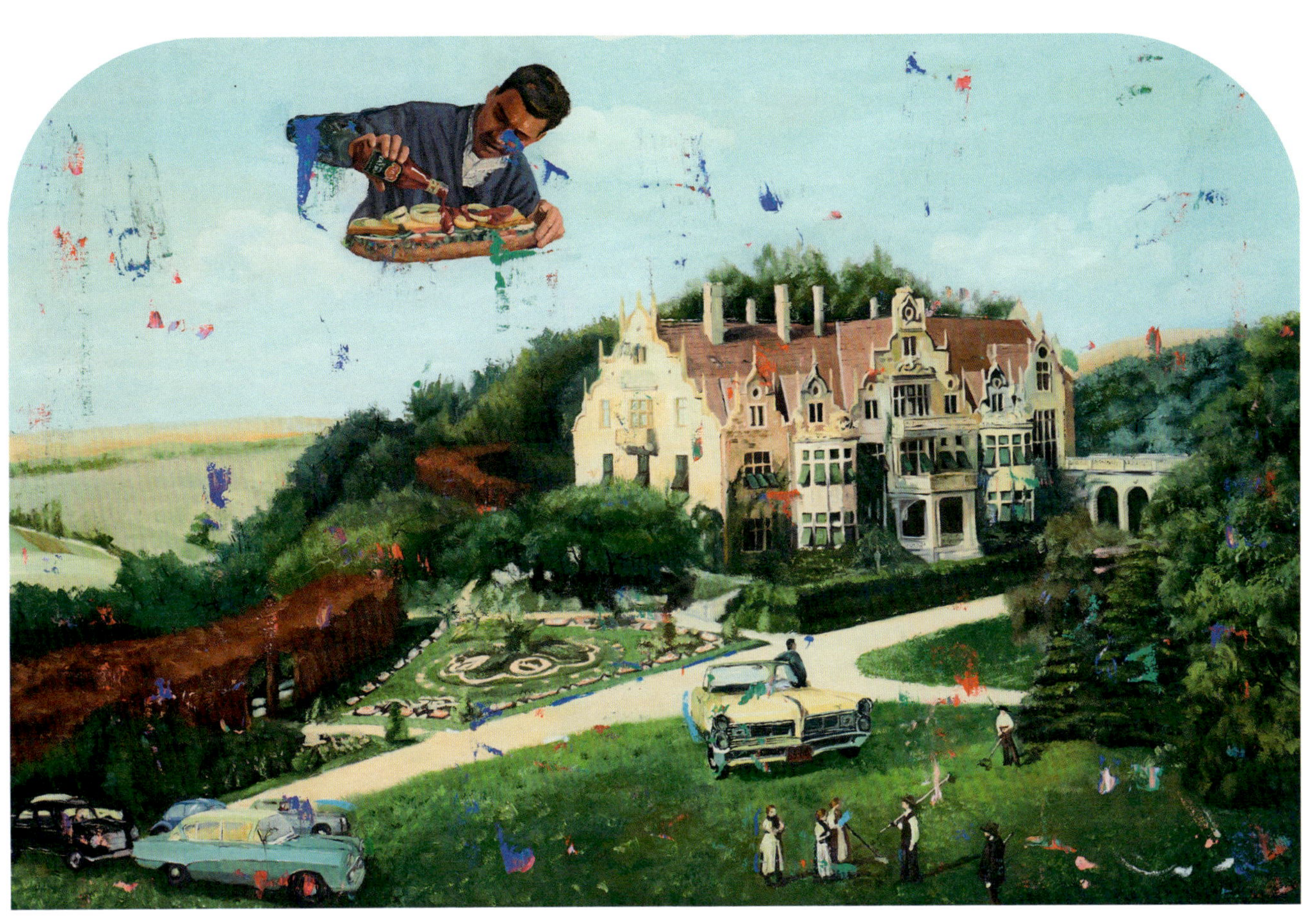

Lifelong Beauty - Life as Vibrant as Ketchup, 2023–24
oil on canvas, 100 × 150 cm

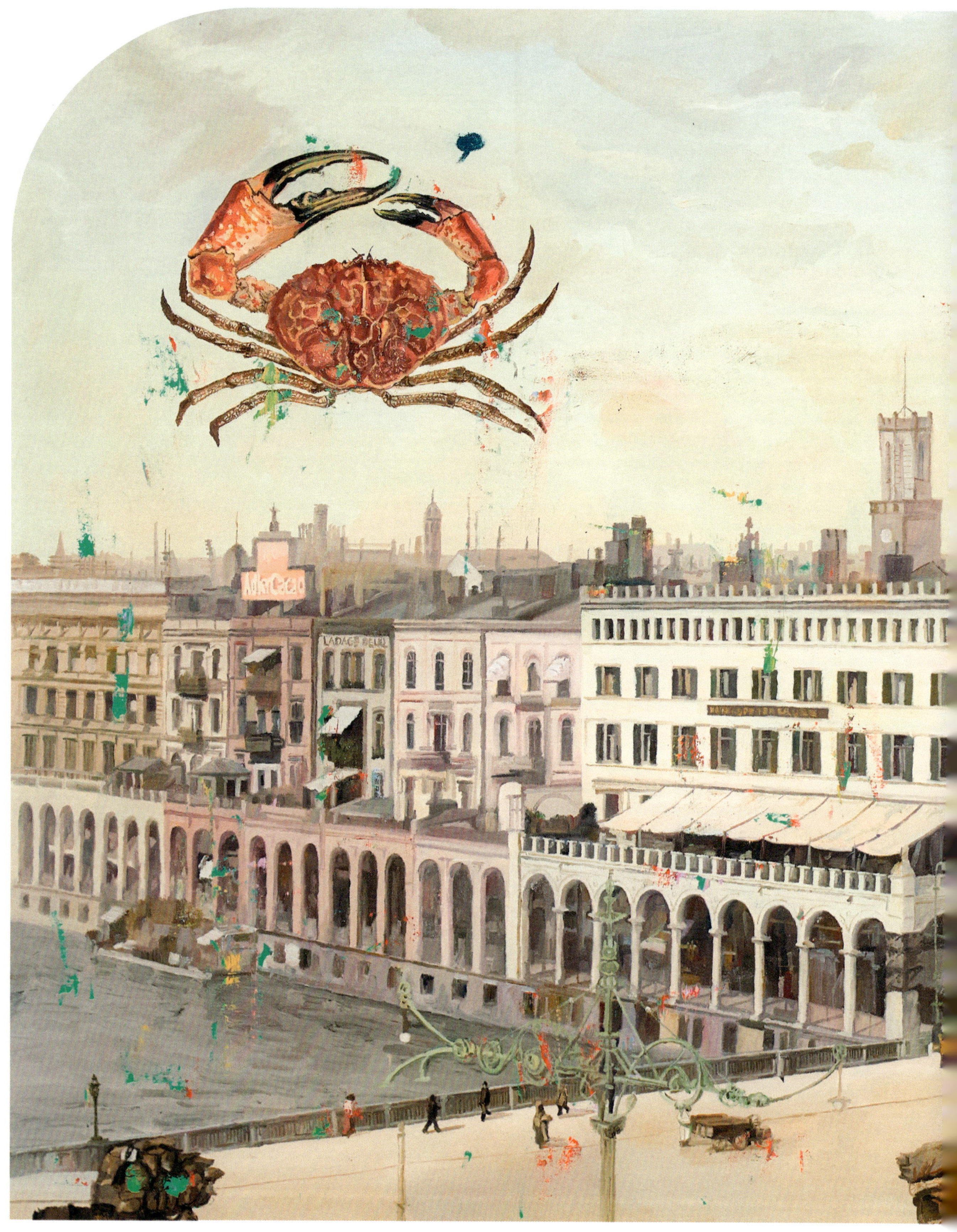

Lifelong Beauty - Encounter, 2023–24 oil on canvas, 115 × 160 cm **96**

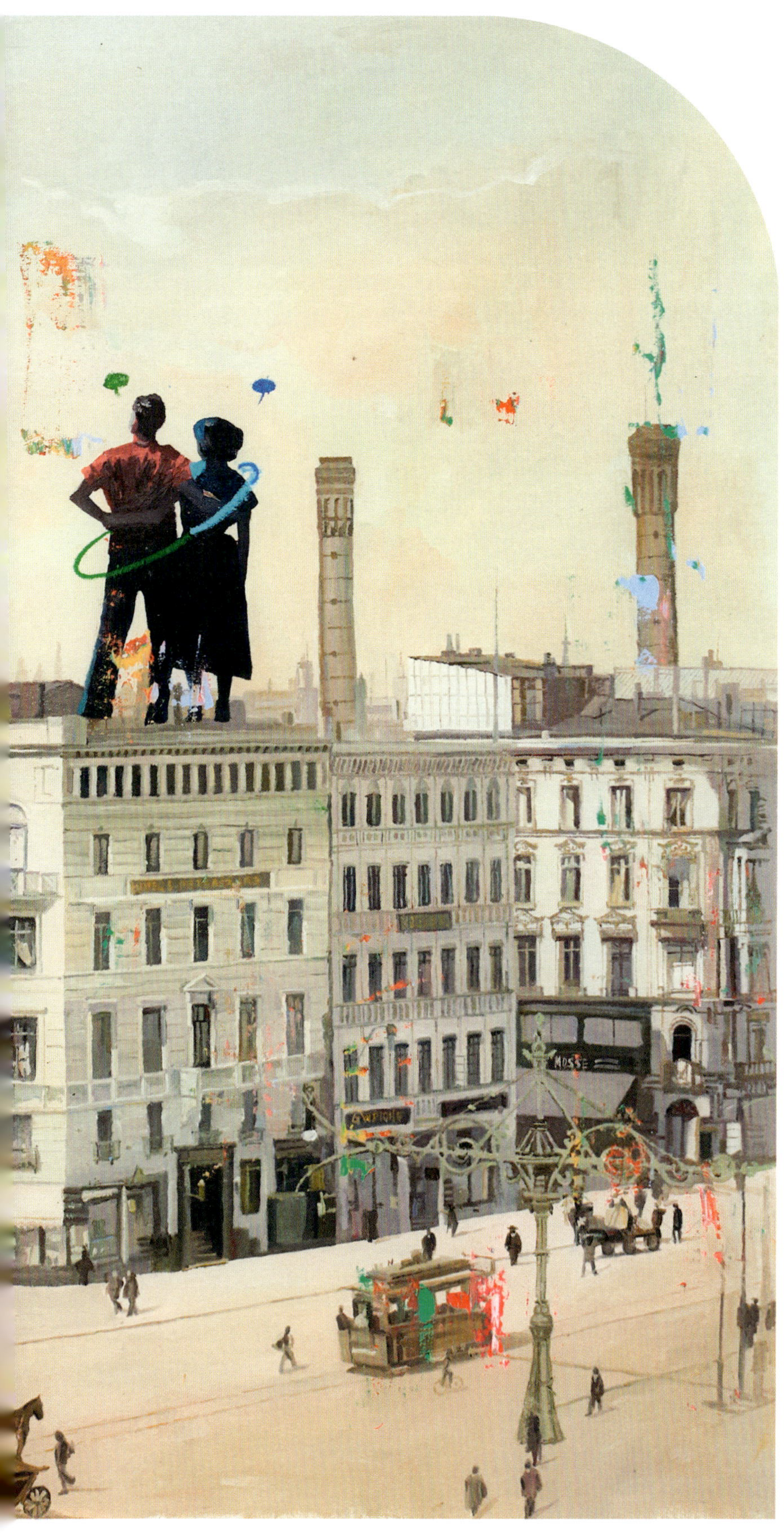

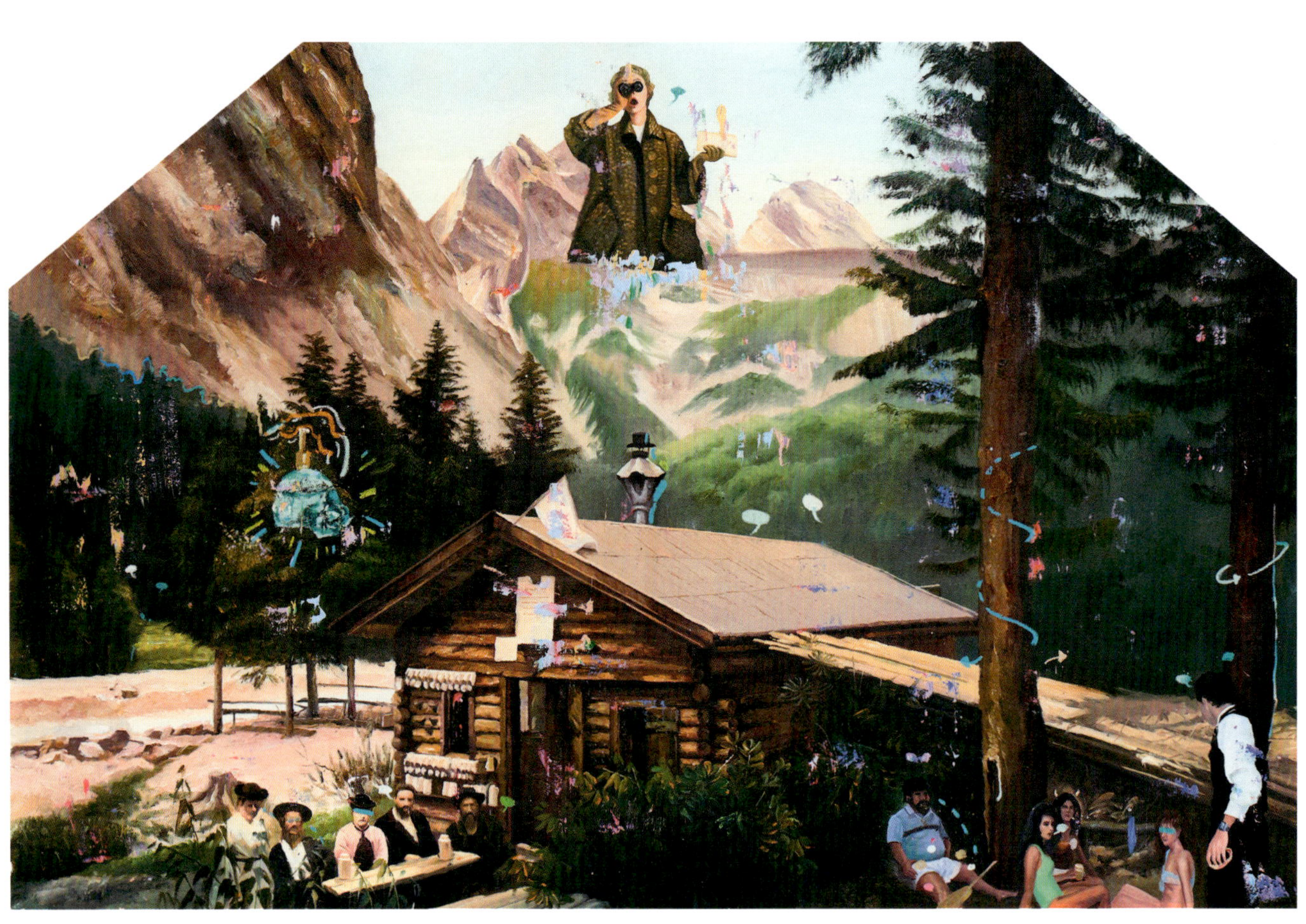

Lifelong Beauty - Fragrance in the Forest, 2023-24
oil on canvas, 100 × 150 cm

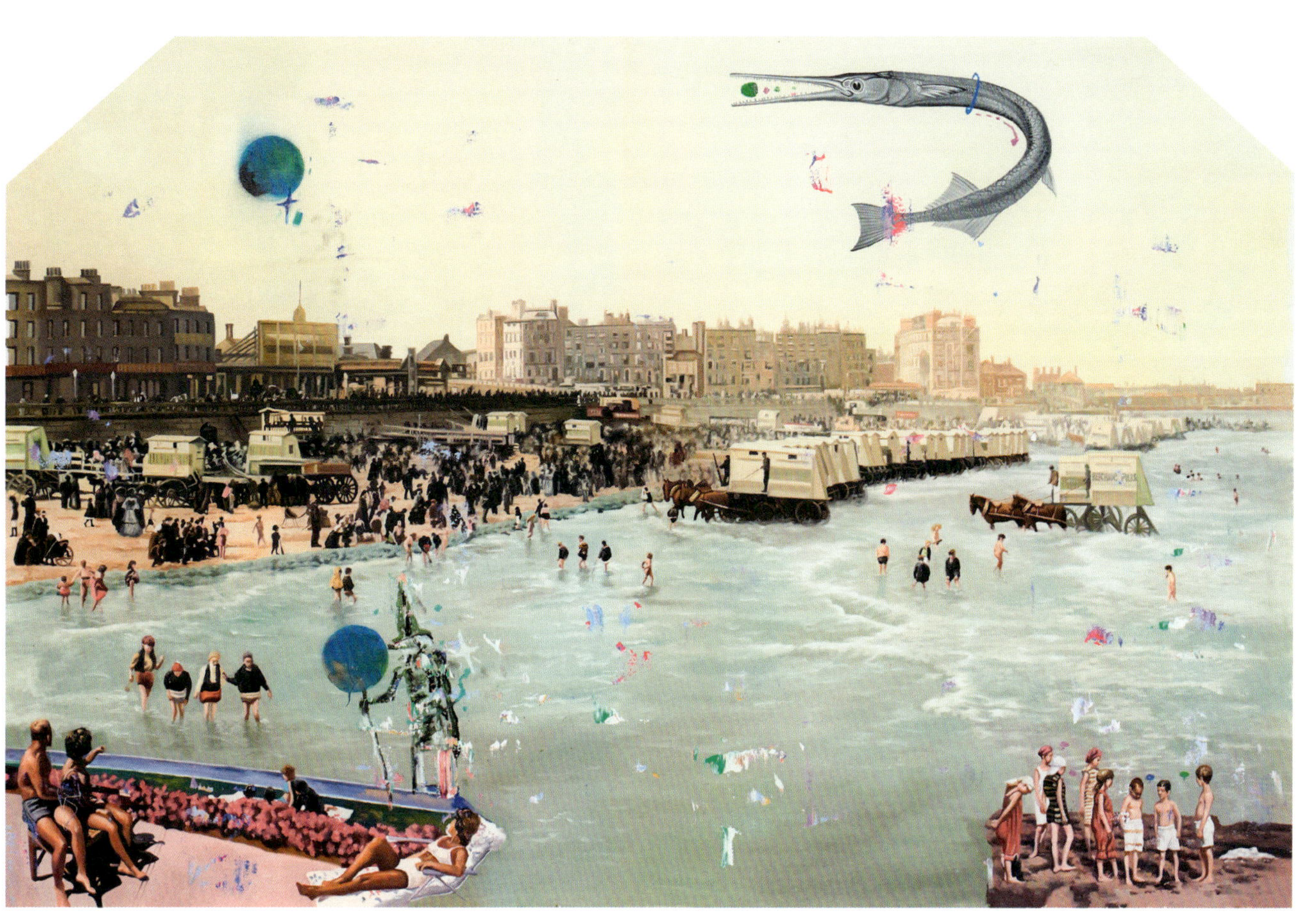

Lifelong Beauty – Obsessed with Hormones, 2023–24
oil on canvas, 100 × 150 cm

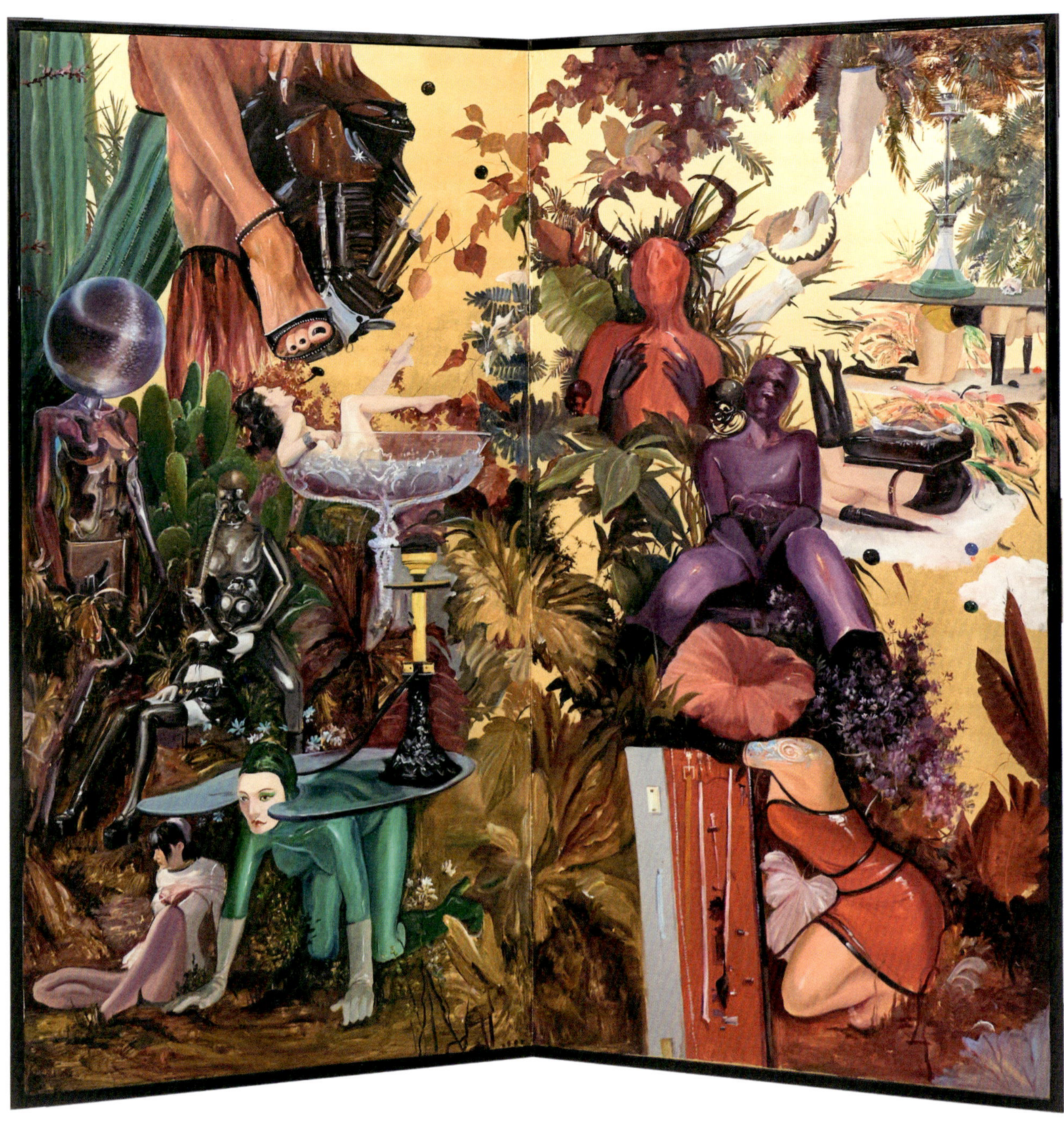

Lifelong Beauty – Tropical Tale, 2023–24
oil and gold foil on folding screen, 173 × 85 cm each panel

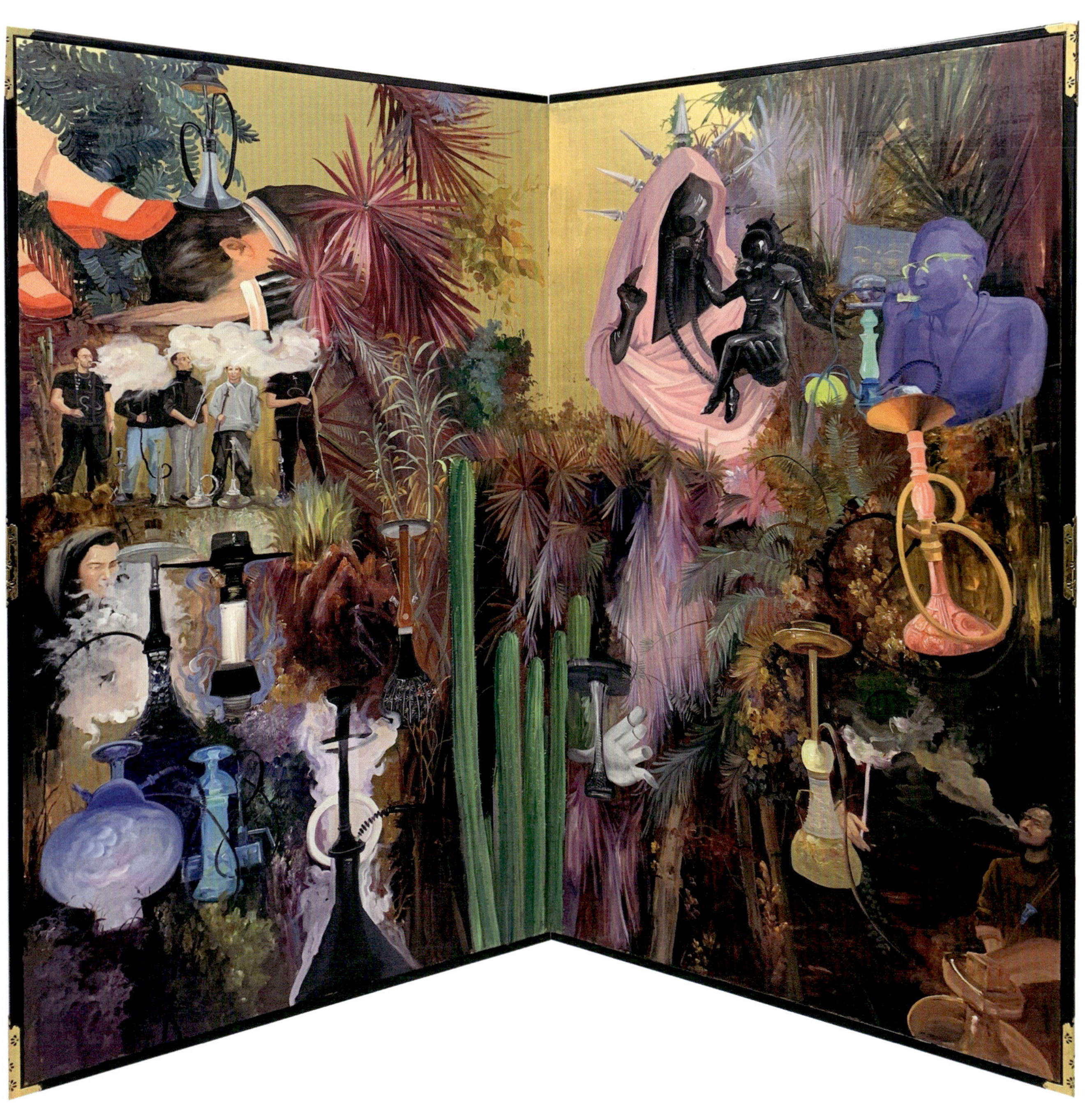

Lifelong Beauty – Compendium of Materia Medica, 2023–24
oil and gold foil on folding screen, 171.5 × 94 cm each panel

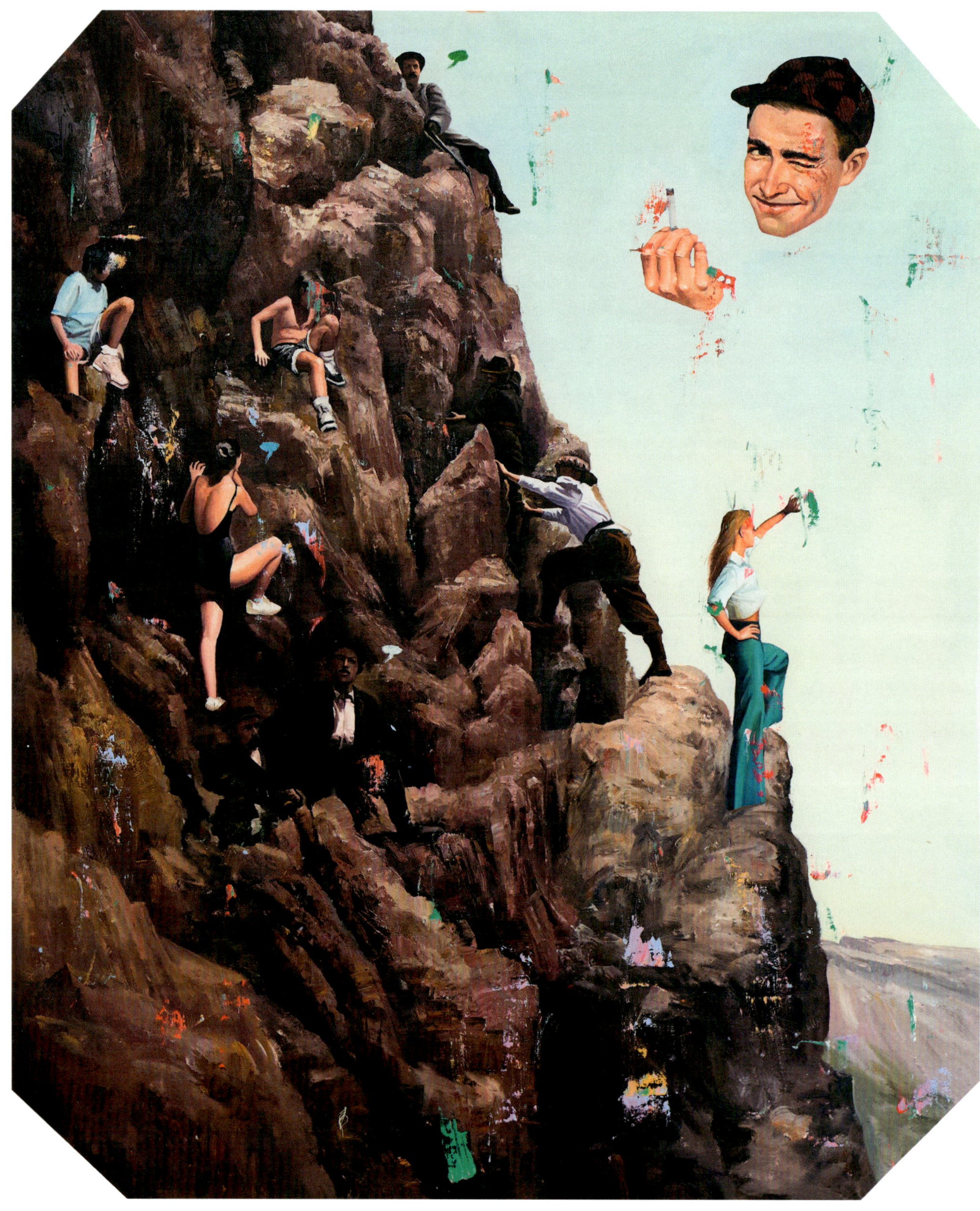

Lifelong Beauty - Side by Side, 2023–24   oil on canvas, 150 × 120 cm   102

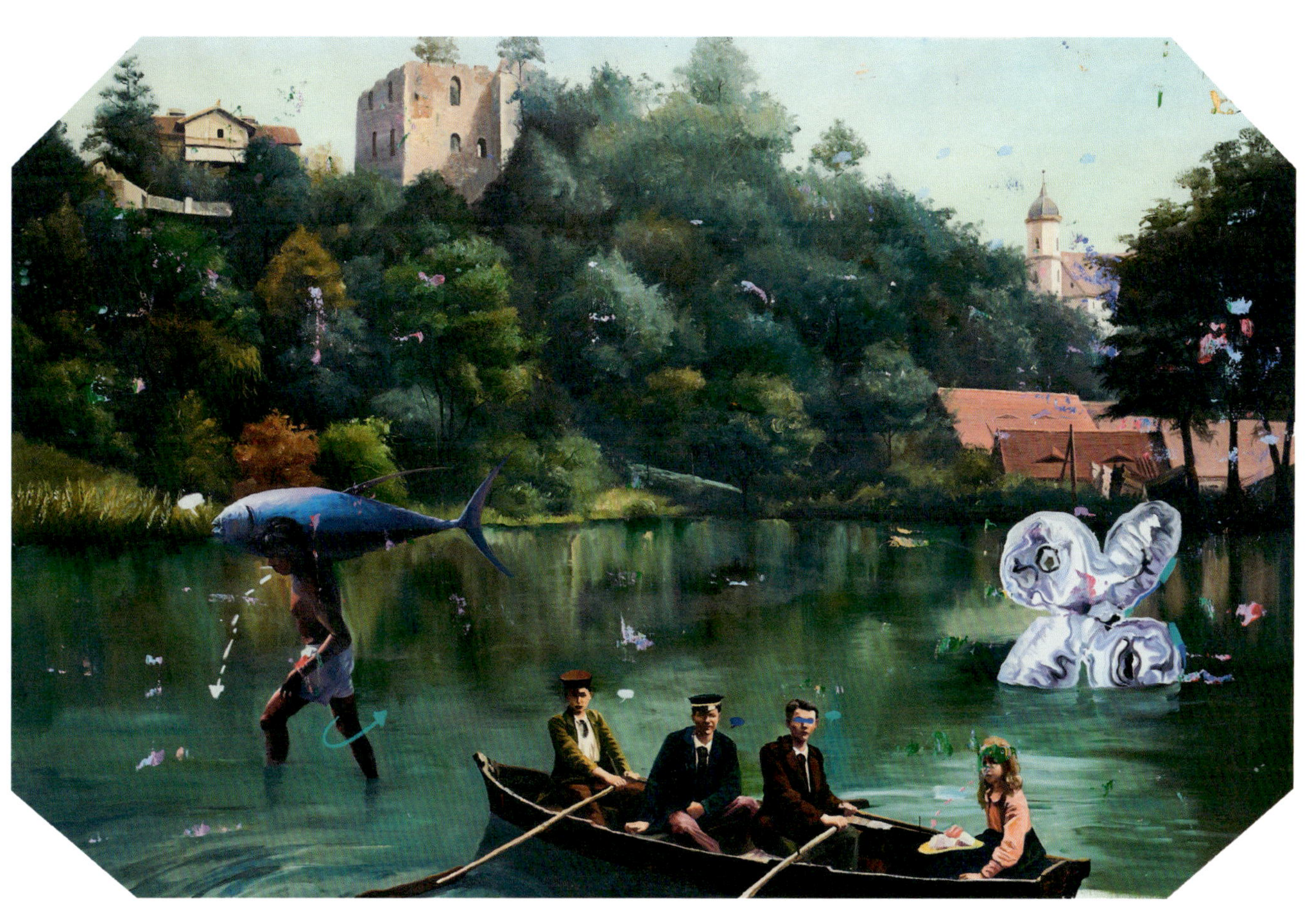

Lifelong Beauty – Having Both Fish and Bear's Paw, 2023–24
oil on canvas, 120 × 180 cm

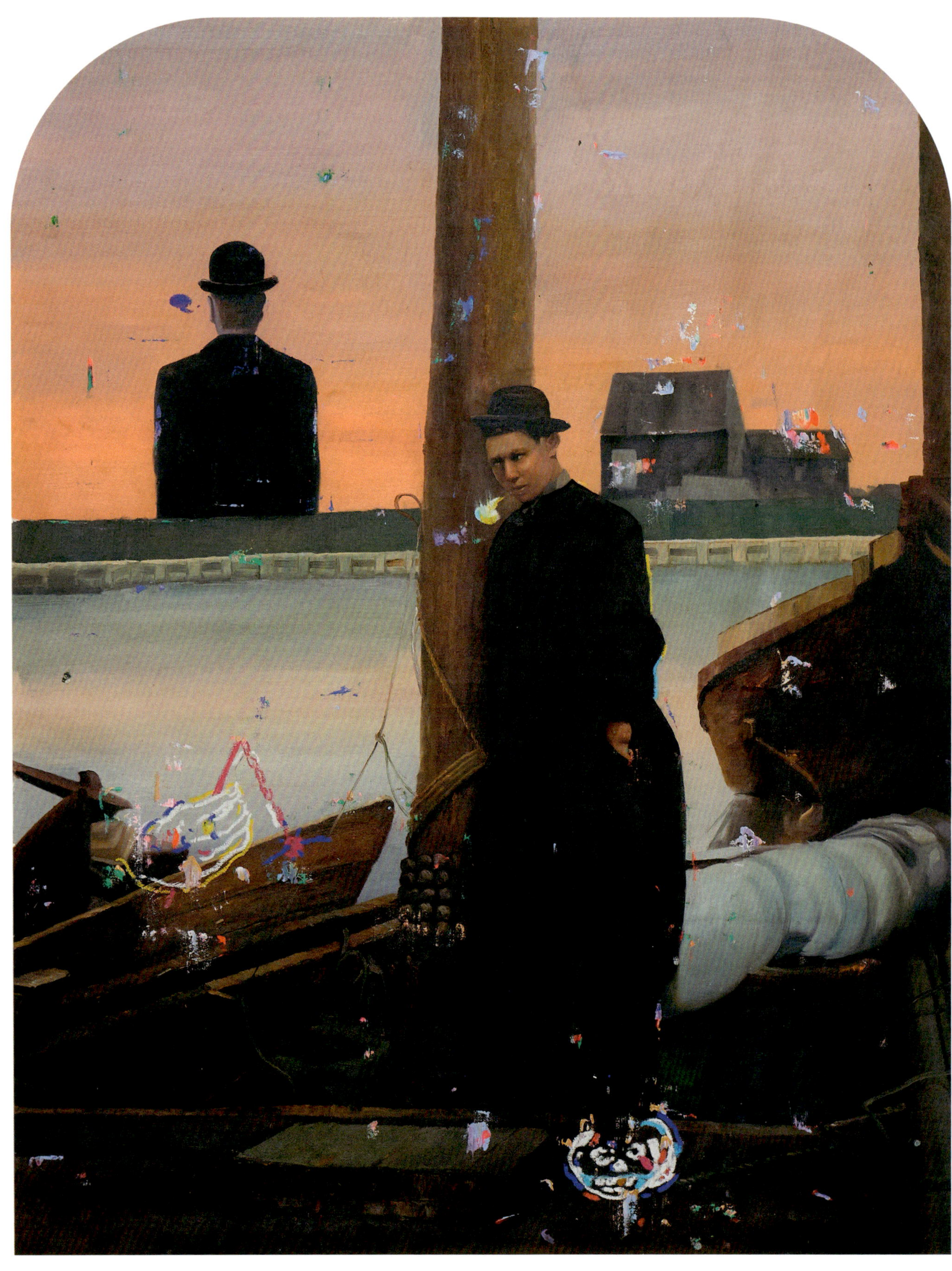

Lifelong Beauty – A Young Man's Longing for Magritte, 2023–24
oil on canvas, 130 × 100 cm

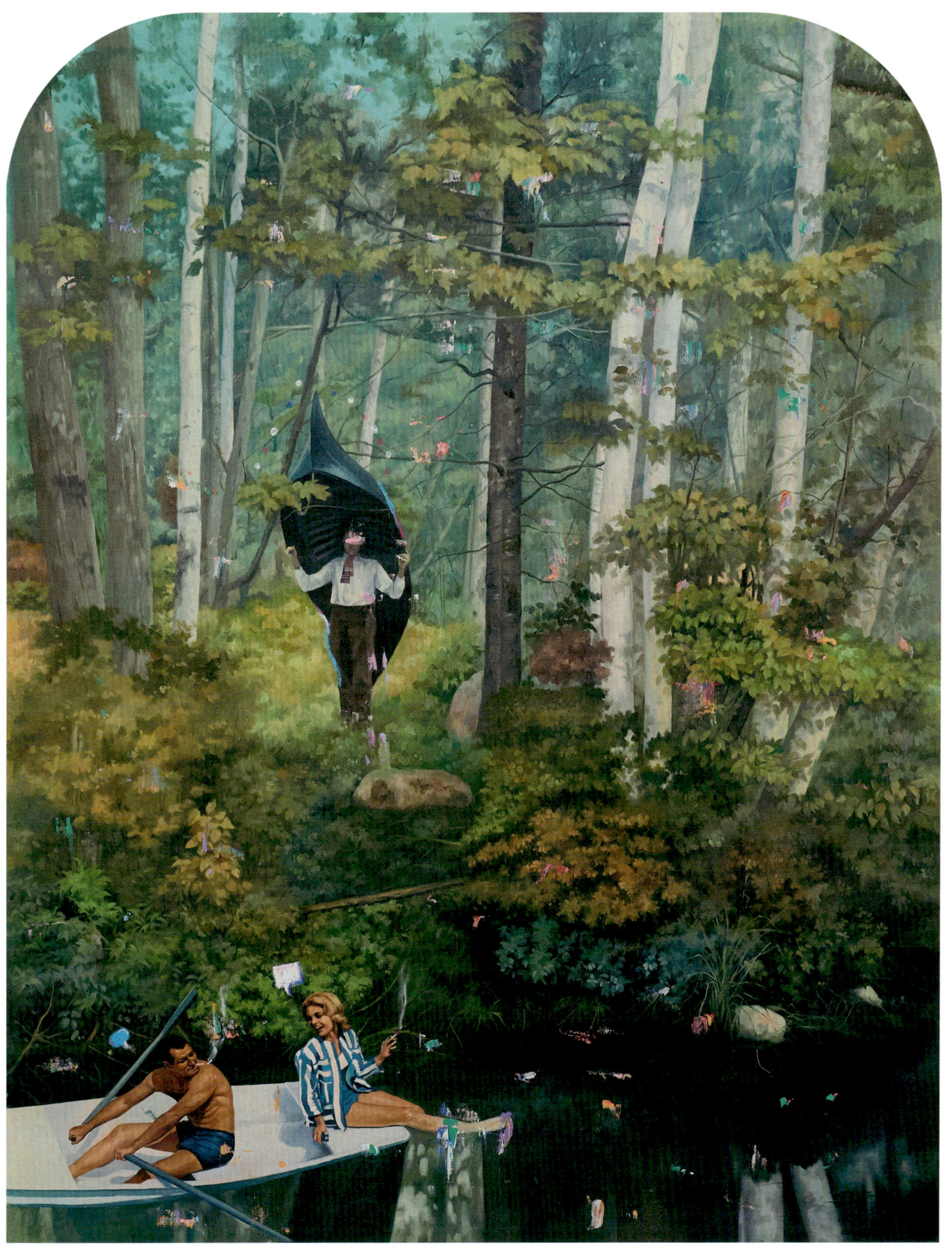

Lifelong Beauty – Rippling, 2023–24
oil on canvas, 160 × 120 cm

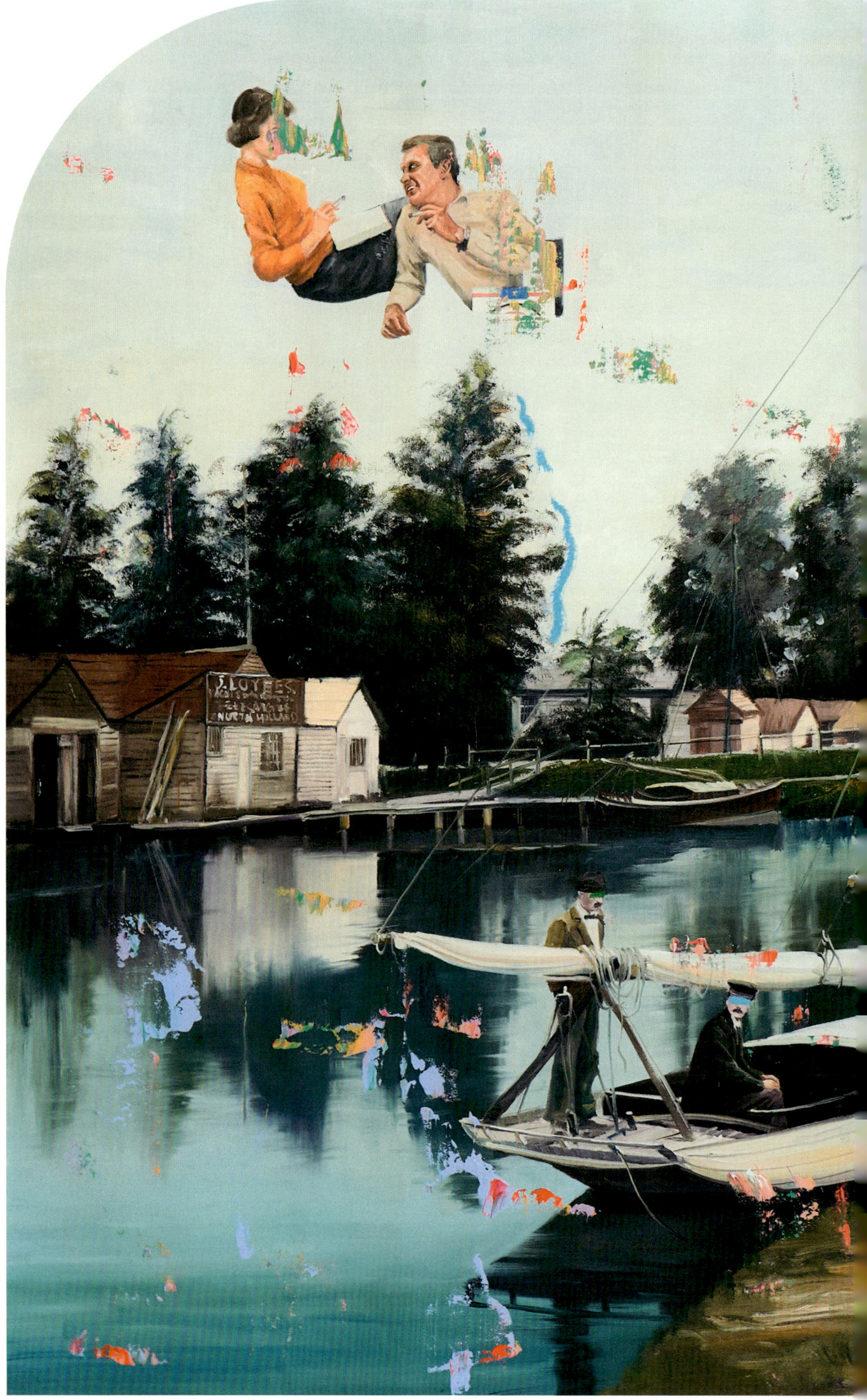
LOYEES
NORTH HOLLAND

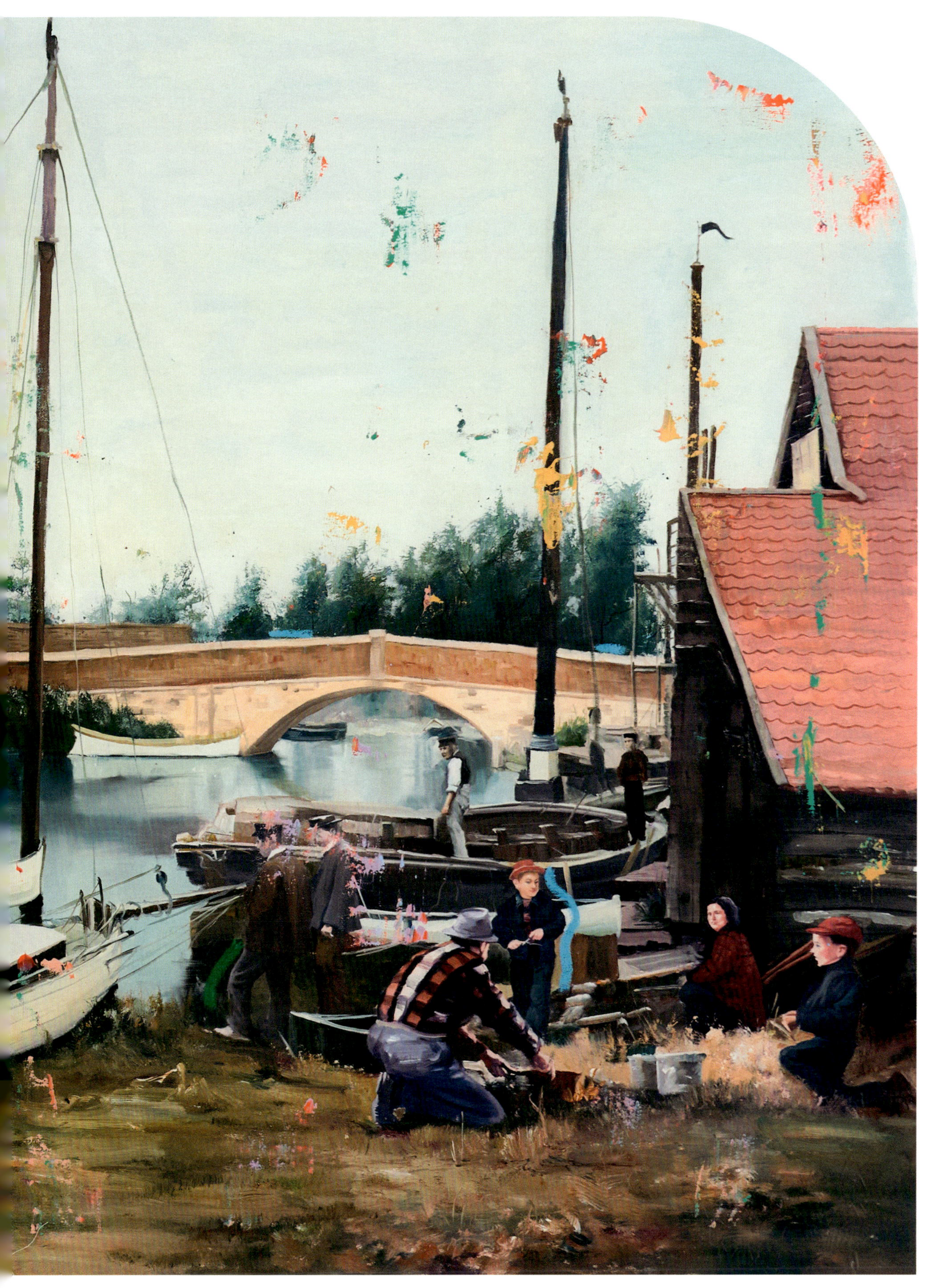

Previous pages *Lifelong Beauty – Reading
with a Kindred Spirit*, 2023–24   oil on canvas, 115 ×160 cm

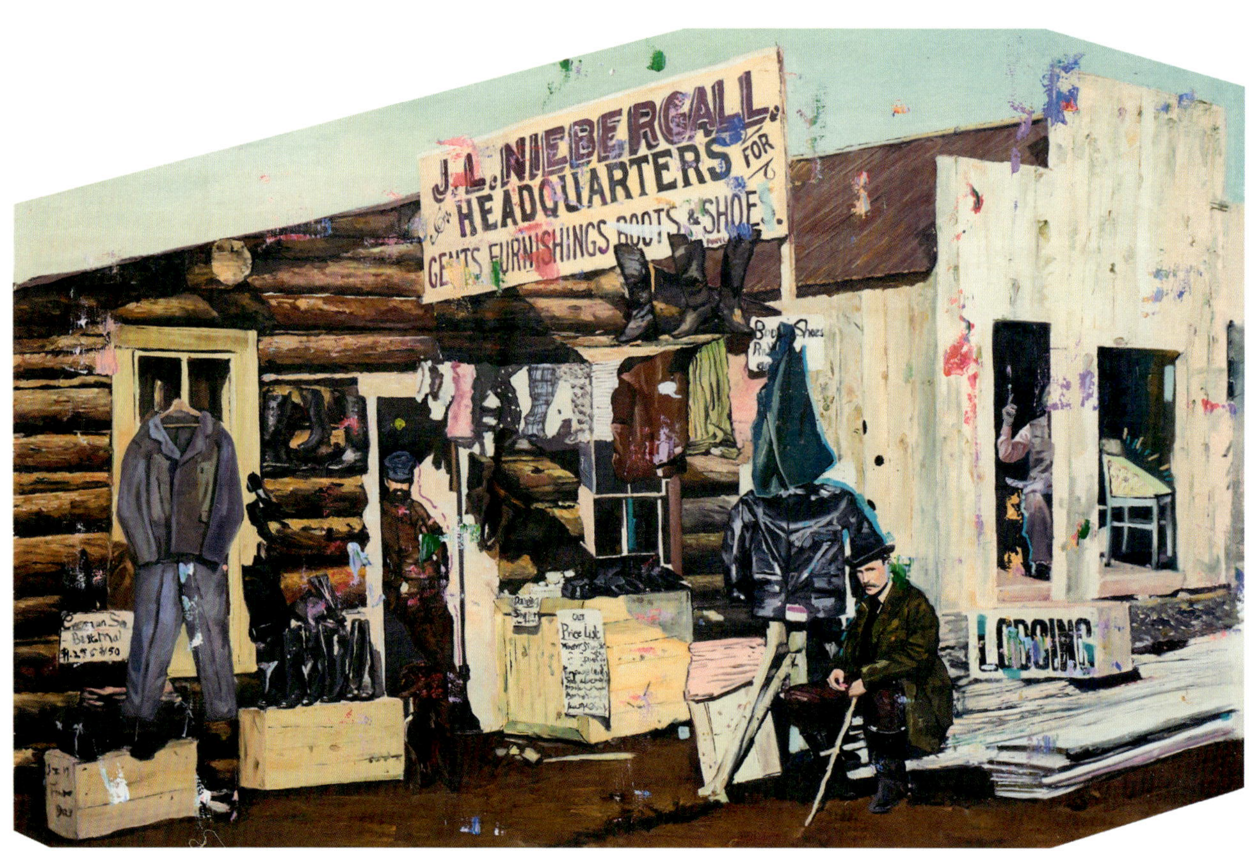

Lifelong Beauty – Beuys' Dressing Room, 2023–24
oil on canvas, 100 × 150 cm   **108**

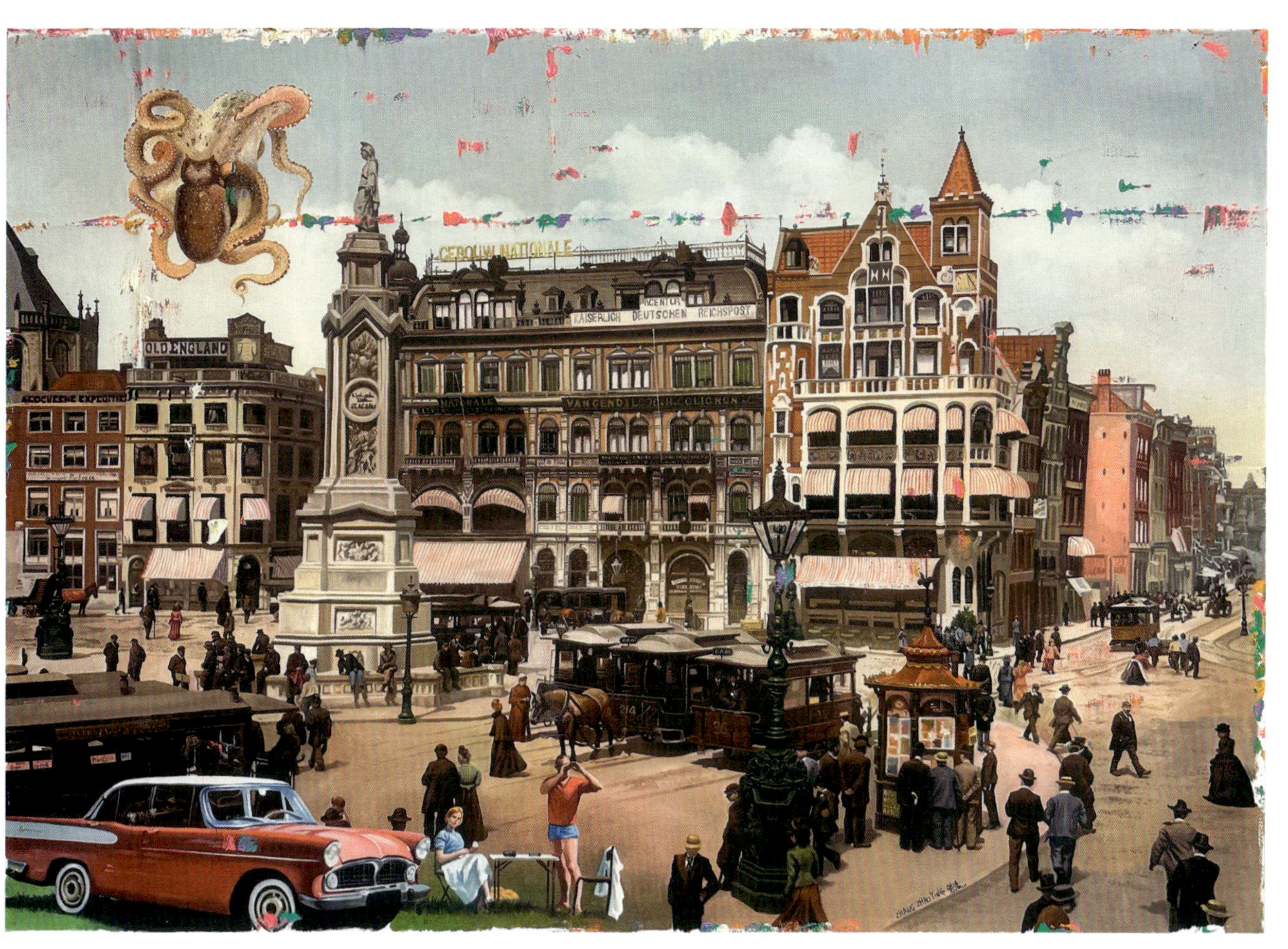

Lifelong Beauty – A Small Town Story, 2023–24
oil on canvas, 110 × 150 cm

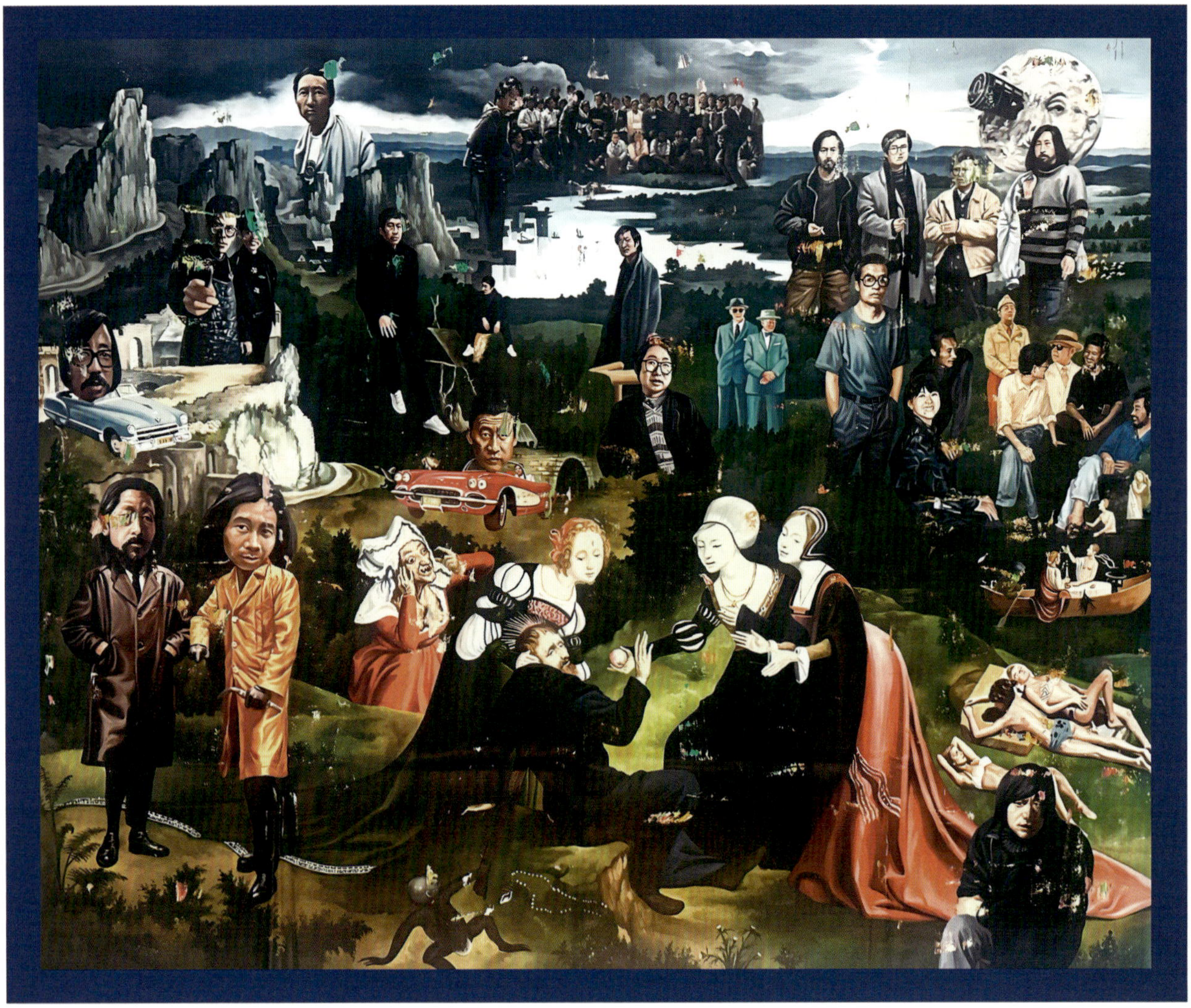

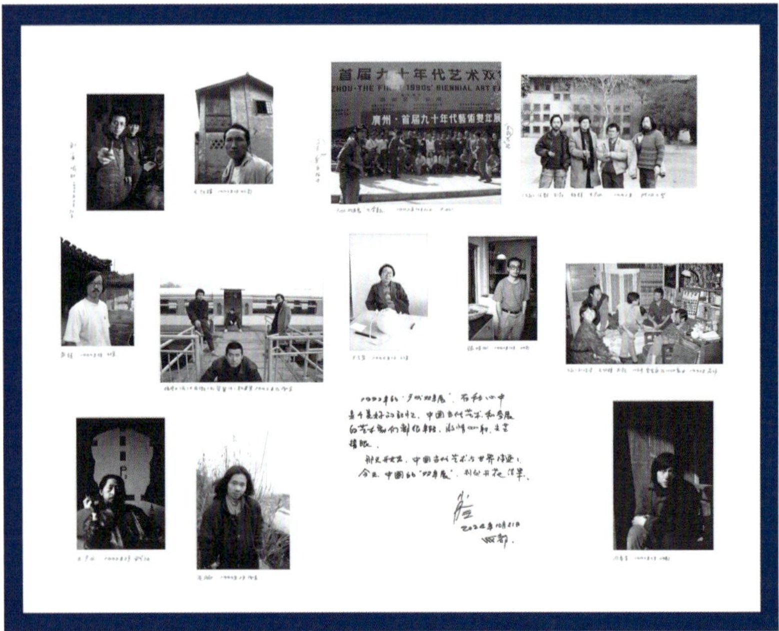

Xiao Quan & Zhang Zhaoying, *This Generation – Art Island A*, 2024
oil on canvas and archival-grade photo paper, Painting, 160 × 200 cm
Photograph, 80 × 100 cm. Unique edition

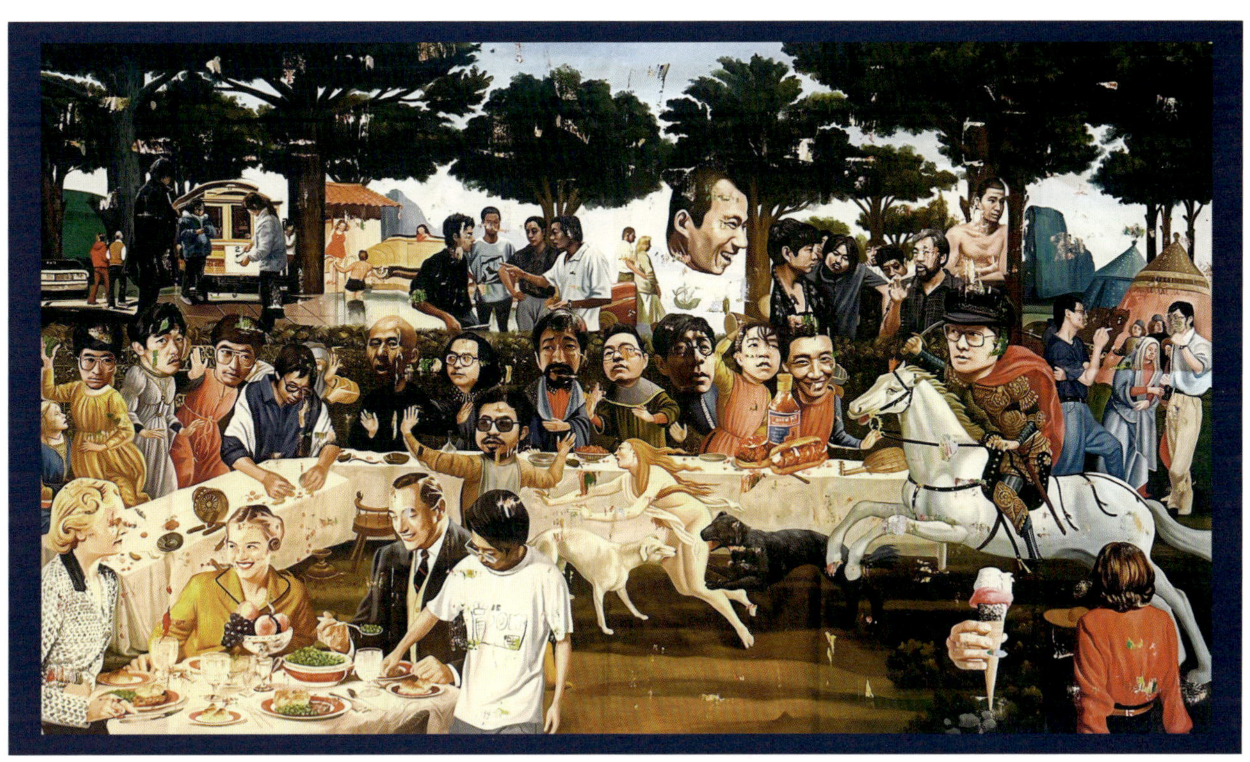

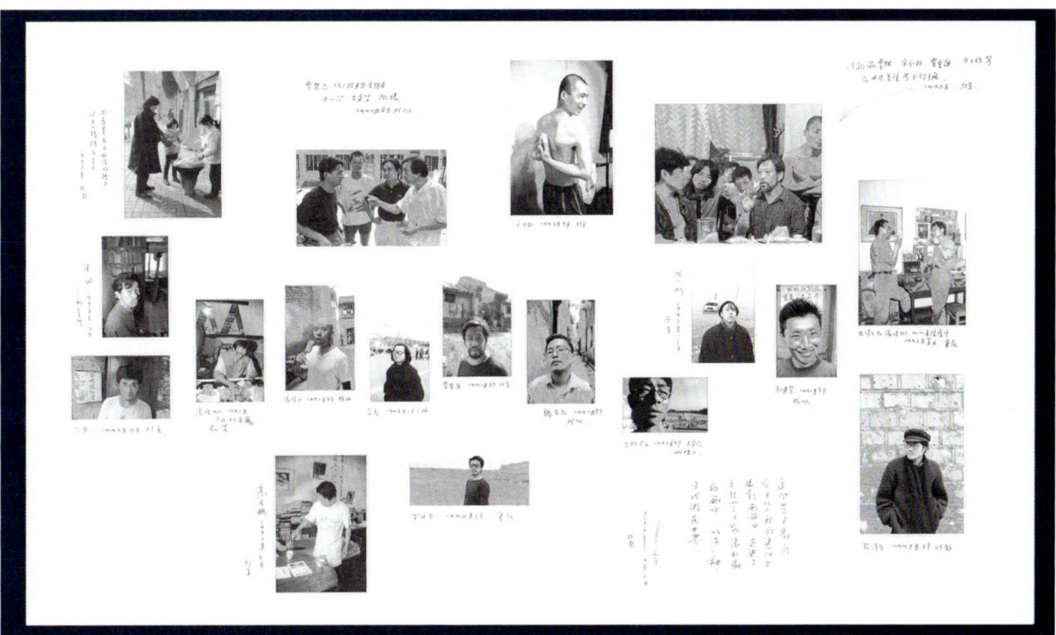

Xiao Quan & Zhang Zhaoying, *This Generation – Art Island B*, 2024
oil on canvas and archival-grade photo paper, Painting, 144 × 240 cm
Photograph, 60 × 100 cm. Unique edition

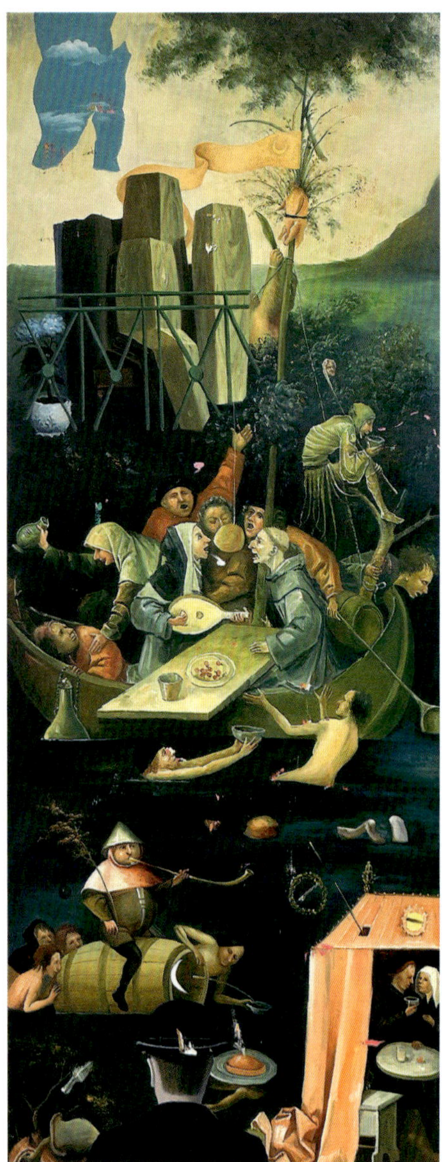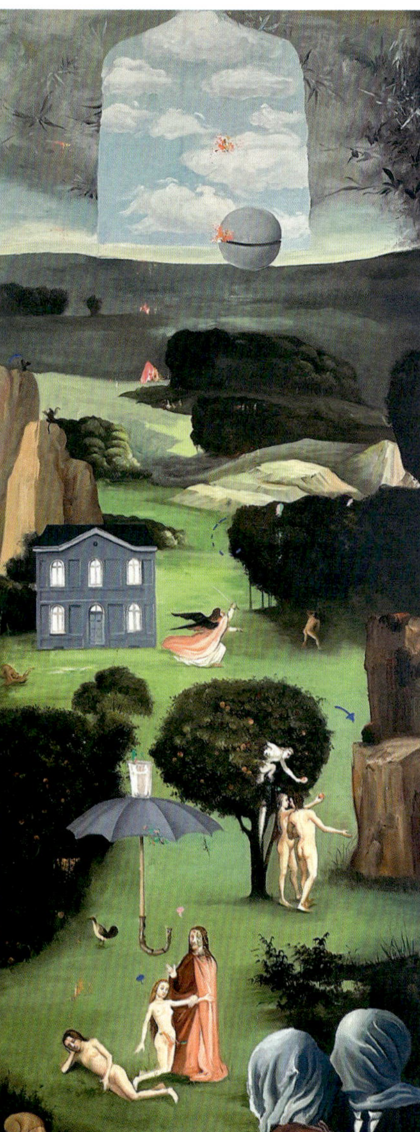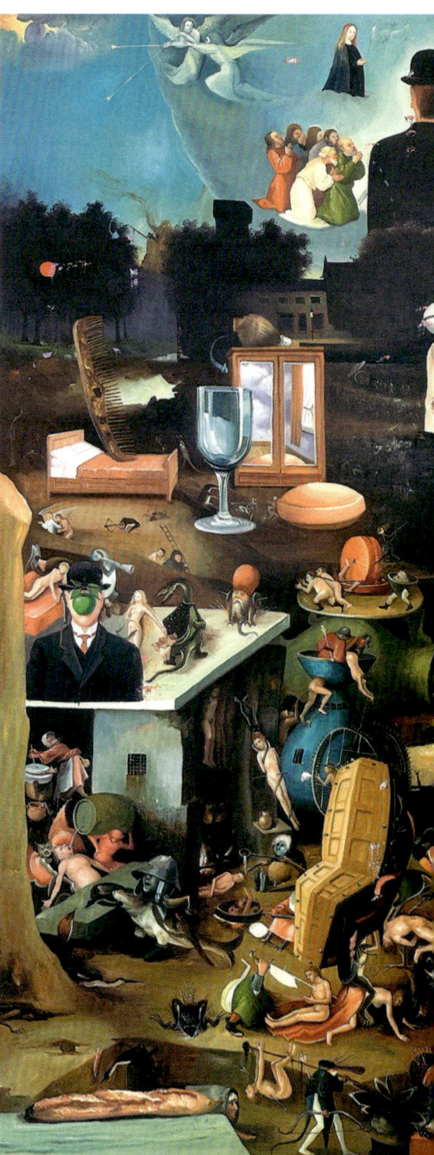

Human World - Magritte in the Persian Realm, 2025
oil on canvas, 203 × 158 cm (central panel), 203 × 78 cm (4 side panels)

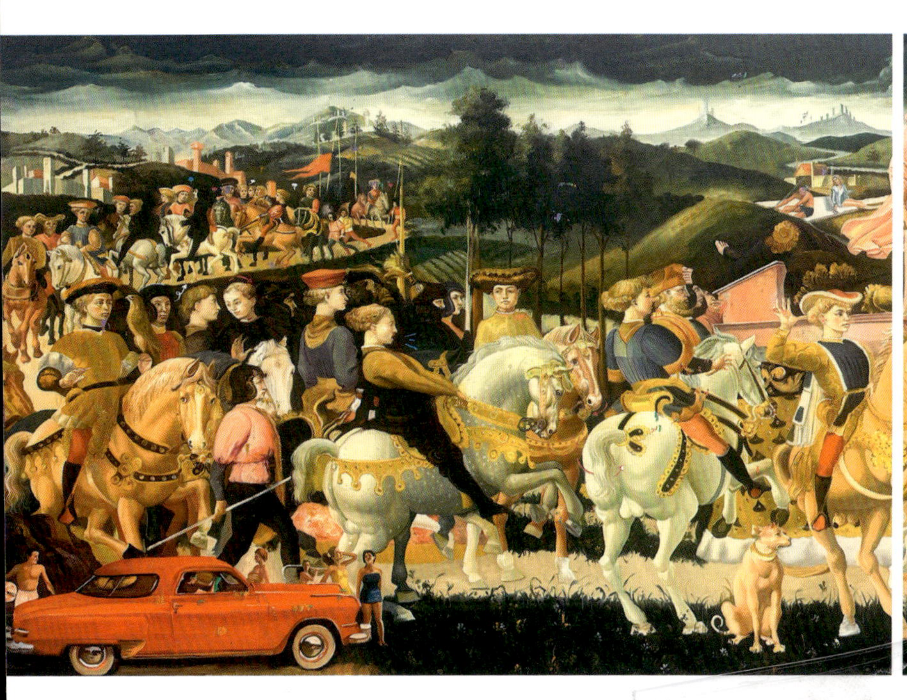
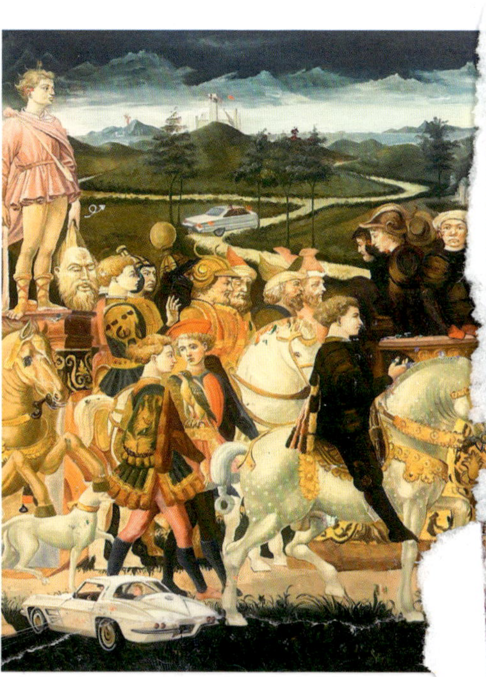

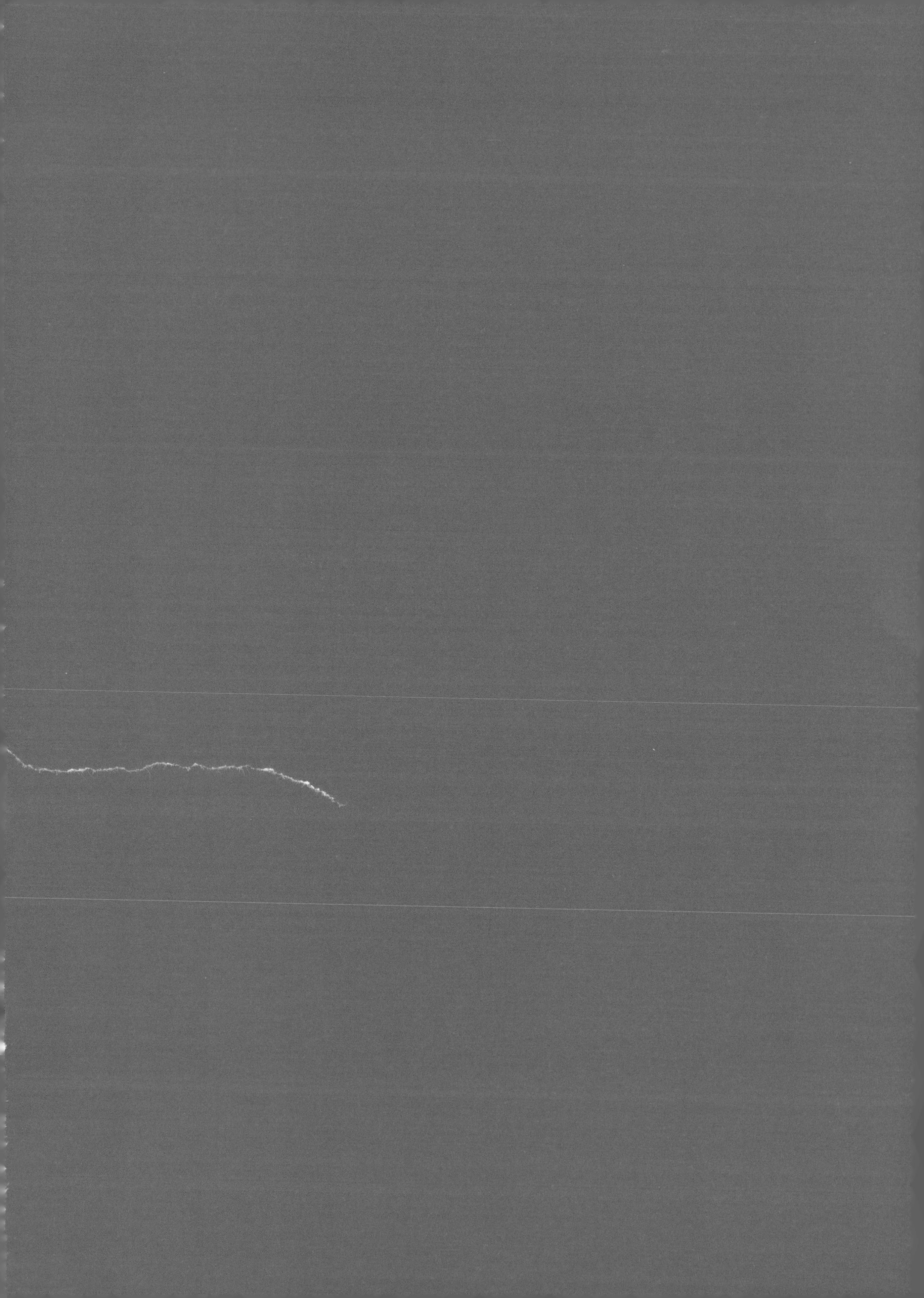

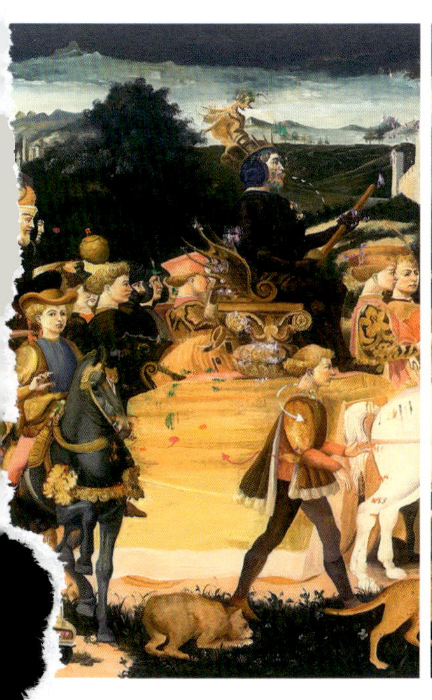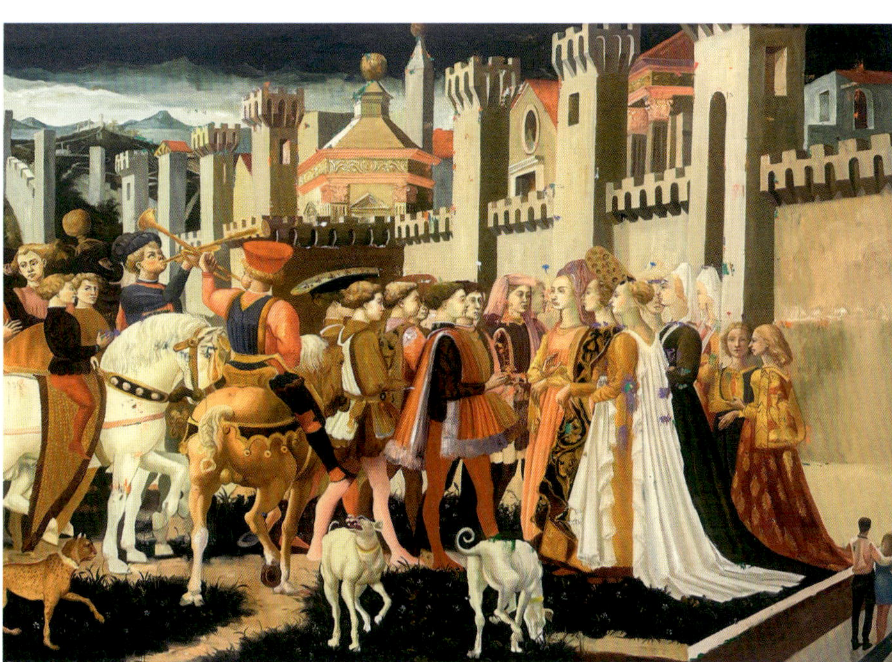

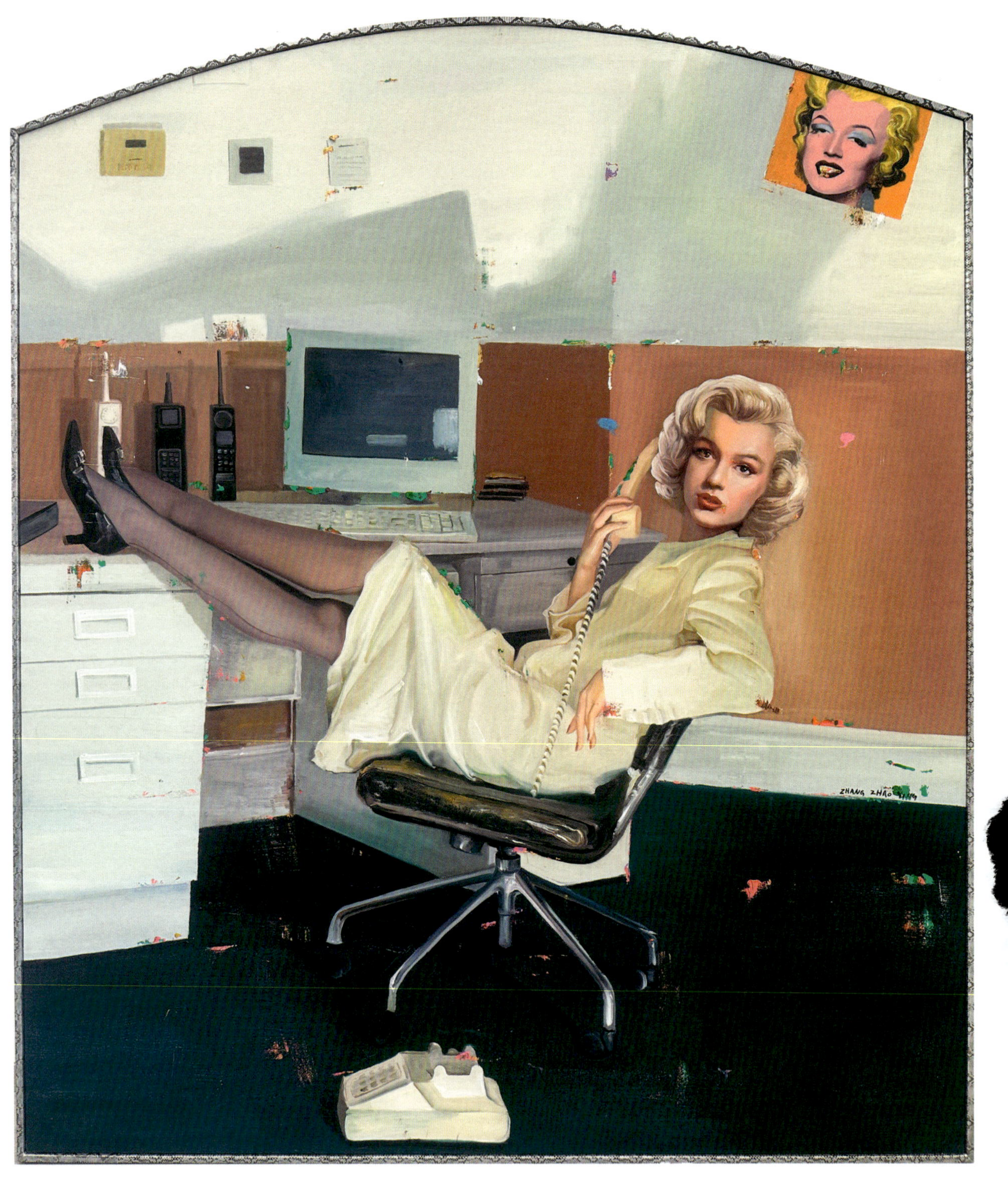

Hello, Monroe, 2025   oil on canvas, 200 × 167 cm

Image, Theatre, and Civilisational Interplay

Zhang Zhaoying's Painting since 2013

Ever since he first began to form his own unique painting language (*Titan's Banquet*, 2013), Zhang Zhaoying has shown an intense interest in dramatic scenes. This Guangzhou-born artist is naturally sensitive to diverse cultures and hybridic life. These cultural genes rooted in his place of birth have gone on to influence his career development. After his diploma in oil painting at the Sichuan Fine Arts Institute, he studied abroad in Brussels and at the Macau University of Science and Technology. During his stay in Belgium, he majored in stage art and the theatre of the absurd. These overlapping backgrounds no doubt helped push the artist toward a highly dramatic painting. Of course, his keen perception of the times was also an important factor behind his pictures becoming so dramatic.

Globalisation, consumerism, social media, video shorts, and AI technology have all made the world appear different. It brought an explosion of information, showing us a never-before-seen spectacle: images from different civilisations, systems, and visual constellations, all rushing towards our retinas like a tsunami. While allowing us to enjoy visual pleasure from diverse cultural sources, it also brought perplexity, especially for those who work in the visual field. When we are faced with such rich visual resources – an overflow – what methods should we employ to face it? Which images should form connections to our creations? Which images can represent the soul of this era? Which images are real, and which images are false? There are no easy answers to these questions, and no simple choices. Zhang Zhaoying thus chose a different approach. He gave up on strict selection, and refrained from seeking out socially microcosmic or representative images, turning instead to adopt a broader, more satirical attitude – casting himself as the "director" of images. Facing so many images, he carries out his own periodical research, rearranging and compiling them to express his own intentions. Sometimes, he also employs appropriation methods, directly transforming images he has collected into pictures. In this way, Broadway plays, circus performances, artists in art history, and famous historical figures can all become images seen in his pictures.

Of course, the artist is not out to become a compiler of montages or a curio cabinet artist. He uses this method to create a series of spectacularised worlds or events through which to respond to changes in the outside world, to catch a glimpse into the mysteries of contemporary society, and discover the connections between the individual and this world. He thus approaches from a variety of angles in his different series: mythology, history, religion, economics, philosophy, or art history, giving rise to works such as *Titan's Banquet* (2013), *Large-Scale Production* (2014), *Custom-Made Youth* (2015), *Private Space* (2015), *Museum of Treasures* (2016), *Big Winner of Production* (2017), *Embroidery Soap Opera* (2014 and 2018), *Eastern Theatre* (2019), *Myth Party* (2017–19), *Faith Props* (2018–19), *Letters* (2019–20), *Lifelong Learning* (2019–21), *Life Props* (2021–22), *Appropriation and Use* (2023), and *Lifelong Beauty* (2022–24). When we look at these works as a whole, these images coalesce into single "stories". These stories seem to have a high level of truth to them, as if the artist is recreating a particular scene. But in fact, most of them are just "plays" composed for the viewer, meticulously crafted "visual traps". The artist's aim is that the viewer will be able to enter these stories, to experience his thoughts, what he sees, and what he perceives. To this end, though the artist does not present a clear viewpoint or answer in his works, he does inspire the viewer to reexamine and rethink those things we once thought of as settled and unerring: whether it is religion, the news, or certain historical images, are they "real", or are they worlds of deception carefully crafted for us by others?

This is the case with *Titan's Banquet*. The story is adapted from a Renaissance tale, in which little people use a banquet to capture a giant "titan". The artist is like a director, painstakingly arranging painting, video, installation, and sculpture on the stage. He meticulously lays out the scene as if recreating a real historic case. In reality, however, it is just an absurd myth, the artist merely presenting the brutal actions of people at a banquet to speak of the distorted humanity and "cannibal" mentality in society.

Meanwhile, in the *Letters* series (2019–20), Zhang Zhaoying has fictionalised a graphic exchange with a photographer as a correspondence in letters: a photographer sent fragments of photographs to Zhang, who used them as the basis for paintings, which he then sent back to the photographer. Through the production of images, this apparently meaningless exchange reveals the unease in the depths of the contemporary mind. For instance, in *Letters – Les Fleurs du mal*, a head made from a wooden mask and fresh flowers gives off an indescribable sense of terror. In *Letters – Aristocrat*, a figure wearing a scary mask and a lion doll with wide open jaws in his hand creates an unsettling feeling. As for the source of this unease, that requires the viewer to think for themselves. The artist provides no answers.

Zhang Zhaoying's 2021–22 *Life Props – Heading to an Exhibition of Resplendent Colour Fields* is also a great example. In this artwork, the artist devised a scene of people going to an exhibition of American artist Jackson Pollock. But there is a powerful contrast between the bustle of the scene and people in reality. At that time in China, due to the pandemic, people were often confined to their homes, unable to leave, let alone travel abroad for an exhibition. This should have been an utterly normal thing in our era of highly developed transportation and communications, but turned it into a nearly insurmountable challenge. The artist wanted to use a humorous, romantic flight of fancy to realise his yearning for freedom. It also seems as if he wanted to use this method, and its contrast with reality, to show that the life we find so normal can, at some particular time, against some special background, turn into an incomprehensible theatre of absurd reality…

Through this, we can see how Zhang Zhaoying's work proposes a way of using the traditional means of painting to reveal the independent thinking of an individual in this chaotic world, even while accepting the conventions of current society. And while he does not resist the influence of technology and new materials on artistic creation – in fact, he has made many creations using installation and video techniques, as was the case in *Titan's Banquet*, which combines video, sculpture, installation and lighting – his painting methods and his employment of images show that painting still has the power today to stand up to the challenge of AI and other technologies. After all, those technologies that lack the weight of flesh, that never experience growing up, that have no understanding of death and rebirth, and no experience of the fragility of life, could never replace the brains and hands of artists to directly convey the rich, subtle, and constantly changing emotional history of humanity.

This point is clearly on display in the series *This Generation – Art Island* (2024), made in collaboration with photographer Xiao Quan. Here, the artist has painted Xiao Quan's photographs of famous figures active in the 1980s and '90s, framing them in a completely new visual experience through arrangement and collage. For instance, *This Generation – Art Island B* is based on numerous photographs of art historians and critics, which Zhang has painted and placed at a dinner table, evoking *The Last Supper*, though the artist has given these figures different clothing, accessories, and postures, breaking the solemn atmosphere of Da Vinci's painting to create an air of absurdity and humour. While this method subtracts to a certain extent from the seriousness of the historical figures from the original photographs, it also reveals their unique personalities in a more vivid and faithful visual form.

Zhang Zhaoying's painting since 2013 reveals certain important traits of China's new generation of painters. The grand perspectives and collective narratives have mostly disappeared from the works of young artists born in the 1980s and '90s. They have also gradually departed from stylism and regional artistic phenomena. Instead, they work in more individualised linguistic worlds, within a global field of knowledge, to complete their creations. The motifs that appear in Zhang Zhaoying's paintings, the cathedrals, entertainment centres, games, karaoke parlours, letters, soap operas, and art history elements are not limited by region or nation. Likewise, figures from completely different times and places, such as Marilyn Monroe, Qi Baishi, Salvador Dalí, and Giorgio de Chirico, are often placed together in his pictures. The cultural conflict between East and West, which had plagued the art world for nearly a century, has become irrelevant in the eyes of these young artists. The question that truly matters to them is how to use painting to respond to this rich world and reveal one's true self. Methods and cultural boundaries no longer matter to them. In the *Lifelong Learning* and *Lifelong Beauty* series, Chinese and international artists are often placed in the same settings, while the urban life of Renaissance Italy and medieval Chinese social scenes are linked together. Through these Surrealist pictures, Zhang Zhaoying has shown us the powerful globalised leanings of this young generation of artists.

Of course, the young generation of painters still faces many serious issues. Aside from the continuous onslaught of technologies and new materials, the secular questions of money and power remain an inescapable reality. But just like the new ideas and new stories constantly emerging in Zhang Zhaoying's painting, the living perceptions of the scene of contemporary life, and the ability to freely pivot between multiple civilisations, have helped these young artists to cast off the burdens and biases of past thinking, and to create entirely new images of our time with freedom and ease.

The Carnival of Images and the Alienation of Time and Space

Zhang Zhaoying's Creative Logic and the Translation of the Times

Looking back from an art historical perspective, the progression of Chinese contemporary art since the 1980s has unfolded in four phases: the referencing and appropriation of Western modernist forms in the 1980s, the experimentation in medium and concept in the 1990s, global market entry in the new millennium, and the synchronous phase of the post-global era. The advancement and iteration of creative ideas is inevitably a reflection of the massive changes taking place in society, civilisation, the economy, and ways of life. The shift from "monolithic" to "diverse" discourse also implies that in our current times we are not only equipped to appreciate the ink styling of ancient Chinese paintings, but can also absorb different values from more distant, more complex civilisational sources. From the traditional to the contemporary, if we follow the linear logic of art historical composition, it inevitably traces a historical line of the "avant-garde" constantly overtaking and replacing the "arrière-garde", but Western art historians warned back in the 1980s of the blind spots and misreadings inherent to such an understanding of artistic development. Thus, looking across the development of Chinese contemporary art, and turning to the understanding of what constitutes contemporaneity, it is perhaps the translation of the times embedded within the individualised creations of the artist. Those images inevitably carry the code to the information within the process, which is to say that the artists' works are their individualised understandings of the times, society, the world, and their own existence.

The works of translators in the 1980s provided nourishment to avant-garde figures born in the 1950s, '60s, and '70s. They feverishly inhaled the hot, heavy air of political and creative freedom, gathering into groups that formed into different schools now repeatedly engraved in the annals of art history. As the older generation of artists gave voice to the tribulations and regrets of their era, the artists born in the 1980s and '90s had been feeding off of the high sugar, high calorie nutrients of the era of material civilisation's global explosion, spending their tender years dressed in clothing branded with Western fashion icons, eating hamburgers washed down with cola. Unlike most artists of the previous generation, who entered the academies for their education in the 1980s, the modern art education of today's young artists can be traced back to the cartoons from various countries that aired on television in their childhood, and in any case, most of them found their lives laid out according to the test preparation track by middle school or even earlier. That specialised, systematic education gave them an outstanding grasp of modelling techniques, and the art academy selection system formed the most familiar criteria in their youth. This framework preparation did not, however, form into an inertial millstone in the years after their graduation. Instead, they all fanned out towards graphic logics and linguistic systems of their own. This is why, when we see their works today – at once both realist and abstract, stressing rationality while altering time and space, emphasising form while not precluding narrative – they cannot be summed up using any one school that emerged in past art history, but can propose a new understanding of creative logic: the arbitrary compilation and pruning of any images that interest them, and placing them together with or without intentional meaning to form new informational semantics and perceptions of the times.

Zhang Zhaoying, who was born in the 1980s, is a representative case study in this generation of young artists. His experience and his understanding of the contemporary are reflections of the liberalist air that flowed through the 1980s and '90s, and point to a redefined global art landscape in the digital era. The birth of ChatGPT and other AI technologies is an inevitable product of our entry into the networked era. Beginning in the early 2000s, the internet gradually moved from large desktop computers to the small handheld terminals we have today, and the cities in which we live our everyday lives have become fantastical worlds filled with digital advertising screens. A chaotic mess of information pervades our everyday lives. In one second, we may be browsing historic visions of Renaissance Italy, and in the next second, watching anthropomorphic robots serving humans. An hour ago, we may have been in Shanghai, only to fly off in the next to any other city in the world. Compared to the previous generation of artists, whose youth was marked by a paucity of information, the information environment experienced by Zhang Zhaoying and his peers is described without exaggeration as an "explosion". In the blink of an eye, images gather in the occipital nerves, accumulating in great numbers to form the vision of an era. This is also why we can see not only the latest industrial products in Zhang Zhaoying's works, but also cultural signs from the Middle Ages or even earlier, all placed together on pieces of canvas of different sizes, bordered areas expanding into a boundless sea of information. He rarely uses only one graphic element in an artwork, instead manifesting as a carnival of multiple genres of filtered images stacked atop each other.

From his 2013 Master's thesis series *Titan's Banquet*, to the series *Fuse – One Piece of News a Day*, created during his studies in Belgium, and on to the *One Small Theatre a Day*, *Lifelong Learning*, and *Lifelong Beauty* series, though he has sometimes used three-dimensional media (such as installations), the same creative logic of visualisation has continued to this day. Rich forms, magical spaces, saturated colours, complex narrative logic, bizarre facial expressions, and absurd masses are common recurring elements in Zhang Zhaoying's creations. The development of art, from literary narrative to the purification of art and then back to narrative, has been a long but purposeful evolution, from the mysterious ancient Greek form of Apollo to the iconographic evolution of the gospels in medieval religious painting, on to modernism's attempts to cancel the requirement that images carry out linguistic tasks.

Now, contemporary art is once again elevating narrative to intellectual blocks optimised for human comprehension. In the creation of narrative images, the artist draws from his keen observations of reality and his abstract literary compilation abilities, acting as the director to adjust the lighting (light and shadow values), colours, positions, blocking, and forms into a complex structure on the limited space of the blank canvas that forms into a graphic sonata. The viewer roams through the information channel formed by the images, closing the creative loop from "information compilation" to "information reception". Bertolt Brecht said that people like theatre because they seek defamiliarisation. The most accustomed aspects of everyday life are rendered unfamiliar. This unfamiliarity provokes thought, which gives rise to new observations and judgements. In his shifts between social theatre, life theatre, and individual theatre, Zhang Zhaoying is referencing a return from the comprehension of his era back to the inner observation of the self. In a creative period spanning more than a decade, his painting has never provided a conclusive explanation, but has instead revolved around procedural experiments and methodological trials in response to the question of what actually constitutes an individualised means of expression for a new generation of youth.

"Post-'80s generation" emerged on internet forums in the early 2000s as a catchall term referring to a group of young writers, and while the fame of this group of artists was mainly rooted in a critical attitude, in any case, after more than a decade moving from youthful scepticism to hard-won experience, the post-'80s artists already out in the world have seemingly never cared about what people on the outside had to say about them. This generation that came up breathing free air have naturally surged toward the construction and declaration of individuality.

During his studies in Belgium, Zhang Zhaoying consciously chose to major in stage art, a natural progression of his interests as an undergraduate. At a time when many artists choose graphic subtraction as a method, he begins with addition as he forms the gatherings in his images, a deliberate individualised choice, using the "falsehood" of theatre to adorn the "truth" of life. This is why he chooses to create large assemblages of complex elements in his works, because he aims to establish a world stage under his own direction, a subjective truth with no need for confirmation from objective reality. From the perspective of graphic truth, perhaps no recreated image can be the absolute truth, much like how there have been so many images of God created in the Middle Ages and the Renaissance, but which one is God's true portrait? In order to affirm the truth of these fabricated images, Zhang Zhaoying embodies a certain naivety in his painting technique. Overall, he uses realist painting techniques that are familiar to viewers, even when his subjects are bizarre and fantastical. If individuality of image is the characteristic trait of this era, then Zhang Zhaoying's creations are the perfect encapsulation of that. Unlike pure expression of sentiments, his painting presents a rational combination of images that is neither cathartic nor compassionate, not conveying information through the speed of the brush or the tension of the colours, with only the combination of images and the alteration of their sources to serve as the energy field to carry the information.

Meanwhile, unlike the previous generation of artists, who had a very concrete experience of life, today's young artists mostly gain their experience through indirect means. Steven Spielberg's 2018 movie *Ready Player One* created a virtual future world, a technological post-human era in which everything humans did aside from eating and drinking could be completed by indirect means. Even at the time of its release, the film wasn't entirely fiction. Our own primary channels of information today no longer follow the traditional model of one person to another; everything can be obtained indirectly. We are already enmeshed in an information cocoon, but our conscious preferences have synthesised a new living fluid that channels the indirect straight into the brain.

Zhang Zhaoying's specialised education experience was largely the same as that of his peers. They began to home in on art in middle school, and had to maintain constant, intense focus on their major and general humanities courses. After gaining admission to the academies, their studies and everyday explorations largely relied on their teachers and class readings (as well as books and the internet, of course). The context encountered by the previous generation of artists in the 1990s was the spread of the free market, while Zhang Zhaoying and his peers encountered the social phase of soaring markets. The material and informational riches left this generation with no choice but to be swept up by the trends of the times. They rapidly absorbed all manner of information from everywhere, processing and transforming it in their minds. This kind of indirect experience manifested in their painting as a cold gaze, as seen in the series *Lifelong Learning*, which he chose as a title for a series of motifs threaded with assemblages and appropriations of images from art history, cultural history, shared social signs, and popular advertising. He alters and combines public image semantics into a new visual method for understanding, one marked by parody and satire, as well as absurdity and confusion, while his bookish research habits are perhaps a result of the rote memory teaching his generation was subjected to.

This is an era of the breaking of traditional conventions, as well as an era of the establishment of new ways of life, of shifts from the country to the city, the lost villages replaced by cultural tourism destinations, and the cities becoming a site for the production and exchange of information and values between groups. The previous generation still retains inherent cultural habits, but the young generation, in this atomised social spectacle, seeks out fragments of the era that can be pieced together into a self. The various image elements that appear in such series as *Soap Opera of Life* and *Life Props* form an unfamiliar time and space as they are arranged in their new setting. Jean-François Millet's *Gleaners* continue to "work overtime" as dusk sets in over the ruins; portraits of famous critics and artists take on a classical air on *Art Island*; political figures, celebrities and philosophers appear before a bustling downtown skyline; cartoon characters join in on an extravagant feast. The use of "realist" painting techniques to fabricate truth is a visual trap Zhang Zhaoying sets in his creations. The visual atmosphere is the most familiar spatial setting for the masses, but the artist also uses spatiotemporal alienation to warn the viewer: that primally anticipated aesthetic moment will not materialise. "I recreate classic sculptures and architectural spaces as physical carriers for time. When facing the original classics, we have an entirely different visual experience. This is a double transformation of the visual experience by temporal painting in the image era: when images and signs are refracted into our visual system, this is the first 'input'; the visual impact brought by the chronological progression of the original classic then alters the original 'program', while also altering our understanding of the accretion of time, breaking the notion of the 'eternal' in time." This is how Zhang Zhaoying explained his understanding and thinking on the displacement of time and space in his creations, in an essay entitled "Magician of Time: On Temporality in Artistic Creation".

Painting is the theatre woven by the artist. In this theatre, the appropriation of any image or sign is a reference to a new surreal style, somewhere between the truth that is seen with the eye and the illusion of the knowledge system, but if we take quantum mechanics a step further, perhaps within multidimensional space-time, all so called truth can be rewritten by another truth. The artist's creation merely aims to propose a re-editing of time and space. This alienated visual perception is precisely the era in which we now reside: the onslaught of information and digitisation enhancing the depth and density of globalisation and cultural exchange, social inequality and immobility producing cultural affinities and identity conflicts, efficiency-focused KPIs mechanising humanity, and mental stress and solitude giving rise to unconscious fatigue. Zhang Zhaoying has used images to create an individualised visual world, taking a performative approach to participating in the observation of young life. The fragmentary context tells us that our present no longer follows a single, linear living logic, while the proliferation of information speaks of the contradictions and conflicts of a rapidly shifting society.

The clash of civilisations that unfolded in the last century has seen surface-level mitigation in this century (though contention in certain areas still continues). The new century began with deep homogenisation. The struggle between East and West was gradually replaced by specific regional cultures. The so called "Third World" of the past has become a growth point for global GDP and cultural diversity. Fast food culture stimulates people who have no time for deeper thinking, while perfectionism and "take it slow" mentalities can no longer handle today's life. In our present day, flooded by the confounding interpretations of bland Conceptual Art, perhaps the ancient art form of painting is the thing humanity truly needs inside. Kenneth Clark came to believe that genius artists possess God-given talent. This flies in the face of modern society's routinised cultivation, but limited art history truly only does select the seeds that demonstrate individuality.

Since 1978, the new Chinese art history has unfolded within stylistic cycles, shaping the myths of the elitist arena of Chinese painting. The cultural contention between East and West, which had long plagued artists, is no longer a topic of major concern for today's young artists. What they face is a rich, complex world that moves in easy lockstep with the entire globe. Markets, discursive power, rates of appearance, new vision, money…these are the issues of the era that this generation cannot avoid. Zhang Zhaoying's painting provides us with such a pictorial vision: topical creation has vanished from the world of the youth, who have also discarded so called "stylism"; meanwhile, they strive to create an individualised world, an ideal shrine free of constraints and limitations, where Qi Baishi and Da Vinci can stand together as peers, a utopia where bars, banquet halls, stages, art history, letters, and theatre can all find their place, where the subaltern, scoundrels and knights, Marilyn Monroe and religious figures, all join together in heralding the coming of the era of art history composition as globalised theatre.

Toward an Encyclopaedic Palace

Zhang Zhaoying and the Flowing Energy of His Art

To analyse Zhang Zhaoying's art through a particular series or a single piece of artwork is, for me, honestly, an exceedingly challenging undertaking. Unzipping the compressed file of his artwork feels like releasing an entire universe, each folder leading to a distinct parallel universe of his creation. Consequently, I find myself curious about the energy within him: Where does this energy originate? How does he manage the relationships between its varied forms? He reminds me of Duan Yu, a character from Jin Yong's novel *Demi-Gods and Semi-Devils*, who absorbed internal energies from martial arts masters and merged them within himself. Yet initially, even Duan Yu was unable to fully integrate these powers.

To seek answers, one must contextualise Zhang Zhaoying and his art within his era and view them through the lens of his personal and cultural experiences.

The East has been imagined in diverse ways through a global, multicultural lens. One is that of the distant East: a magnificent ancient civilisation epitomised by porcelain and silk, a China defined by archaeology and Chinese studies. Another is a symbolic China, the mysterious China of tangible symbols prevalent from 1949 to the 1980s. Lastly, there is post-2000 China, a rapidly growing society full of raw energy. The world imagines distinctly different versions of the East according to various historical stages and scopes.

Zhang Zhaoying's generation of artists grew alongside China's rapid globalisation. Collective memories of China's successful bid for the Olympics, its accession to the WTO, and the national football team's first World Cup appearance created an uplifting national image at the dawn of the new century. In 2008, Beijing successfully hosted the Summer Olympics, signalling China's readiness to open fully to the world. This was a time when globalisation profoundly influenced everyday life in China; never before had its effects felt so tangible. In 2009, Zhang Zhaoying graduated from the Attached High School of Guangzhou Academy of Fine Arts and enrolled in the Sichuan Fine Arts Institute in Chongqing. Transitioning from familiar Cantonese culture to Bashu culture marked his first significant cultural flux. Upon graduating in 2013, he moved to Brussels for further studies, experiencing a second cultural flux: this time from a localised environment to a truly global context. This period coincided with the peak of globalisation in contemporary Chinese art, during which numerous biennials and large-scale group exhibitions that emphasised global consciousness among young artists emerged. Notably, Zhang Zhaoying participated in the *CAFAM Future* exhibition held by the CAFA Art Museum alongside some of the finest contemporary artists of his generation. In my view, this exhibition represented the final rehearsal of global consciousness among artists of that generation, as subsequent youth exhibitions in China never quite matched the scale or the systematic exploration of the young art ecosystem exemplified by *CAFAM Future*. In 2015, Zhang returned to China after graduating from the Académie royale des Beaux-Arts in Brussels, experiencing yet another cultural flux. He taught at the Sichuan Fine Arts Institute until 2023, after which he moved to the Tianjin Academy of Fine Arts, encountering his fourth major cultural flux from Bashu culture to Tianjin culture. His journey – spanning Guangzhou, Chongqing, Brussels, back to Chongqing, and finally, Tianjin – clearly illustrates the complexity and multilayered experiences that define his generation of artists, especially when correlated with various stages of his creative output.

Professor Wu Hung shares an intriguing anecdote in the book *Interviews on Chinese Civilization* (*Zhongguo Wenming fangtan lu*). Professor Bagley, after reading Wu Hung's article in *Art Research* (*Meishu Yanjiu*), commented that it "did not seem written by a Chinese scholar", a remark loaded with implications. Zhang Zhaoying's paintings evoke similar feelings in me; they hardly seem painted by a Chinese artist. Bagley's comment left Wu Hung uncertain whether to feel pleased or disheartened, but perhaps this ambivalence mirrors the unique circumstances faced by Wu Hung's generation, the first scholars from post-1949 China to engage internationally. These scholars and artists retained a wild yet romantic passion shaped by China's unique historical context of the 1960s. They developed their global consciousness during the extraordinary 1980s and stepped onto the international stage in the late '80s and early '90s, a period marked by the rise of global multiculturalism. Zhang Zhaoying's generation, however, grew up already integrated into this global consciousness. Unlike earlier generations, post-2000 China experienced globalisation alongside rapid urbanisation, making cultural flux and transitions commonplace, thereby infusing the Chinese social landscape with a dynamic energy that feels both abundant and surreal.

The flux and migration of China's population generated intense social energy, which immediately found expression in art characterised by raw, romantic, melancholic, turbulent, and angry emotions. The "scar generation" grappled with sorrow stemming from the rural-urban migration and flux of the 1960s, while sixth-generation filmmakers depicted narratives of rural youth migrating into urban areas. Zhang Zhaoying's millennial generation, born in the 1980s and maturing during the "post-Olympic era", experienced the dreamlike, dizzying growth of the early 2000s, followed by a decade of relative stability and rationality and today's retreat from globalisation. This historical rollercoaster brought uncertainty and a sense of losing control into their artistic development. His personal experiences of mobility and cultural flux are even more intricate than those of his contemporaries. The interplay between China's multicultural regional dynamics and his transition from local to global contexts imbues his art with raw energy and cross-cultural hybridity, making his works particularly challenging to categorise.

The difficulty in categorising Zhang Zhaoying's work arises from the fact that, since 2013, he has been creating an encyclopaedic palace of artistic wonders. Such a monumental project demands extraordinary creative energy from an artist. Critics may question whether such an extensive and systematic construction, which makes possible the artist's diverse visual styles and artistic narratives, is a self-undermining weakness. However, in my view, artistic complexity and diversity far outweigh symbolic consistency. Imagine him presenting a retrospective exhibition years from now. It would be great if his work were presented as a palace of encyclopaedic wonders; it would far surpass exhibitions limited by singular concepts, styles, narratives, or media. While his art may appear blended and diverse, is this not reflective of the China of great flux he has personally experienced? For me, it is insufficient to view his individual artworks in isolation; instead, they must be understood within the larger system he is carefully crafting. He is not only the palace's architect but also its curator and librarian, accurately organising and shaping his complex artistic universe. His art thus embodies the contradictory tension between nearly chaotic creative energy and structured, meticulous order.

Zhang Zhaoying's work also explores many other tensions, such as those between myth, allegories, and social reality; the sublime and its bathos; the classical and the modern; the historical and the real; popular culture and eternal monuments; and the past and future. The artist skilfully weaves together these seemingly contradictory elements, generating energy akin to that of flux, the central theme in his artwork. These relations, in essence, reflect conflicts between personal experience and cultural knowledge. Zhang Zhaoying rarely incorporates overtly autobiographical elements, choosing instead to conceal himself behind layers of cultural references and public imagery. Rather than directly engaging in personal storytelling, he prefers to narrate observations deeply rooted in the social landscape. This distinguishes him from many of his contemporaries. In other words, as a painter, he appears to stress public consciousness even more strongly than one might expect from a public artist. This emphasis is particularly evident in his frequent use of public imagery and shared cultural experiences, which suggests his enduring curiosity about depicting the world. Although the relationship between imagery and painting has been increasingly discussed in recent years within the Chinese art community, the specific relationship between public imagery and painting remains underexplored. Zhang Zhaoying implicitly addresses this crucial but often overlooked subject in his work. In today's context of social media and artificial intelligence, the way artists negotiate between public and personal spaces is reflected in how they approach the relationship between public imagery and personal artistic expression. Zhang Zhaoying undoubtedly provides one of the best case studies for this inquiry.

Just as sixth-generation Chinese filmmakers obsessed over personal narratives before the generational framework dissolved, the new generation of Chinese artists increasingly conceal their stories behind their art. In essence, the energy in Zhang Zhaoying's art reveals a public consciousness, which is reflective of the global flux and shifts he experienced and the energy of the Chinese social landscape. Additionally, he is essentially his own best critic, much like filmmakers who say Jia Zhangke is "his own best film critic". For example, Zhang Zhaoying succinctly describes his artistic method as "displacing the temporal dimensions within images and weakening the concept of time on a shared plane". This simple yet profound statement provides critics with ample material for contemplation. Further discussions, such as those regarding theatricality in his works, are beyond the scope of this essay. As aforesaid, Zhang Zhaoying skilfully compresses vast amounts of information into his artworks. His "marathon-like" painting process and exploration of temporality open yet another doorway, revealing a compelling contradiction: his works reflect a public panorama, yet his research looks inward. Perhaps this tension is precisely the source of his artistic energy.

ANDREA B. DEL GUERCIO

Zhang Zhaoying: "From the Apartment of Memory"

My first encounter with the work of Zhang Zhaoying came in 2023, as part of that exemplary exhibition route laid out within the expansive spaces of the Museo di arte moderna e contemporanea di Trento e Rovereto. Given the choral dimension of a title that succeeded in co-ordinating individual expressive personalities and in describing those distinctive cultural areas that were specified through an extension of the pictorial heritage across both East and West (*Global painting. La Nuova pittura cinese*),[1] Zhang Zhaoying's particular interest in the "social history of art" – to re-use Arnold Hauser's title[2] – and in its "impossible" relations with that unit of time which encompasses both the modern and contemporary seasons, was not lost on me.

In the wake of an observation that concentrated, in a collective context, on two single works, I had the opportunity to come into contact with the developments of a new phase of painting, with Zhang Zhaoying giving a major boost to an intimate and intense linguistic process, based on that experience which comes out of a process of iconographic contamination. Just like a literary story marked out by the principle of sequential events and the permeation of memories and emotions, he constructs a form of painting that is the fruit of a persistent, urgent aggregation of the infinite variability of those values that he finds accumulated in the tradition of artistic images, before going on to bring out, in the orchestration phase, those expressive nuances – from the languor of intimacy to the excitement of pleasure – that are to be found in social conduct in the phase of aesthetic perception.

We can talk about an engagement with – which becomes a veritable "conquest"[3] of – the culture of art and the history of painting, whereby we can chart the extrapolation not only of the "cultured" dimension (*A Perfect Match*) but also, and above all, of the complete transcription of those data that describe the architecture and landscape of Europe, its collective customs and private notes, from the centrality of food to its parlour games (*Lifelong Beauty – The Feast of Mr. Pan*). It amounts to a narrative process, conducted today as yesterday through figurative texts of "a religiously inspired art in which the spiritual and secular elements are more or less fused into a single whole, and in which those who experience it at first hand are not always aware of the distinction between the ecclesiastical and secular purposes behind it."[4]

In perfect harmony with that wide expressive area, transversal across the generations and geographies of East and West, and geared up to reconstruct those linguistic dynamics on which the centrality of a style and an iconographic culture is redefined, Zhang Zhaoying attributes to his own output those data that place it in qualified relation with the sphere of perception, rebuilding that ancient accord, now strained, that bound the artist to his "reader". It is a linguistic operation targeted at the recovery of that classical equilibrium whereby every iconographic fragment is a testament to, and an elaboration of, a new state of beauty, the upshot of the affirmation of transitoriness and instability – "*Persuade tibi hoc sic esse, ut scribo: quaedam tempora eripiuntur nobis, quaedam subducuntur, quaedam effluunt*"[5] – while, with the support of memory, everything leads to the precious kaleidoscope of the present.

1   *Global painting. La Nuova pittura cinese*, edited by Lü Peng and Paolo De Grandis (Milan: Skira, 2023).

2   Arnold Hauser, *The Social History of Art* (1951) (New York: Vintage Books, 1957).

3   "The intellectual restlessness of later Romanesque art is expressed, among other things, in the constant widening of the field covered by pictorial representation, which leads to the conquest for artistic purposes of the whole range of Holy Scripture." Hauser, *The Social History of Art*, p. 172.

4   Ibid., p. 167.

5   Seneca, *Letters on Ethics*, trans. Margaret Graver and A. A. Long (Chicago: Chicago UP, 2015). "Convince yourself that what I write is true: some moments are snatched from us, some are filched, and some just vanish", p. 25.

The exhibition sequence of the most recent paintings, imposing in their dimensions, leads our eye into an extraordinary museum route entirely shorn of temporal limits, grasping what can effectively qualify contemporary perception, preparing for and impacting on the definition of taste and synchronising with a competent sensibility.

I fully share the logic that determines Zhang Zhaoying's expressive process, arising from his cultural engagement with the history of art, but at the same time entirely independent with respect to a still too widespread and "reductive" sequence of styles and aesthetics. Every painting is, indeed, the outcome of a choice that led him to enter into a direct dialogue with the private kaleidoscope of art – at which we look carefully and in which we recognise ourselves – and with the stratification of his iconographic recollections, produced by means of the transcription of the drawing, through the "gift" of the pictorial gesture…when, as Wittgenstein put it: "A picture depicts reality by representing a possibility of existence and non-existence of states of affairs."[6]

Based on these observations, we can state that the painting of Zhang Zhaoying, on passing across that frontier which inexorably divides the sayable from the unsayable, places itself in that area of the contemporary art system that is independent of the responsibilities of investment value, being instead the "ripe fruit" of the "emotional dividend". This is crucial vis-à-vis the definition of a season that is witnessing the return to centrality of a judgement founded, in terms of priority, on "fascination", on "pleasure", having had its origin in the introspection of beauty in relation to a painting that "plays" with the culture of art. We can recognise that Zhang Zhaoying has positioned himself in perfect synch with all of those creative processes which in every period of history have played their part in the throwing into crisis of harmonic expressive systems, in order to reach a new emotional state. As Mario Praz stated on visiting Paul Marmottan in his apartment at No. 2 Rue Louis-Boilly in Paris, which would become the Musée Marmottan Monet: "For me, all of this décor of sober classicism got lost in the long night of the soul, in that nebulous region of sensibility in which the paths of aesthetic beauty and love seem to be still merged as one."[7]

The Works

In terms of the published works, I follow here the same "sequence" as showcased in the exhibition, and I observe the various dimensions, lingering on the ancient variables set by the format of the canvases, between curvatures and the cut of the corners. I recognise narrative modalities and the insistent sequence of details and fragments extrapolated from a museological pictorial process, which belongs to and binds together traces of the strict German medieval panels and the elegant Italian Renaissance frescoes – *A Perfect Match*: visual "memories" scattered along an ideal European Grand Tour in the 19th and 20th centuries, animated by that ascientific freedom that is part of a private aesthetic experience which only antiques can give to the collector's sensibility: "Jacob chairs, Boilly paintings, Savonnerie rugs, 'en Sarreguemines' chandeliers and Thomire bronzes were his family."[8]

6   Ludwig Wittgenstein, *Tractatus Logico-Philosophicus* (1921), trans. David Pears and Brian McGuinness (London: Routledge, 2001), 2.201, p. 10.
7   Mario Praz, "Vecchi collezionisti", in *Voci dietro la scena* (Milan: Biblioteca Adelphi, 1980), p. 203.
8   Ibid., p. 206.

1. Hendrik Voogd, *Italian Landscape with Umbrella Pines*, 1807, detail Rijksmuseum, Amsterdam

2. Zhang Zhaoying, *Lifelong Beauty – Rippling*, 2023–24, detail

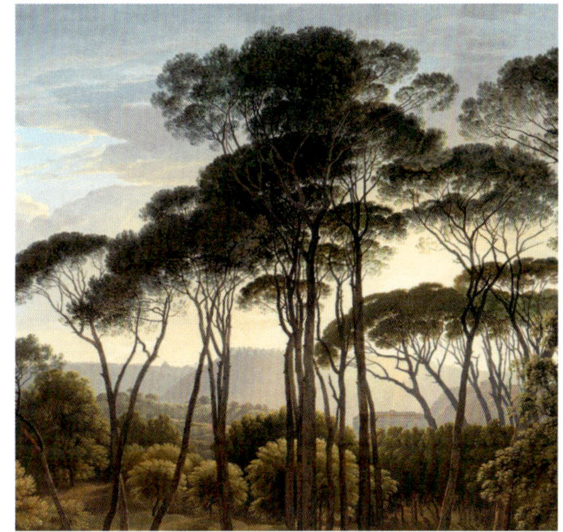
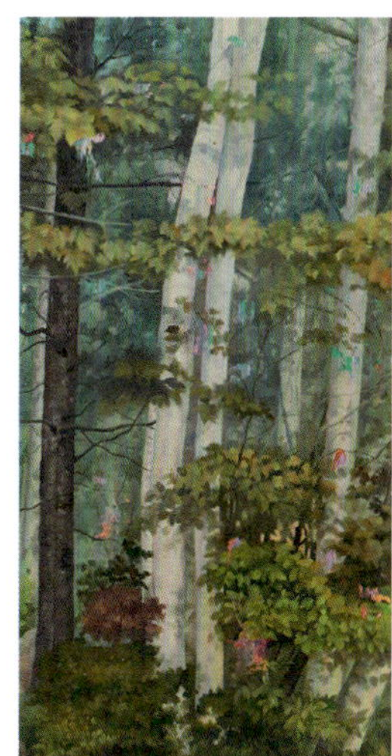

Of apparent instrumental significance is the presence in most of the paintings of a chromatic disintegration very similar to smears of fresh paint; traces left rather than streaks. They could look like involuntary, casual abrasions, but in reality they tend to evoke both the "antique" dimension of surfaces worn away through the circulation of the work in the world, and the incompleteness of the painting – i.e. that which it awaits in order to be finished, but which in turn could remain in the "timeless" space of the "unfinished" (figs. 1–2).

Entirely analogous to an extensive monographic exhibition, our eye participates, then comes to rest, and then becomes immersed in every single "window" opened by Zhang Zhaoying, recognising in his "figurative texts" the reaching of that perfect equilibrium that runs between intellectual experience, born of the need for engagement with the culture of art, and the pleasure of a creative frequentation, dictated by curiosity, in the persistent vitality of the pictorial tradition. It is a process both theoretical (the cultural responsibility of the artist) and technical (the linguistic skills of painting) that confirms how essential the "live" gaze of the present is in generating "living testaments" to the past.

If the large-scale painting is installed in the space, catalysing our attention with its vibrant inner articulation, reminiscent of the suggestions of a *Wunderkammer*, then a relentless sequence of works, which the visual memory succeeds in conjoining, opens up that all-encompassing and involving experience that leads to the typology of the "Panorama Museum" – Salzburg, Innsbruck, Bad Frankenhausen – before summoning up the shift from the centrality of photography to the development of cinema (figs. 3–4).

Zhang Zhaoying's expressive action – which was certainly shaped by his direct experience of living in Belgium while studying for his Master's degree at the Académie royale des Beaux-Arts (a period that must have brought him into contact with Flemish painting and with the Surrealism of René Magritte, as quoted in *The Youth's Yearning for Margarete*) – ranges widely, the spatial and temporal dimensions

139

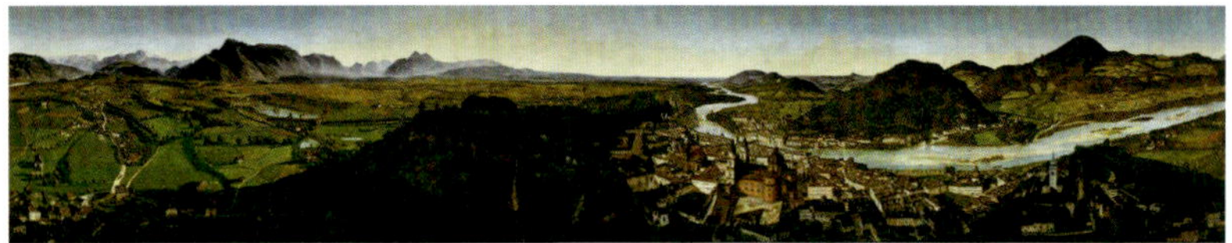

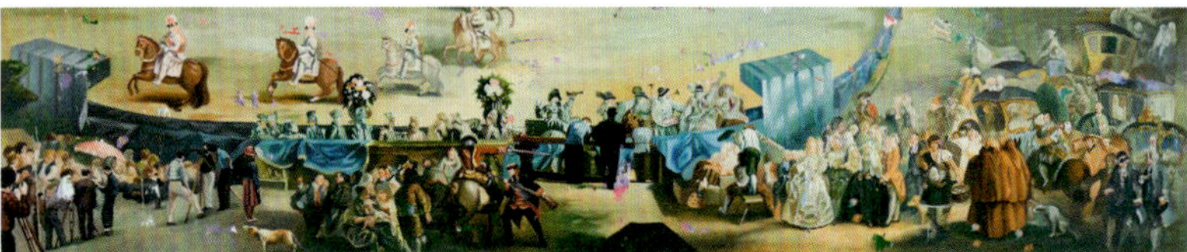

3. Johann Michael Sattler, *Panorama of the City of Salzburg*, 1825–29, detail
Salzburg Museum

4. Zhang Zhaoying, *Seeking a Beautiful Life*, 2023–24, detail

criss-crossing, involving alternately Nature and Architecture, developing an iconographic synergy between the internal and external landscapes, constantly supported by a technique that in certain cases bursts into glorious technicolour and is qualified through the abundance of food (*Lifelong Beauty – The Feast of Mr. Pan*) whereas in others he pursues a monochromatic languor (*Encounter* and *Blue-Blooded Nobility*). Our eye remains fixed on the ensemble and on each detail, uncovering the interweaving of quotations and experimenting with the opening up of new cultural and emotional experiences, addressing abundance in the still lifes and in the long tables, laden with food, dating from the 17th and 18th centuries, encountering various states of memory, from Mitteleuropean culture, via photograms of social relations typical of the 1950s and '60s, all the way to the transcription of those many moments of family serenity and affective adventures (*Waver* and *Lifelong Beauty – Reading with a Kindred Spirit*) experienced within brief, sweet moments of leisure; traces of the form of cinema that still knows how to document, mindful of that infinite series (from Giorgione's 1506–08 painting *The Tempest* to Caravaggio's 1597 work, *Rest on the Flight into Egypt*) and of the myriad versions of *Le Déjeuner sur l'herbe*[9] (figs. 5–6).

In the impossibility of controlling and managing the complexity of the heritage being channelled into the creation of a number of the large paintings, our attention risks getting lost within a kaleidoscope in constant movement. Exemplary in this regard is that "new version" of Jan Brueghel the Elder's 1613 work, *The Entry of the Animals into Noah's Ark*,[10] which stretches across more than two-and-a-half metres. The horizontal development encompasses two directions, which from the edges gravitate towards the centre, where they meet, marked by the lighting up of the "yellow" colour, the "twenty-four-hour" man and the "grey" horse. Not by chance, the horse in question is one of the subjects chosen by the artist in which many others before him have also shown a particular interest, due to its expressive power, from Sandro Botticelli in the cycle of *Nastagio degli Onesti*, painted in 1483, to Peter Paul Rubens in his *Equestrian Portrait of the Duke of Lerma* from 1603,[11] right through, bordering on frenzy, to Giorgio de Chirico (figs. 7–8).

For me, it is an extraordinary, utterly perfect painting, encapsulating Zhang Zhaoying's entire expressive process, offering a summation of

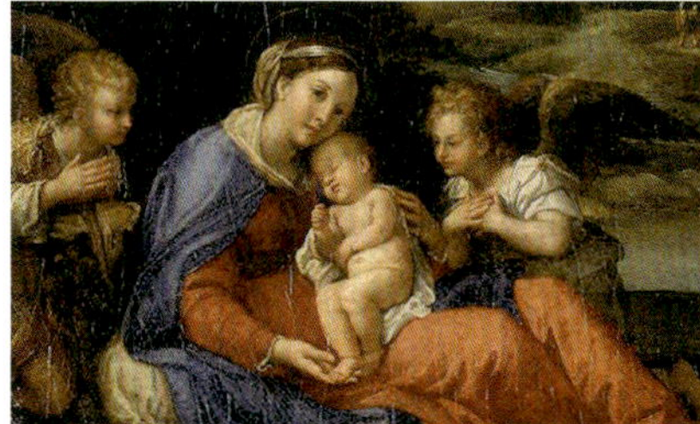

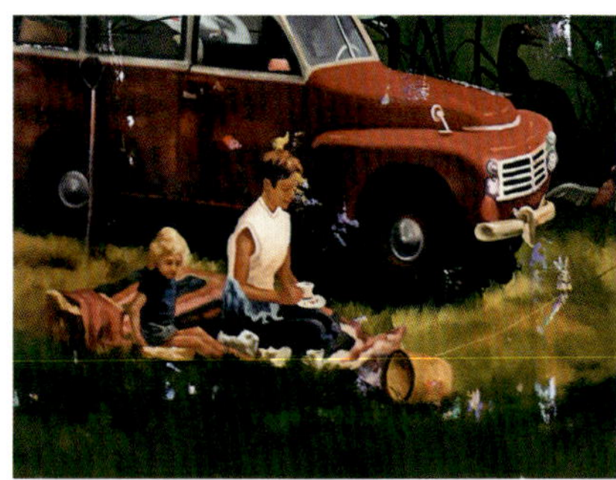

5. Annibale Carracci
The Holy Family, c. 1604, detail
The State Hermitage, Saint Petersburg

6. Zhang Zhaoying, *Lifelong Beauty — The Pursuit of Happiness*, 2023–24, detail

9   Édouard Manet, *Le Déjeuner sur l'herbe*, 1863, Musée d'Orsay, Paris.
10   Jan Brueghel the Elder (1568–1625), *The Entry of the Animals into Noah's Ark*, 1613, oil on panel, 54.6 × 83.8 cm, J. Paul Getty Museum, Malibu.
11   The two works are held at the Museo Nacional del Prado, Madrid.

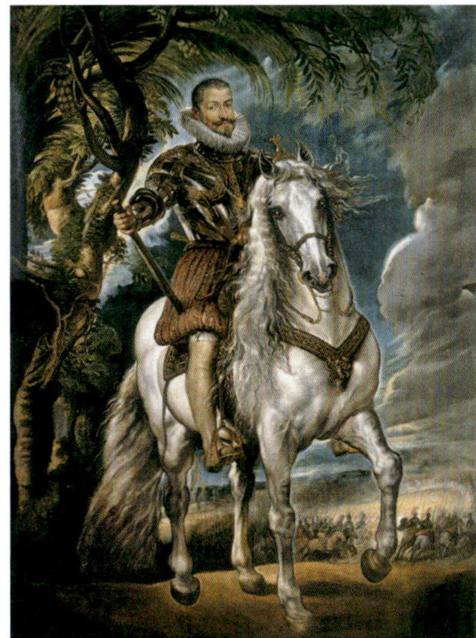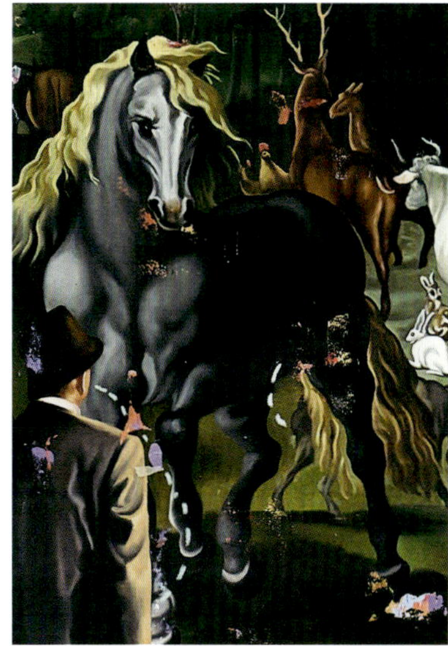

his cultural, technical, aesthetic, and compositional qualities. This "choice" on the part of the artist appears even more significant if it is framed and placed in close relation to the content found in the testimony of Cardinal Federico Borromeo (1564–1631), who had Jan Brueghel as his guest in Milan between 1595 and 1596: "On questioning Brueghel, who was staying in my house, as to the identity of his master in art, he answered, 'Sir, it is nature, from whom I learn every day.' It was true. He was astonished, forever gazing upon things, before expressing them in painting, whence came his excellence."[12]

12   Federico Borromeo, *Miscellanea
     Adnotationum Variarum*, Biblioteca
     Ambrosiana, Milan (Milan: Gruppo
     Editoriale Zaccaria, 1985).

Lü Peng is a leading Chinese art curator, critic, and historian.
Born in Chongqing, Sichuan, in 1956, he graduated in Political Studies
from Sichuan Normal University in 1982. From 1982 to 1985, he was
the chief editor of *Theater and Film* magazine, and from 1986 to 1990,
he served as Deputy Secretary of the Sichuan Dramatists Society.
In 1992, he was appointed Artistic Director of the First Guangzhou
Biennial Art Fair, China's first art biennial.
Lü's notable curatorial projects include *A Gift to Marco Polo*,
a collateral event at the 2009 Venice Biennale; *Reshaping History*
(Beijing, 2010); *Pure Views: New Painting from China* (Louise
Blouin Foundation, Frieze, London, 2010), followed by *Pure Views*
at the Asian Art Museum in San Francisco in 2011; the 2011 Anren
Biennale; *Passage to History: 20 Years of La Biennale di Venezia
and Chinese Contemporary Art*, co-curated with Achille Bonito Oliva
at the 55th Venice Biennale (2013); and *Global painting. La Nuova
pittura cinese* at the Mart in Rovereto (2023).
Lü has also authored several important publications, including
A History of Art in 20th-Century China (Charta, 2010); *A History of Art
in Twentieth-Century China* (New Star Press, 2013); and *Storia
dell'arte cinese dal XX al XXI secolo* (Rizzoli, 2024).
Currently, Lü is an Associate Professor in the Department of Art
History and Theory at the China Academy of Art in Hangzhou, as well
as at the Sichuan Fine Arts Institute, and the Xi'an Academy of Fine
Arts. Since 2017, he has served as President of L-Art University.

Zhang Zhaoying was born in Guangzhou, China, in 1988.
He earned a Bachelor of Fine Arts degree from the Oil Painting
Department at the Sichuan Fine Arts Institute in Chongqing
and a Master of Fine Arts from the Académie royale des Beaux-Arts
in Brussels. He later completed his PhD at the Macau University
of Science and Technology and currently teaches at the Tianjin
Academy of Fine Arts. He is also a postgraduate supervisor
at Sahmyook University.

Zhang Zhaoying is considered one of the leading figures among
artists of the post-1985 generation, distinguished by a highly
internationalised perspective. His works reflect a hybrid mentality,
crossing various media, languages, and temporalities, and are
nourished by deep iconological research. His work focuses
on the reconstruction of a "personal domain" through subverted
and reinterpreted discourses.

He has exhibited his works in numerous solo exhibitions, including
at Yibo Gallery in Shanghai in 2021 and the Art Museum of Nanjing
University of the Arts in 2019, as well as in various galleries and
exhibition spaces across China. His work has also been featured
in significant international group exhibitions, including *Global painting*
at Mart Rovereto, the Chengdu Biennale, and exhibitions
in Germany, Switzerland, and New York.

His works are part of prestigious collections such as Mart, Rovereto,
the National Art Museum of China, Beijing, the White Rabbit
Gallery, Chippendale, Australia, and the Today Art Museum, Beijing,
among others. His ability to blend traditional elements with modern
influences and to explore universal themes such as desire and
human struggle makes him a unique and highly relevant artist in the
contemporary art scene.

Solo Exhibitions

Museo di Palazzo Grimani,
Venice, 2025
Yibo Gallery, Shanghai, 2021
Art Museum of Nanjing
University of the Arts, Nanjing,
2019
MAO Space, Shanghai, 2019
Yima Gallery, Chengdu, 2018
L-Art Gallery, Chengdu, 2016
Yi Yuan Space, Wuhan, 2016
EGG Gallery, Beijing, 2015

Group Exhibitions

Global painting, Mart Rovereto,
2023
Chengdu Biennale, Chengdu,
2021
Tang Contemporary Art,
Bangkok, 2019
*New Art History: 2000–2018
Chinese Contemporary Art*,
MOCA Yinchuan, 2019
*Zoom-In Chongqing: Malerei und
Video an der Hochschule
der Künste Sichuan*, Kunsthalle
Darmstadt, Darmstadt;
travelling Germany and
Switzerland, 2017
*Social Theatricality: The 5th
Chongqing Biennale for Young
Artists*, Art Museum of Sichuan
Fine Arts Institute, Chongqing,
2017
*Closer to the Beautiful World:
Asia Contemporary Art Week
(ACAW)*, Klein Sun Gallery,
New York, 2017
Utopia, UCCA Centre for
Contemporary Art, Beijing,
2016
Opening Exhibition of ARTRON,
ARTRON Art Centre,
Shenzhen, 2016
*Painting: Twenty Multiplied by
Twenty*, Poly Art Museum,
Beijing, Hong Kong and Macao,
2015
*The 2nd CAFAM·Future
Exhibition*, CAFA Art Museum,
Beijing, 2015
*In the Tide: An Exhibition of Young
Artists*, Sanya Art Festival,
Sanya, 2014
*Exhibition for Luo Zhongli Prize
Awardees*, Chongqing Art
Gallery, Chongqing, 2014

Collectors

Mart Rovereto
National Art Museum of China,
Beijing
White Rabbit Gallery,
Chippendale, Australia
Today Art Museum, Beijing
Jan van der Togt Museum,
Amstelveen, The Netherlands
Chongqing Art Gallery,
Chongqing
Luo Zhongli Memorial Gallery,
Chongqing
Art Museum of Nanjing
University of the Arts, Nanjing
Ivy Art, Nanjing
L-Art Gallery, Chengdu
Yi Yuan Space, Wuhan
MAO Space, Shanghai
Capsule Shanghai, Shanghai
Mr. Guangyi Wang, Mr. Haitao
Wang, Mr. James Wang,
Ms. Dan Yu, Mr. Shoutai Cheng,
Mr. Fanzhi Zeng, Mr. Fan'gang
Zhang

Cover
*Lifelong Beauty – The Temptation
of Giorgio de Chirico*, 2023–24, detail

Page 2
Warrior – Marx's Commitment, 2025, detail

Project Manager
Costanza de Bellegarde de Saint Lary

Art Director
Luigi Fiore

Design
Anna Cattaneo

Editorial Coordination
Manuela Schiavano, Eva Vanzella

Copy Editor
Doriana Comerlati

Layout
Evelina Laviano

Translations
Jeff Crosby (texts by Lü Peng, Li Guohua,
You Yi, Duan Shaofeng)
Gordon Fisher, Traduzioni Liquide
(text by Andrea B. Del Guercio)

Photo Credits
© Alamy Stock Photo: fig. 3 p. 140
© 2025. Fine Art Images/Heritage Images/
Scala, Florence: fig. 5 p. 140
© 2025. Museo Nacional del Prado © Photo
MNP/Scala, Firenze: fig. 7 p. 141
Photo Heather Wong: p. 43

Part of L-Art Group, which curates
contemporary art exhibitions worldwide
and is expanding art education across Europe,
L-Art Book is the group's publishing arm,
dedicated to high-quality art publications.

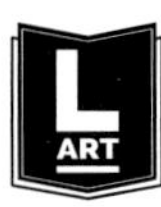

Acknowledgements
I would like to express my sincere gratitude
to Zhi Yi (Shanxi) Cultural Investment Co., Ltd.
for their generous support.
Special thanks to Yang Xiaoqing, Hou Yihang,
and Ma Junjie, for their exclusive sponsorship.
I am also deeply grateful to the entire team
who worked tirelessly on this project,
particularly Costanza de Bellegarde de Saint
Lary, Manuela Schiavano, Manuela Calandra,
Anna Cattaneo, Eva Vanzella, Evelina Laviano,
and Doriana Comerlati.